AN AEROPLANE CONVOY.

Foodships successfully convoyed by seaplanes in clear weather when submarines were easier to detect.

THRILLING STORIES
of the GREAT WAR

HEROIC INCIDENTS AND STARTLING
EVENTS OF THE WORLD WAR ON
LAND AND SEA, IN THE AIR AND
UNDER THE WATER

By
CAPTAIN LOGAN HOWARD-SMITH
with Special Chapters by
THOMAS F. TRUSLER
Third Brigade Canadian Artillery
and
VISCOUNT JAMES BRYCE

———

Profusely Illustrated with Photographs,
Maps and Drawings

———

British Library Cataloguing-in-Publication Data
A catalogue record for this book is available from
the British Library

INTRODUCTION

THE DEFENSE of Home and Country has always called forth the noblest instincts in man. Patriotism is a magnet that draws men to planes of heroic endeavor, of consummate devotion to principle, where the sacrifice of physical comfort is nothing, and the giving up of life itself a trifle.

The moments of supreme courage, effort, and achievement in the life of man have been when he has shouldered arms and faced the invader and persecutor.

War is a horrible and hateful thing; at best it is a terrible, lamentable necessity. But it does not make cowards of brave and honest men; it does frequently inspire the timid and hesitating with the fire of valor and resolution to a degree undreamed of.

So it is that in war we find stories of intrepidity, and deeds palpitating with heroism, such as only the crises of supreme danger and necessity could inspire; and we treasure these stories as part of the priceless heritage of humanity, that children and grandchildren may remember the valor of their sires; we tell and retell them, we preserve them in the volumes of the historian, on the canvas of the artist, we chisel them in stone, that men may remember the price paid for liberty and virtue.

CONTENTS

CONTENTS

CONTENTS

9

CHAPTER I

STORMING THE MESSINES RIDGE

CAREFUL WORK OF PREPARATION—WONDERFUL WORK OF THE BRITISH GUNS AND AIRMEN—THE GREAT EARTHQUAKE—GERMAN DEFENDERS ANNIHILATED—BRINGING UP THE GUNS—HEAVY GERMAN LOSSES.

AFTER THE British and French had consolidated the territory won from the Germans in the Battle of Arras there was a lull in the fighting and the world waited with eager expectation for the next offensive on the Western front. Two months were to elapse before the Allies were ready for another mighty blow. For over two years and a half the Germans had suffered a checkmate in the Ypres salient. But they held the Wytschaete-Messines Ridge which gave them complete observation of Ypres and of the British entrenched forces in their front. During this long period they had harrassed their enemies with continuous gunfire and had constructed a system of trenches, dugouts, and wire-entanglements which they thought impregnable. What they had, they felt confident of being able to hold until the end of the war. But General Haig had made preparations on a huge scale and early in June was ready to launch an offensive that was to capture the German position and straighten out his line from Hill 60—made famous

11

by the heroic defence of the Princess Patricia's in 1915—to Ploegsteert Wood north of Armentières.

CAREFUL WORK OF PREPARATION

By the 1st of June the vastest concourse of British guns so far assembled at one point during the war was fronting the Wytschaete-Messines Ridge. For the next six days these heavy guns and light field-guns played on the heights and on the lines of communication in the rear. Flocks of British airplanes flew over the German lines driving back enemy squadrons, daring incredible deeds to blind their foe. The Germans knew that this increased gunfire, this air activity meant the launching of a powerful offensive. To meet it they rushed forward reinforcements, but so terrific was the long range fire of the British artillery that supply columns and battalions approaching the ridge from the East were decimated. The Germans on the ridge were pinned to their trenches and dugouts and with the memory of the Somme and Vimy Ridge in their minds had misgivings regarding the impregnable character of the position. Had the whole truth been known to them their fears would have been increased one hundredfold.

For two years British sappers had been burrowing under the ridge and had succeeded by patient perseverance in constructing nineteen mines containing more than 1,000,000 pounds of ammonite. The Germans were living in fancied security on a quiescent volcano. On the night of June 6th the work of the sappers and electrical engineers was completed and everything was in readiness for touching off the volcano.

12

Nature seemed in harmony with the spirits of the contestants. On the night of June 6th a thunderstorm swept the battle front with ominous rumblings and fierce flashes of lightning. When the storm passed, through the darkness men and guns and "tanks" moved forward from the British reserve line to the battle zone and waited patiently for the signal to assault the enemy. By 3 A. M. on the 7th the guns were in full play and at 3.10 the battle began in earnest. Philip Gibbs, the war correspondent, gives the following account of its appalling opening:

WONDERFUL WORK OF THE BRITISH GUNS AND AIRMEN

"For five days at least many Germans were pinned to their tunnels as prisoners of fire. No food reached them. There was no way out through these zones of death. A new regiment, which tried to come up last night, was broken and shattered. A prisoner says that out of his own company he lost fifty to sixty men before reaching the line. For a long way behind the lines the British heavy guns laid down belts of shell fire, and many of the enemy's batteries kept silent.

The British gunners smothered the German batteries whenever they were revealed to the airmen. Those flying men have been wonderful. A kind of exaltation of spirits took possession of them, and they dared great risks and searched out the enemy's squadrons far over his lines. In five days from June 1 forty-four separate machines were sent crashing down, and this morning very early flocks of airplanes went out to blind the enemy's eyes and report the progress of the battle.

In the darkness queer monsters moved up close to the lines, many of them crawling singly over the battle-fields under cover of woods and ruins. They were the tanks, ready to go into action on the great day of the war, when their pilots and crews have helped by high courage to a great victory.

Last night all was ready. The men, knowing the risks of it all (for no plans are certain in war), had a sense of of oppression, strained by poignant anxiety. Many men's lives were on the hazard of all this. The air was heavy as if nature itself was full of tragedy. A Summer fog was thick over Flanders and the sky was livid. Forked lightning rent the low clouds and thunder broke with menacing rumblings. Rain fell sharply, and on the conservatory of the blg Flemish house, where officers bent over their maps and plans, raindrops beat noisily.

But the storm passed and the night was calm and beautiful. Along the dark roads and down the leafy lanes columns of men were marching and brass bands played them through the darkness. Guns and limber moved forward at a sharp pace. "Lights out," rang the challenges of sentries to staff cars, passing beyond the last village and nearer to the line. Masses of men lay sleeping or resting in the fields before getting orders to go forward into the battle zone.

All through the night the sky was filled with vivid flashes of bursting shells and with the steady hammer-strokes of guns. From an observation post looking across the shoulder of Kemmel Hill straight to Wyts-chaete and Messines Ridge I watched this bombard-ment for that moment when it should rise into a mad

14

fury of gunfire, before the troops, lying in those dark fields, should stumble forward.

The drone of a night flying airplane passed overhead. The sky lightened a little and showed great black smudges like ink blots on a blue silk cloth where the British kite balloons rose in clusters to spy out the first news of the coming battle.

The cocks of Flanders crowed, and two heavy German shells roared over Kemmel Hill and burst somewhere in the British lines. A third came, but before its explosion could be heard all the noise there had been, all these separate sounds of guns and high explosives and shrapnel were swept into a tornado of artillery which now began.

THE GREAT EARTHQUAKE

The signal for its beginning was the most terrible, beautiful thing, the most diabolical splendor I have seen in the war. Out of the dark ridges of Messines and Wytschaete and that ill-famed Hill 60 . . . there gushed up enormous volumes of scarlet flame from exploding mines and of earth and smoke, all lighted by flame spilling over into fountains of fierce color, so that the countryside was illuminated by the red lights." The earth trembled and quaked; the British soldiers waiting to rush the first line trenches were "rocked up and down, this way and that," as if "in an open boat in the rough sea." The gigantic explosion, which was heard by Lloyd George at his country home in England, 140 miles away, levelled hills, made mincemeat of trenches, dugouts, and wire entanglements and blew the defenders high in air

15

or buried them under tons of earth. Simultaneously with this volcanic eruption the guns, great and small, subjected the salient to the most intense shellfire of the whole war. The fire lifted and close behind its "infernal rain," the infantry under General Sir Herbert Plumer dashed forward with fixed bayonets, and in a few minutes the entire front line of the enemy's trenches was won. The Germans remaining on the ridge were sending up distress signals frantically and in the early dawn, white, red, and green lights blazed among the exploding shells. But they were of no avail; the heavy British guns playing over the hills prevented reinforcements from coming up.

GERMAN DEFENDERS ANNIHILATED

The scene of destruction that met the conquerors was appalling. Only bits of trenches and a few traverses here and there and concrete emplacements, knocked sideways above the closed entrances of deep tunnels and dugouts remained among the shell craters. Scattered amid "this vast midden of war" were the gray-clad forms of dead Germans. Only a few, however; "most of those killed were buried as they died, buried under the masses of earth flung up by exploding shells, buried in their tunnels, . . . buried by the wild upheaval of mines which opened the earth beneath them with yawning chasms a hundred yards wide and sixty feet deep." Hill 60 was obliterated and its site was quickly seized by some English troops. Below Mount Sorel and Armagh Wood groups of Germans were still alive, and these Wurttembergers and Jagers, shaking with terror from the

EXPLOSION OF LAND MINES UNDER MESSINES RIDGE.

For two years British sappers had been burrowing under the ridge and had succeeded in constructing nineteen mines containing 1,000,000 pounds of ammonite. The explosion rocked the earth and was heard by Lord George at his home 140 miles away. The destruction in the German trenches was appalling. Only bits of trenches and concrete emplacements knocked sideways remained. Most of the German dead were buried in the ruins. (*Ill. L. News copr.*)

SAPPING AND MINING THE ENEMY'S TRENCHES.

When the hostile trenches are near together an open zig-zag trench is dug to a point very close to the enemy's line, then a covered gallery is excavated to a point almost under the hostile trench.

ORGANISATION OF DEFENCES BY JOINING CRATER WITH SHELL-HOLES

SECTION FROM C TO D.

LIP OF CRATER

SECTION OF GALLERY.

GAINING A FOOT OF GROUND PER HOUR.

Here a charge of explosive is placed and fired from a distance by an electric wire. At the same instant the men charge over the ground and occupy the ruined trench of the enemy. (*Ill. L. News copr.*)

RUSHING A GUN TO THE FIRING LINE. With the Royal Horse Artillery in Flanders. Always the guns follow closely in the wake of an infantry advance to break up counter attacks and speed the fleeing Germans on their way.

effects of the explosion, came forward extending trembling hands and, with the usual cry of "Kamerad," plead for mercy.

BRINGING UP THE GUNS

The winning of the front line trenches ended the first phase of the battle. The peak of the ridge had still to be stormed, but in less than three hours after the battle began the whole sector south of Ypres from Observation Ridge to Ploegsteert Wood was won and the position was being rapidly consolidated. Now came the third and final stage of the battle. For two and a half years the British guns had been stationary in front of this battleground. The commanding position of the Germans had, during all this time, enabled them to harass the crews by shells fired by direct observation, but now that the British infantry were in possession of the high ground so long held by the enemy a command was passed along to all batteries; guns were limbered up and in quick order the drivers were urging their horses up the slopes. As they rushed to the top of the ridge the infantry stood by to let them pass and cheered them wildly. Now began the assault of the rear defences which ran across the base of the salient formed by the ridge itself. Here was experienced the only strong resistance to the British attack during the battle, but by night-fall the victory was complete and the whole rear position, on a front of five miles and to a depth of three miles, was in the hands of the victors. Never was a more decisive victory won; all that the British troops set out to do was accomplished. Not only was the supposedly safe ground of the Wytschaete-Messines Ridge won from the enemy, but so paralysing was the blow struck that it was not until forty hours had passed that the Germans were able to concentrate for a counter-attack, but with the British guns dominating the eastern approaches to the ridge the attack completely failed.

HEAVY GERMAN LOSSES

The victors paid but a small price for their triumph, less than 10,000 men were killed or wounded and of these fully 7,000 were light casualties. Official information places the German losses at 30,000 and of these 7,000 were valid prisoners. This victory, significant in its immediate results, was far reaching in its effects. It taught the Germans that their fortresses were of no avail against the British artillery, it took from them their last commanding position on the west front, and it gave their foes perfect command of the region surrounding the important city of Lille.

CHAPTER II

TURNING BACK THE HUNS AT THE SOMME

A SCENE OF DESOLATION—BRAVERY OF THE ALLIES—HOW THE BRITISH STORM TRENCHES—SOMME RIDGES AND MARSHES—MARVELOUS BRETON RESERVISTS—HOW BECQUINCOURT WAS WON—GREAT GAINS AT SMALL COST—FRENCH ADVANCE IN SINGLE FILE—PROGRESS OF THE BATTLE.

IT IS probable that the concerted offensive against the German lines in Picardy, begun July 1st after the most terrible bombardment known even in this war of high explosives, will go down into history as the battle of the Somme.

A correspondent who visited the French army in its position near Peronne gives us this glimpse of the country over which the battle had swept:

"As far as the eye can see the view is utterly the same; utterly monotonous, nothing but desolate slopes that once were a thickly populated French countryside. The complete inhumanity of outlook strikes one tremendously. Here two great armies are at death grips, yet apart from the incessant tumult of cannonade and the never-ending rows of little smoke clouds—new ones forming before the preceding ones have time to melt—one might be thousands of miles from civilization. Our maps are of little assistance. Here should be Feuillers, there Flaucourt, further on Assevilliers, but one can distinguish nothing save heaps of blackened stones that appear through the glasses. Even the roads have been swept away by the bombardment. Nothing but ditchlike trench lines mark the presence of humans

BRAVERY OF THE ALLIES

"Suddenly voices cried: 'Look over there, you can see soldiers.' About half a mile before us one sees groups of men like ants working busily on the hillside. Through the glasses one sees that they are sheltering themselves with extraordinary care. Some have strange oblong shields like the ancient Roman legionaries. Others are grouped under a kind of casemate on wheels whose roof touches the ground in front rising in a curve behind to give room for the workers. Still others hide behind a ripple of ground or hillocks.

"All are working furiously with picks and shovels. I have been told that the British losses have been heightened by an utter disregard of danger. Even when not engaged in attacks our allies seem still not to realize the necessity of unremitting caution. But the French have learned the lesson that Verdun hammered home—that the best soldier is he who regards his life as belonging to France, something precious, never to be risked save when sheer necessity demands it. That, combined with the magnificent artillery service, is the reason why the French losses in this battle have been less than half—I speak from intimate knowledge—those in any previous French offensive in proportion to the number of troops engaged."

20

HOW THE BRITISH STORM TRENCHES

The British method of storming trenches, which has won the admiration of French officers, is to combine the smashing of concrete shelters under heavy shell fire with a system of night raiding by scouting parties. The raiders locate hidden machine-guns and finish the destruction of barbed-wire entanglements, thus opening the way for the usual charges of infantry.

The fire of the French and British guns, which were used for the tremendous preliminary bombardment, was increased in fury on June 29th, the date first fixed for the assault. But no order was given to the troops, either because the bombardment was not thought to be sufficient, or more probably because the rumor as to the date of the movement had been deliberately allowed to reach the enemy and induce him to pack his reserve trenches. During the last two days of the bombardment these reserve trenches were subjected to an especially terrific fire, and several zones of shrapnel were maintained over all the enemy's routes of supply and reinforcement. According to a German statement, every place within ten miles of the firing-line was smitten with heavy shell and incendiary projectiles. Then in the morning of Saturday, July 1, 1916, the British and French infantry forces climbed out of their trenches and advanced into the German lines.

General Fayolle's army connected with the British Army north of the Somme at the village of Maricourt. Here, General Balfourier, the army-corps commander of the Twentieth Corps, had his troops of the Twenty-ninth Division—the incomparable Iron Division—stretched down to the river at Vaux. Then by the canal-locks in the river valley, at Eclusier, another famous French African force, the Colonial Division, with which General Pétain had conquered the Hand of Massiges in Champagne, extended southward towards Fontaine-les-Cappy, where a fine Breton force was arrayed against the enemy.

SOMME RIDGES AND MARSHES

The crux of the position was the dividing line of the Somme Valley, separating the Ironsides from the Colonials. The small split stream of the Somme ran through marshes from one to two miles broad, the marshes being cut by a canal as well as by the river. Above the wide, winding zone of the marshes rose on either side a rampart of chalk. The river cliffs were in turn dominated by ridges, from three hundred to four hundred and fifty feet high, occupied by the Germans northwest and south. All the hamlets, woods, and fields in the large southern angle of the Somme running to Péronne were dominated by the main German heavy batteries on the slopes of Mont St. Quentin north of Péronne; and at Villers Carbonnel, four miles south of the town, there was another important mass of long-range German siege-guns. The consequence was that, although Péronne was only about six miles from the trenches of the French Colonial Division, there was no chance of storming into the town by a direct frontal attack. For the great, curving, marshy river valley turned sharply south by the old, grey, lovely, walled city, and if the French troops had there crossed the stream, canal

22

and marsh they would have had to work through a large stretch of low ground westward, which was surrounded by an amphitheater of downs, on the farther slopes of which the Germans had placed guns by the hundred. In other words, the wedge of lowish, seamed tableland extending from the southern French sector to the enemy's railhead at Péronne, was a great natural trap. Troops who stormed into it from the west would be held up by the river and exposed to a cross-fire of artillery. This was no doubt the reason why General von Einem thought that the allied bombardment on the southern side of the Somme was merely a distracting demonstration, and that General Foch and his able Staff intended to launch their real assault at Roye and Chaulnes.

MARVELOUS BRETON RESERVISTS

At half-past nine on Saturday morning the French Colonial and Breton troops advanced to the attack. The Bretons were middle-aged reservists, who had distinguished themselves in some fine defensive work at Quennevières alongside the Zouaves. Quiet, settled, steady married men, they had borne themselves calmly under bombardments and rush attacks in the sedentary life of the trenches, but only their own commander seems to have been strongly convinced that they would show great driving power in attack. Nearly all the other attacking French and Colonial regiments were led by battalions of fresh young troops, directed by old, experienced officers and supported by battalions of the finest veterans. The extraordinary reservists of Brittany, however, equaled the best

23

active troops in endurance, skill and charging power.
Kinsmen of the Welsh who emigrated from Britain
in the days of King Arthur, these middle-aged Celts
were transformed by the fury of battle. Half an hour
before the advance they asked permission to sing, and,
chanting the "Marseillaise," they went forward in
platoons with their lines straighter and steadier than
they would have been at maneuvers in peace time.
They captured the hamlet of Fay, and, between Fay
and Soyécourt, they advanced to the outskirts of
Estrées, which was a vast subterranean fortress the
approaches of which were drenched with shells by a
park of heavy German guns at Villers Carbonnel,
four miles directly in front of Estrées. Villers Carbonnel, south of Péronne, and Mont St. Quentin north
of the town, were the two grand artillery positions of
the enemy, each comprising hundreds of siege-guns
that swept all the Santerre promontory. Months
had to pass before Villers Carbonnel was even remotely
threatened by the French troops. It was the main
rallying-point for all the German forces south of the
Somme, and though seldom mentioned in communications, was one of the most important places in the
European War. Many of its guns were destroyed
by the terrible plunging shells from the new monster
French artillery. But the Germans managed to
transport new howitzers at night across the river
valley and maintain the strength of the position. The
gallant Bretons dug themselves in near Estrées and
swung their northern wing forward towards Belloy
and Assevilliers. Behind them were some regiments
of the famous Foreign Legion, who afterwards relieved

24

them when they had gallantly won and held the most difficult and most critical position in the allied line of advance.

Meanwhile, the Colonial Division, with its colored troops, renowned for their terrific ardor in attack, enjoyed itself in an amazing fashion. On this point of the front, between Frise and Dompierre, the Germans had not expected to be attacked, and were completely taken by surprise. This was the chief reason why the French Colonial Division, forming the center of General Fayolle's army, had an astonishingly easy task in the morning of July 1st.

HOW BECQUINCOURT WAS WON

Neglecting the village of Frise, in a marshy loop of the river on their right, the Colonial troops marched into the ruins of Dompierre and Becquincourt, which formed together a large mass of shattered buildings the size of a town. The cellars in the chalk plateau were originally deep, and for nearly two years the Germans had burrowed deeper and linked up their caverns with tunnels until the two connected villages were transformed into a subterranean Gibraltar. But the new French monster siege-guns had smashed in many of the thick vaults, choked the entrances, broken the armor that had protected machine-guns and artillery, and destroyed practically every wall above ground. Among the French gunners were men picked from other sectors because they were natives of the places on which their guns were trained. In particular, there was one young farmer of Becquincourt who took a savage pleasure in destroying his own fine old farm buildings and getting his huge shells well down into his own cellars. When the village was won, and he contemplated the unrecognizable heap of stones representing the house of his birth, he said, with the professional pride of an artilleryman, "What splendid shooting!" After so extraordinarily devastating a bombardment as this there was no infantry battle, but merely a walk-over. The remnant of the garrison of Dompierre, consisting of two hundred men and officers, was captured by the French Colonials at the cost of only one man killed on their side. The hamlet of Bussus, south of Dompierre, was also carried with little loss. The casualties of the entire Colonial Division numbered only six hundred and forty, after breaking through the entire system of the first German zone of defenses and reaching the second zone, between Herbécourt and Assevilliers, in the evening of July 1st.

GREAT GAINS AT SMALL COST

Yet the hostile organizations were extremely elaborate. At Dompierre, for instance, the attacking troops had to cross in the first place the German fire-trench; in the second place two twin trenches, a hundred yards behind, protected by fields of barbed-wire; in the third place the Wolff trench, with another zone of wire entanglements a hundred yards farther; and in the fourth place the village itself and the connected ruins of Becquincourt, with their underground maze of fortified works. One large cavern, west of Dompierre, was equipped with two great vats for the manufacture of poison gas. From the vats pipes ran into the fire-trenches. But the heavy French shells had broken the gas system before a favorable wind could be used by the enemy. It was creditably reported that the two Colonial regiments engaged in surrounding all this German system of works had five men killed and sixteen wounded while working through the first four rows of trenches, losing afterwards, as we have already stated, one men in Dompierre itself.

At Estrées, farther south, the Breton reservists avoided a frontal attack, and, rapidly working round the village on both sides, enveloped it and stormed it from the rear. Their casualties, though somewhat larger than those of the skilled attackers of the Colonial Division, yet remained exceedingly small when compared with the former allied average of losses in conquering intensively fortified trench systems. The miraculously insignificant number of casualties among the French south of the Somme was not entirely due to the fact that the enemy in this sector was taken unawares. His routine system of artillery defenses was very formidable. After the terrific bombardment he was still able to bring into action hundreds of guns which he had kept silent and concealed during the hurricane French fire.

FRENCH ADVANCE IN SINGLE FILE

But among other things, such as aerial infantry, General Fayolle had thought out during his experiences in Champagne a new method of deploying troops. Each assaulting regiment advanced in single file through the zone of hostile shell fire. The target they thus presented was scarcely more than three feet wide. Near the enemy's fire-trench the thin stream of blue-

27

clad figures changed formation, and went forward
in slow, long waves of attack in very open order. If
any machine-gun that had escaped destruction then
opened fire upon them, all the men fell down and
sought for cover in the shell-holes. Their officers
would not allow them to charge, and often prevented
them from trying to creep cautiously round an active
center of resistance. There was, indeed, some trouble
at first, especially with some of the French Colonial
troops, accustomed to swift, fierce, hand-to-hand bomb
and bayonet conflicts in former offensive movements.
But the strangely loud drone of propellers at once
confirmed the orders violently shouted by the French
officers, and the troops understood why they had to
tumble into cover at the slightest sign of hostile
resistance. The novel aerial infantry of France was
operating just in advance of each attacking wave, at a
height varying from three hundred to a hundred feet.
Some of the pilots came low and shot down, from the
rear of the enemy machine-gun positions, the German
crews, and then signaled their own infantry to advance.
Other pilots, who could not bring their guns to bear on
some deadly knot of resisting Germans, dropped
smoke-bombs upon them, or wirelessed their position
to the French artillery. Then above the heads of the
sheltering attacking troops screamed a shower of well-
aimed shells, which blasted away all opposition. The
troops then arose and walked onward, preceded by
their aerial scouts, enskied machine-gunners and celes-
tial bomb-throwers. Naturally the French staff
work was of almost superhuman perfection, for each
regimental brigade, divisional army corps, and head-

28

quarters staff had alert and finely-trained eyes aloft and in advance of its troops, and wireless messages told the chiefs in the rear more about the state of affairs in the breaking German line than was known to the men who were actually breaking the line.

PROGRESS OF THE BATTLE

Thus began the great Battle of the Somme, which was destined to last for months—a tremendous war of itself, as wars were once reckoned. At the end of two days the German lines were penetrated to a depth of two miles. Montauban, Mametz, Fricourt, Dompierre, Becquincourt, Herbecourt, Fay, Curin, and Frise, were among the fortified places captured, and 10,000 prisoners were taken. In the succeeding few days the positions gained were firmly consolidated, German counter-attacks repulsed, and an important gain made by the capture of Hardecourt at the junction of the British and French lines. On July 11th the important defensive position of Contalmaison was stormed for the second time, and held. By the following day the whole first system of the German defense along a line of about eight miles had been captured, four miles of the second line were taken, and the third line was pierced. Then followed constant, fierce attack and counter-thrust, and at the end of the first month's fighting the whole of Longueval and the important Delville Wood were in the hands of the Allies.

The ensuing progress was substantial, if less spectacular, both British and French forces advancing their sectors and obtaining possession of many villages and towns, until the high ground commanding

29

the plain in which Bapaume lies was reached, giving them artillery command of this important point.

Late in February of 1917, the Germans voluntarily abandoned their trenches on the North or Ancre face of the Somme salient and took up new positions along the Bapaume ridge. On March 17th, after a powerful drive by both the British and French forces, the important military base of Bapaume fell together with the powerfully fortified German front between the rivers Ancre and Oise. Allied successes continued throughout March and early April on this front, with the German resistance gradually stiffening. This seemed to indicate that the German lines had been shortened sufficiently for adequate defense and had reached the lines on which a determined stand was to be made.

AFTER A DRIVE ON THE SOMME

British advancing over the captured German trenches, after heavy artillery fire had reduced them to tangled ruins and

One of the Famous British Tanks

Land battleships equipped with rapid-fire and machine guns and built to travel unhesitatingly over trenches, shell craters:

CHAPTER III

THE NEW FIGHTING MONSTERS: THE BRITISH "TANKS"

AN IMPORTANT FACTOR IN THE OFFENSIVE—HOW
THE WHEELS WORK—THE MONSTERS IN ACTION—
A DESPERATE ENCOUNTER—CARRYING OFF THE
WOUNDED—TERRIBLE ENGINES OF WAR.

THE MOST terrifying engine of destruction which the war has developed is the British armored motor car, or "tank," as the soldiers have named it. These formidable machines were first mentioned in the official disptaches of September 16, 1916, and were brought into use with important results in the battle of the Somme. Subsequently they figured daily in the war news and have became an important factor in the offensive. The cars are capable of moving in shell-torn areas and can negotiate a roadless wilderness of trenches.

This land-dreadnought is an adaptation of the American caterpillar farm-tractor. Several thousand unarmored cars were bought by the British Government, which added the armor and armament. The cars are about 23 feet long and 9 feet wide over all. They weigh, unarmored, from 18,000 to 25,000 pounds, develop 120 horse-power, and move from 2½ to 4 miles an hour. Each machine has two fore wheels, used only for guiding purposes. No weight rests on these wheels. The main weight is carried on two chain belts, or caterpillars, having corrugated surfaces, on the inside of which are two lines of steel rails, jointed in short sections and operated by sprocket wheels. As the endless belt turns, the forward sprocket wheel lays down the track and the rear one picks it up again. On the rails thus laid down roll the wheels of the machine. The rails are set extremely far apart, being near the edges of the shoes so as to avoid any possibility of twisting the track, even when traveling over the roughest ground, and in addition, the truck rollers are provided with alternate inside and outside flanges.

HOW THE WHEELS WORK

The pressure on the ground under the caterpillar—the string of steel plates seven feet long and two feet wide on which the entire weight of the machine is supported—is said to be less than that caused by the foot of a horse or even of a man. And owing to the construction and location of the engines the center of gravity of the whole machine is near the back of the caterpillar and not more than eighteen inches off the ground. For this reason the machine can roll along without danger of tipping over on an almost incredible slope, and it can run considerably more than half its length forward over a chasm without any support at all.

When it moves across a trench the front wheel, on which normally no weight rests, crosses first. The front end of the caterpillar then moves forward over the open part of the trench, and the machine is sup.

ported by the rear of the caterpillar, where most of the weight is concentrated, while the guide wheel on each side in front acts as a stabilizer. Then by the time the rear part of the caterpillar has reached the edge of the trench the forward part will already be across and there will be very little displacement of the machine. In this way the machine can cross a trench almost as wide as the ground length of the caterpillar, and by lengthening these for war purposes the British are able to get across almost any trench or shell crater with little difficulty.

THE MONSTERS IN ACTION

Vivid stories come from the front of the "tanks" in action, and from the mass of material it is clear that the cars strike terror into the hearts of the enemy and accomplish useful and important results. The *London Times* correspondent describes the exploits in one day's fighting near Combles as follows:

"The pilot, whose steering gear went wrong, found himself astride a German trench on the outskirts of Combles—a little out of his reckoning. Here he halted, enfilading the trench repeatedly, until a chance shell of large dimensions hit the car, making it impossible to move forward or back. For five hours the crew of the 'tank' worked their guns while parties of German and British bombers lobbed their missiles across from opposite sides. Eventually the Germans were killed or driven off, and the crew of the 'tank' returned safely through a deadly enemy barrage.

"A second 'tank' traveled about half way up Bouleaux Wood until in a position enabling it to enfilade the enemy's trenches. Then the commander discovered that the infantry were not coming up behind him, so he went back for them. Again he went forward, with the infantry following, passing over enemy trenches and continuing his journey to the outskirts of Morval. Subsequently the commander found that he was again alone. Not wishing to keep all the fruits of victory for himself, he again turned and went back to find the infantry for whom he was acting as a kind of chaperon. He made a return journey of more than 1,500 yards in their direction, and then discovered that the infantry had been held up by a group of machine guns which had been turned on them from a trench previously reported as unoccupied. Calmly hoisting itself astride the trench, the 'tank' took a hand in the firing, knocking out one machine-gun after the other until the trench was unoccupied—save by bodies.

A DESPERATE ENCOUNTER

"Unfortunately, the 'tank' became wedged in an unusually deep crater, and the crew could not extricate it, even though they emerged and tried to dig it out—with the enemy firing at them from another trench seventy yards away. Then the fun really started. Parties of German bombers worked around to one side of the car, while British bombers from the infantry took cover on the opposite side. The ensuing duel lasted an hour and a half. The Germans tried to drop their bombs on the roof of the 'tank' without success. A corporal of the 'tank's' crew seized a German bomb which fell among his companions, and tried to fling it back, but it exploded, blowing him to pieces. Eventually the German bombers were driven off, and the crew returned to the British lines.

"In one group of advancing 'tanks' eight out of ten reached the point to which they were directed at the beginning of the offensive. Northwest of the Ginchy Telegraph one of this group silenced a group of six machine-guns in a redoubt, concentrating its fire on one after another. All of them did useful work in clearing other machine-gun parties out of craters. The enemy had poised his guns on the far lip of the crater, and it was extremely difficult to spot them in the tumbled earth. Another 'tank' in this group captured a trench full of Germans just east of Delville Wood. The pilot saw a white flag waving violently and advancing toward him as he was about to halt his 'tank' on the trench and sweep it from both sides. Behind the white flag streamed a long procession of unarmed Germans with their hands in the air. The 'tank' accepted their surrender, and told them to pass back to the British lines. Early in the fighting a 'tank' 'steamed' into a redoubt where a strong detachment of German machine-gunners were holding up one part of the British advance, and calmly cruised about, firing in every direction. The enemy took cover, and, being unable to capture the entire position alone, the 'tank' finally came back.

CARRYING OFF WOUNDED

"One 'tank' cleared a trench near Delville Wood, and then started on another mission in a northeasterly direction. This accomplished, it halted in a region

35

thickly strewn with British wounded. The crew alighted, and for three hours worked under heavy shell fire, tending the fallen men and helping carry them into shell craters. The 'tank' that silenced a battery outside Gueudecourt had first made a lonely tour through that enemy-held village, advancing from the direction of Flers. No Germans were found in the village—they must have fled to their dugouts when the monster hove in sight—so it came back again, and on the return journey found the field guns referred to. The guns were silenced, but a shell, which must have been aimed point blank from another hidden battery, knocked the 'tank' out of action. When the commander was last seen he was standing beside the wrecked car dressing his wound, and a machine-gun was playing on the group.

"A curious experience befell the crew of a 'tank' that helped to clear the Germans out of Foureaux (High) Wood. It climbed into the enemy trenches in the wood and did terrible execution with its guns, when the occupants tried to bolt to their support trenches. After raking the ground for half an hour, the commander found that the infantry had not arrived in accordance with his plan. He and the crew got out to reconnoitre, and while in the German trench some of the enemy reappeared. The commander made them surrender at the point of the revolver, and just then the infantry arrived to take charge of the prisoners. It was an awkward moment, for otherwise he could not have taken them back in the car, and they might have realized that these few men were absolutely alone. Another 'tank' engaged in the clearance of Foureaux Wood was told to silence the machine-guns in a great crater on the eastern edge of the wood. When it rolled into the crater the gunners fled in terror, leaving their twenty-five guns. So rapid and thorough was the execution that Foureaux Wood was quite free of the enemy in an hour from the time the 'tanks' began to work."

TERRIBLE ENGINES OF WAR

Philip Gibbs, in describing the operations of the "tanks" in the Somme region, proceeds as follows:

"A 'tank' had been coming along slowly in a lumbering way, crawling over the interminable succession of shell craters, lurching over and down and into and out of old German trenches, nosing heavily into soft earth, and grunting up again, and sitting poised on broken parapets as though quite winded by this exercise, and then waddling forward in the wake of the infantry.

"Then it faced the ruins of the château, and stared at them very steadily for quite a long time, as though wondering whether it should eat them or crush them. Our men were hiding behind ridges of shell craters, keeping low from the swish of machine-gun bullets, and imploring the 'tank' to 'get on with it.' Then it moved forward in a monstrous way, not swerving much to the left or right, but heaving itself on jerkily, like a dragon with indigestion, but very fierce. Fire leaped from its nostrils. The German machine-guns splashed its sides with bullets, which ricochetted off. Not all those bullets kept it back. It got on top of the enemy's trench, trudged down the length of it, laying its sandbags flat and sweeping it with fire.

"The German machine-guns were silent, and when our men followed the 'tank,' shouting and cheering, they found a few German gunners standing with their hands up as a sign of surrender to the monster who had come upon them.

"One of the most remarkable 'tank' adventures was in the direction of Gueudecourt, where our troops were held up in the usual way—that is to say, by the raking fire of machine-guns. They made two attacks, but could not get beyond that screen of bullets.

"Then a 'tank' strolled along, rolled over the trench, with fire flashing from its flanks, and delivered it into the hands of the infantry with nearly 400 prisoners, who waved white flags above the parapet. That was not all. The 'tank,' exhilerated by this success, went lolloping along the way in search of new adventures. It went quite alone, and only stopped for minor repairs when it was surrounded by a horde of German soldiers. These men closed upon it with great pluck, for it was firing in a most deadly way, and tried to kill it. They flung bombs at it, clambered on to its back, and tried to smash it with the butt-ends of rifles, jabbed it with bayonets, fired revolvers and rifles at it, and made a wild pandemonium about it.

"Then our infantry arrived, attracted by the tumult of the scene, and drove the enemy back. But the 'tank' had done deadly work, and between two hundred and three hundred killed and wounded Germans lay about its ungainly carcass. For a little while it seemed that the 'tank' also was out of action, but after a little attention and a good deal of grinding and grunting it heaved itself up and waddled away.

"These things sound incredible. . . . They are true; and though I write them in fantastic style, because that is really the nature of the thing, it must not be forgotten that these 'tanks' are terrible engines of war, doing most grim work, and that the men inside are taking high risks with astonishing courage."

CHAPTER IV

EARL KITCHENER DIES A HERO'S DEATH

BRITAIN'S GREATEST SHOCK—ADMIRAL JELLICOE'S
REPORT—ON MISSION AT RUSSIA'S REQUEST—
SPIES BLAMED FOR CALAMITY—NEWS RECEIVED
AMID INTENSE EXCITEMENT—ARMY ORDERED INTO
MOURNING — HOW LORD KITCHENER DIED —
SUNK BY A MINE — LOSS OF THE HAMPSHIRE —
KITCHENER'S PLACE IN BRITAIN'S HISTORY.

THE NEWS received by the world on June 6, 1916, that Lord Kitchener, Secretary of State for War, and his staff were lost off the Orkney Islands the previous night, was the most stunning blow delivered to Great Britain since the beginning of the war.

It was the second great shock which the country had sustained within a week. The first was the announcement of the naval battle in the North Sea in the form of a list of the ships lost, with virtually no way of ascertaining the enemy losses. The bulletin telling of the intimation that there was any compensation in the death of Kitchener gave the country even a greater shock.

Lord Kitchener was the one outstanding personality whom the people talked of and believed in as a great man, nothwithstanding the newspaper attacks, which, at a former period of the war, threatened to undermine his popularity and the public confidence in him.

LORD KITCHENER INSIDE A TURKISH FORT

An inspecting trip to one of the captured Turkish fortifications on the Gallipoli peninsula in company with Colonel Sir

LORD KITCHENER AT SEDDUL BAHR.

The British War Secretary, together with Colonel Watson, the French commander and Colonel McMahon, on his historic

ADMIRAL JELLICOE'S REPORT ON THE DISASTER

A telegram from Admiral Sir John Jellicoe, commander of the fleet, giving the bare facts, was received at the Admiralty on the morning following the disaster. The first official announcement was issued at about

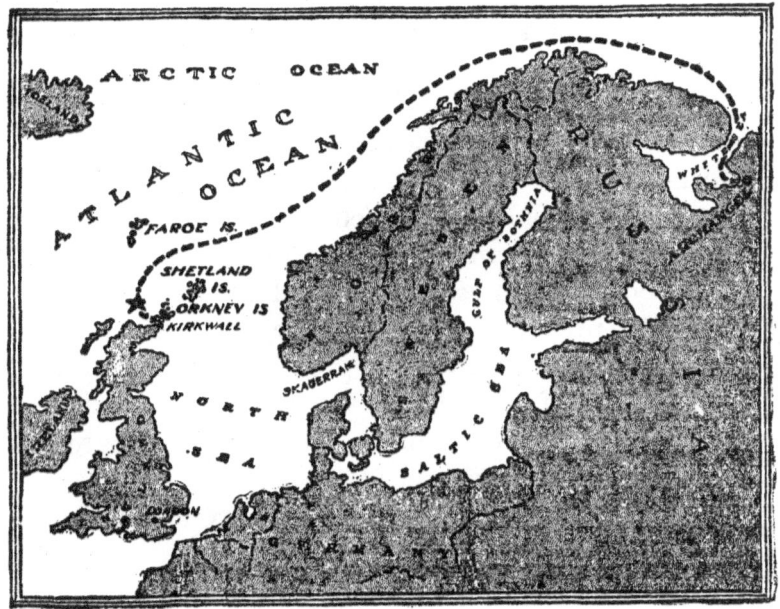

WHERE BRITAIN LOST HER GREAT SOLDIER AND WAR MINISTER

At the time of his death Lord Kitchener was en route to Russia, intending to sail around the northern coast of Russia and land at Archangel, as indicated by the dotted line. The star shows where his ship was sunk.

1.30 in the afternoon. Such news, however, cannot be kept entirely secret even for an hour. Before noon rumors were spreading, and the telephones in the newspaper offices were busy with inquirers anxious to know whether this—one of the many reports circulating in those days of tension—had any foundation.

Admiral Jellicoe's report to the Admiralty was as follows:

I have to report with deep regret that His Majesty's ship Hampshire, Captain Herbert J. Savill, R. N., with Lord Kitchener and his staff on board, was sunk last night at about 8 P. M., to the west of the Orkneys, either by a mine or a torpedo.

Four boats were seen by observers on shore to leave the ship. The wind was north-northwest and heavy seas were running. Patrol vessels and destroyers at once proceeded to the spot and a party was sent along the coast to search, but only some bodies and a capsized boat have been found up to the present. As the whole shore has been searched from the seaward, I greatly fear that there is little hope of there being any survivors.

No report has yet been received from the search party on shore.

H. M. S. Hampshire was on her way to Russia.

ON MISSION AT RUSSIA'S REQUEST

Earl Kitchener was on his way to Russia, at the request of the Russian Government, to discuss important military and financial questions with Emperor Nicholas, including chiefly the supply of munitions for Russia. He intended to land at Archangel, visit Petrograd, and probably go to the Russian front.

Accompanying Earl Kitchener as his staff were Sir Frederick Donaldson, superintendent of the Royal Ordnance Factories at Woolwich and technical adviser to David Lloyd-George, Minister of Munitions; Hugh

42

James O'Beirne, former councilor of the British Embassy at Petrograd and former Minister at Sofia; O. A. Fitzgerald, Earl Kitchener's private military secretary, and Brigadier-General Ellershaw. On board the Hampshire with the British War Secretary were also a number of minor officers.

SPIES BLAMED FOR CALAMITY

In connection with suggestion that information of Earl Kitchener's movements may have been conveyed to the Germans by spies, it is interesting to note that the *Official Gazette,* on the same night on which Lord Kitchener lost his life, contained an order placing new restrictions on passengers landing at ports in the Orkney Islands, and providing that thereafter no person might land at such ports without specific permission of the military authorities at Kirkwall.

The *Daily Mail* gave prominence to the following statement:

"Earl Kitchener's intention to go to Russia was known to a great many persons in London on Thursday. It ought not to have been so known. The news of it may have reached the enemy. The public mind has been quick to associate his death with the work of spies. We have every sympathy with the demand which comes to us from many parts of the country that all alien enemies who are still at large, especially those in high places be interned at once."

The *Morning Post,* discussing the sinking of the Hampshire, said:

"Circumstances point at espionage or treachery, and the country will suspect this the more owing to the singular freedom still allowed to enemy subjects in Great Britain."

Naval officers expressed the opinion that the cruiser Hampshire must have struck a mine, as it would have to be an exceedingly lucky shot for a torpedo to get a ship with her speed and under the condition of the sea which was very rough. The Hampshire was an old boat and not fit for fleet action, but was fast enough for patrol and blockade work.

When Admiral Jellicoe's report finally was issued the fact spread about London some time before the newspapers could get into the streets. There was a crowd about the Stock Exchange which required police reserves to deal with.

NEWS RECEIVED AMID INTENSE EXCITEMENT

At the same time another mass of people was assembling about the Government offices in Whitehall. All the windows of the War Office had the curtains lowered. That confirmed the rumor beyond doubt.

Other crowds gathered around the newspaper offices; when the boys came out with an armful of extras the people fell on them and fought for the papers. In the course of the afternoon the flags on all buildings were flown at half staff.

There was an exciting scene at the close of the Stock Exchange session.

ARMY ORDERED INTO MOURNING

The King hurried from Windsor and sent for Premier Asquith when he heard the news.

A NOTABLE SUCCESS ON THE WESTERN FRONT.

The taking of the village of Loos by British Troops under heavy bombardment from the German guns.

HOODED BRITISH SOLDIERS CHARGING GERMAN TRENCHES.

Gas attacks are so frequent and deadly that every soldier carries two gas proof helmets. At the first alarm of gas he instantly adjusts his helmet, for the yellow cloud steals along the ground with great rapidity, and to breathe it means almost certain death.

By the King's command the following order was issued to the army:

The King has learned with profound regret of the disaster whereby the Secretary of State for War has lost his life while proceeding on a special mission to the Emperor of Russia.

Field Marshal Lord Kitchener gave forty-eight years of distinguished service to the State, and it is largely due to his administrative genius and unwearying energy that the country has been able to create and place in the field the armies which today are upholding the traditional glories of our empire. Lord Kitchener will be mourned by the army as a great soldier who, under conditions of unexampled difficulty, rendered supreme and devoted service both to the army and the State.

His Majesty the King commands that the officers of the army shall wear mourning with their uniforms for the period of one week. Officers are to wear crepe on the left arm of uniform and of great-coats.

HOW LORD KITCHENER DIED

Leading Seaman Rogerson, one of the survivors of the Hampshire, has furnished the following account of Lord Kitchener's last moments:

"Of those who left the ship and have survived it, I was the one who saw Lord Kitchener last," said Rogerson. "He went down with the ship. He did not leave her. I saw Captain Savill help his boat's crew to clear away. At the same time the captain was calling to Lord Kitchener to come to the boat, but owing to the noise made by the wind and sea, Kitchener could not hear him, I think. When the explosion occurred, Lord Kitchener walked calmly from the captain's cabin, went up the ladder and on to the quarter-deck.

"There I saw him walking quite collectedly and talking to two officers, all three wearing khaki. They had no overcoats on. Lord Kitchener calmly watched the preparations for abandoning the ship, which were going on in spite of the heavy sea. In a steady and orderly way the crew just went to stations, obeyed orders and did their best to get out the boats, but it was impossible.

"Owing to the rough weather no boats could be lowered. Those that were got out were smashed up at once. No boats left the ship. What people on shore thought were boats leaving were rafts. Men did get into the boats as these lay in their cradles, thinking that as the ship went under them the boats would float, but the ship sank by the head and when she went down she turned a somersault forward, carrying down with her all the boats and those in them.

"I do not think Lord Kitchener got into a boat. When I sprang to a raft he was still on the starboard side of the quarter-deck talking with officers.

"Of the civilian members of his suite I saw nothing. I got away on one of the rafts and we had a terrible five hours in water so rough that the seas beat down on us and many men were killed by buffeting. Many others died from the piercing cold. I was quite numbed and an overpowering desire to sleep came upon us. To keep this away, we thumped each other on the back, for the man who went to sleep never woke again. When men died, it was just as though they were falling asleep. One man stood upright for five hours on a raft with dead lying all around him; one man died in my arms.

"As we got near the shore the situation grew worse. The wind was blowing on-shore, the fury of the sea dashed the rafts against the rocks with tremendous force. Many were killed in this way, and one raft thrice overturned. I don't quite know how I got ashore, for all the feeling had gone out of me. We were very kindly treated by the people who picked us up. They said it was the worst storm they had had for years."

SUNK BY A MINE

An official statement of the destruction of the Hampshire contains the following account:

"The Hampshire was proceeding along the west coast of the Orkneys. A heavy gale was blowing and seas were breaking over the ship, which necessitated her being partly battened down. Between 7.30 and 7.45 P. M. the vessel struck a mine and begun at once to settle by the bows, heeling over to starboard before she finally went down about fifteen minutes later.

"Orders were given by the captain for all hands to go to their established stations for abandoning ship. Some of the hatches were opened and the ship's company went quickly to their stations. Efforts were made without success to lower some of the boats. One of them was broken in half and its occupants were thrown into the water.

"Large numbers of the crew used life-saving belts and waist coats, which proved effective in keeping them afloat. Three rafts were safely launched, and, with about fifty to seventy men on each, got clear. It was daylight up to about 11. Though rafts with these large numbers of men got away, in one case out of over seventy men aboard only six survived. The survivors all report that the men gradually dropped off, even died aboard the rafts from exhaustion and exposure to cold. Some of the crew must have perished in trying to land on the rocky coast after such a long exposure. Some died after landing."

On board the Hampshire were also a number of minor army officers, and the cruiser carried a crew of between 400 and 500 men.

At the time of the attack by a German submarine on the cross-channel passenger boat Sussex, several months previous to Lord Kitchener's death, there was a report in London that the Germans sought to sink the vessel because they had heard Lord Kitchener was on board. This report never was confirmed, but survivors of that attack admitted that a "certain high official" actually was on the Sussex. The identity of this personage was not established, but it was generally accepted that Lord Kitchener was the man.

LOSS OF THE HAMPSHIRE

The Hampshire was an armored cruiser of 10,850 tons displacement, 450 feet long, $68\frac{1}{2}$ feet beam, 25 feet draught, and an indicated horse-power of 21,508. She was launched at Elswick in 1903 and completed in 1905 at an estimated cost of $4,332,635. She was protected amidships by 6-inch armor, over the vital parts, which thinned down to two inches in other parts. Her deck was protected by armor from ¾ inch to 2 inches ·in thickness, and her bulkheads carried 5-inch armor. Her main batteries were protected by 5-inch armor. She carried four 7.5-inch, six 6-inch, twenty 3-pounders and two machine guns, with two torpedo tubes.

KITCHENER'S PLACE IN BRITAIN'S HISTORY

No doubt Lord Kitchener, who was a soldier before all else, met death as he would have chosen to meet it, in the performance of his duty to his country; but the disaster to the cruiser Hampshire was no less a tragedy of compelling horror. The great commander's life is but one of many sacrificed during the war and from the human point of view it is possible to count it as no more than the rest. Yet, however impartially pallid death may knock, he finds the conspicuous victim at the towers of kings rather than at the cottages of the poor. The loss which England suffered by Lord Kitchener's taking-off cannot be measured in words. In a sense he had fulfilled his destiny. It might even be said that he had begun to outlive his reputation. Perhaps no other man could have done what he did. To him is due the greater share of the credit for organizing the largest volunteer army which the world has ever seen. England was wretchedly unprepared in a military way for the terrible conflict thrust upon her. It was a staggering burden that Lord Kitchener had to bear. Red tape at the War Office, lack of munitions and equipment, strikes among laborers, raw troops ignorant of the very elements of military science, popular ignorance of or indifference to the titanic nature of the conflict—no wonder he made mistakes, no wonder he provoked criticism.

Yet the faith of his countrymen as a whole never wavered; and it was justified. Such an admission does not diminish the substantial service he rendered or detract from his genius. He was undeniably one of the first commanders of his time; and if in this war his duties had taken him to the field there is every reason to believe that he would again have revealed the qualities which first won him fame. No English general in the fighting line has yet surpassed or even equaled him. He had that efficiency which we have come to associate with German officers rather than with English. It was shown in his administrative work in India and Egypt as well as in his campaigns. Having formed his plans, he carried them through relentlessly, not to say ruthlessly. He could not excuse negligence nor forgive failure. He worked hard himself and expected every one else to do so. Duty controlled him, not sentiment. Such a man is bound to do great things.

CHAPTER V

OVER THE TOP AT VIMY RIDGE

THE HINGE OF THE GERMAN RETREAT—CAREFUL
PREPARATION—THE TERRIBLE GUNFIRE—OVER
THE TOP—THE FIRST AMERICAN FLAG—A GREAT
TRIUMPH AT SMALL COST—COLD STEEL WINS "THE
PIMPLE"—SMASHING THE COUNTER ATTACK—THE
FALL OF ARLEUX COMPLETES THE VICTORY. .

EARLY IN March, 1917, the Germans on the western
front south of Arras began what Berlin saw fit to call
a strategical retreat. But they were in reality forced
to take this step. The Battle of the Somme of 1916
had so bitten into their lines that their whole front
was in danger, and to save the situation a retirement
to a safer line of defence was a necessity. There was,
however, one part of their line that they had determined to hold at all cost—the twelve mile stretch of
high land between Arras and Lens. Here, the natural
strength of Vimy Ridge and the fortifications they
had constructed along its top and sides during two
and a half years of war in this region gave them a
feeling of security.

THE HINGE OF THE GERMAN RETREAT

Vimy Ridge, which had already cost thousands of
lives and had, during the progress of the war, been
captured by both French and British troops only

51

AREA OF THE FIGHTING ON THE OLD GERMAN FORTRESS FRONT, BETWEEN LENS AND ARRAS, APRIL 9 TO 14, 1917.

GERMAN ABUSE OF THE WHITE FLAG

An incident showing how a company of British soldiers were cut down by an ambushed enemy. The front rank of Germans had been firing from behind a small ridge. In apparent surrender they stood up in a long row and held up the white flag. The British advanced to receive their guns and take them prisoners, when suddenly the entire line

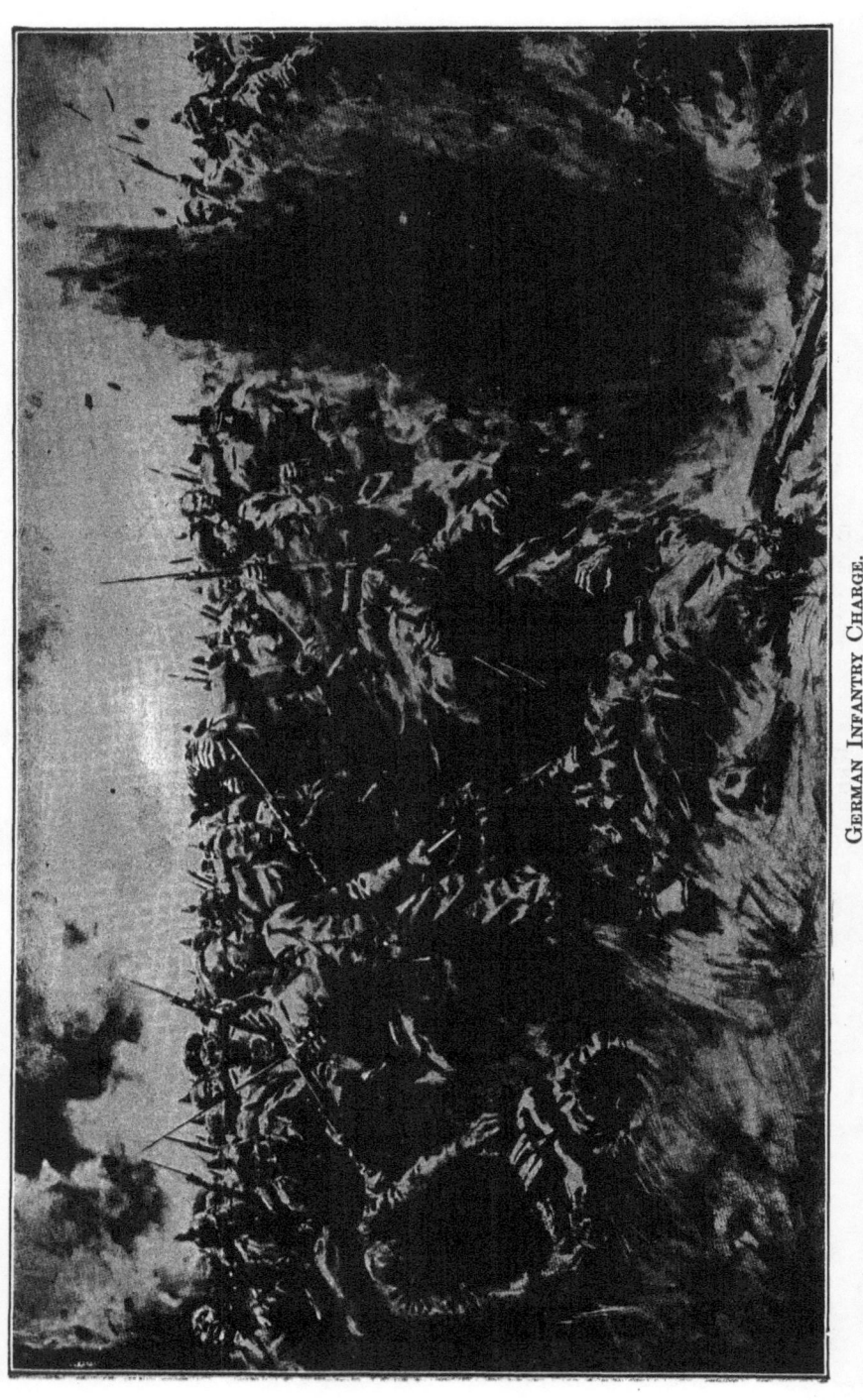

GERMAN INFANTRY CHARGE.

Everywhere along the battle front the Germans have attacked in massed formations, which give the impression of a rush of bar-
baric hordes. Impressive and terrible as is the charge shown here, the Allied artillery, land mines and hand grenades have wrought

to be lost again, is the last promontory of the range of chalk hills which extends from the North Sea to Arras. The ridge has two prolonged summits; the northern one named La Folie, after the farm that lay on its side, now plowed by huge shells and harrowed by shrapnel; the southern one called Telegraph Hill after the old semaphore post on its crest. Between these ridges, over a slight saddle in the range, ran the great Roman road that extends from Arras to Belgium. While the Germans were in full retreat destroying villages and orchards, looting and murdering with inconceivable barbarity, a strong force was left at Vimy Ridge, the hinge of the great "strategical retirement." As the Germans retired, hotly pursued by British and French troops, preparations were made for a powerful attack on Vimy Ridge and the four Canadian divisions were chosen as the spear-point of this attack.

CAREFUL PREPARATION

In the Autumn of 1916 after the Battle of the Somme the Canadians under Sir Julian Byng, who, before taking over command of them, had been in command of a British brigade at Vimy Ridge, were moved to this front. All through the weary winter the new drafts, with a stiffening of the heroes of the second and third Battles of Ypres and Courcelette, endured the hardships of trench warfare, their monotonous life relieved only by raids across No Man's Land. It was with intense relief that about April 1st they learned that a vigorous offensive against Vimy Ridge was to be made. All winter long preparations had been conducted for this attack. The gun factories of England had been working overtime and the ammunition works in England, Canada, and the United States had been turning out millions of shells daily. Vast piles of these were stationed at convenient points behind the lines, and for miles field-guns and "heavies" were almost wheel to wheel in front of the strong system of German tranches, dugouts, and wire entanglements. One detail will be sufficient to show with what thoroughness the work of preparation was done. After a battle, thirst is the most trying enemy of the soldiers consolidating the lines won and of the sorely wounded on the battlefield. To overcome this evil the Staff-Major of the Canadians, during the winter, had carefully collected all used petrol tins and by spring, behind his hut, he had assembled "a pile as large as a church." When the battle began these were filled with water and packed on mules ready to be rushed to the battlefield.

THE TERRIBLE GUNFIRE

All through Holy Week the preliminary work leading up to the Battle of Vimy Ridge—a detail of the greater and more extended Battle of Arras—went on. Guns thundered continuously against the heights, ripping holes through wire entanglements, smashing trenches and dugouts, and cutting off communication from the rear. Squadrons of British airplanes circled in the air over the ridge, photographing the German trenches and gun positions, directing the fire of the artillery and driving back or destroying every German aircraft that spread its wings above the lines. By

Saturday there was not a foot of land on the ridge but was torn by shellfire, and Thelus on the slope of Telegraph Hill immediately southeast of the Roman road had but two houses left standing. All through Easter Sunday the artillery and aircraft kept up their work and on Sunday night the troops received orders to hold themselves in readiness for an assault of the German position at 5.30 on the following morning.

OVER THE TOP

In their sodden trenches and on the wet plains the soldiers of the Canadian divisions slept a disturbed sleep. Just as the first dim light suffused the Eastern horizon they stood to arms, knee deep in mud and in a pelting rain. Suddenly the smashing roar of the "heavies" and the drumfire of the field-guns deafened their ears. In the dim distance trenches were obliterated and the very top of the ridge blown off. The Germans knew what this concentrated fire meant and frantically shot distress signals high in air. But the "heavies" were playing over the top of the ridge and the troops and supplies being rushed up by trains from Lens and Douai were prevented from reaching their objective. The rolling barrage lifted and "over the top" went the Canadians warily following in its wake. From their trenches and shell craters the distance to the ridge top was from 1,200 yards to a mile. As they advanced in three waves they were subjected to a heavy fire, especially from machine guns on the extreme left; but nothing could check them and in half an hour the front line trenches in the center of La Folie Farm

Ridge were won. But the left and right still held.
Many Germans eagerly surrendered, praying for something to eat; so intense had the fire of the past week
been that for days many of them had been without
food or drink. Some of the enemy were in deep
tunnels and as the conquering waves of Canadians
passed over them they came from their burrows and
attacked their foe from the rear with machine guns.
But these were quickly put out of action. At the
Southern end of the battleline, where a British brigade

THE FIRST AMERICAN FLAG

was assisting the Canadian division there engaged,
the fight went on. The shell-battered village of
Thelus was a hard nut to crack, but by noon the
Canadians were in its shattered streets. In the attack
on this village the first American flag used in the
Great World War was carried into action on the
point of a bayonet by a young lad from Texas who
at the outbreak of war had come to Ontario to enlist
in this struggle against militarism. The United
States had, on April 6th, declared that a state of war
existed with Germany. News of this act had reached
the front, and on the 9th this gallant young American
triumphantly bore his country's flag into battle and
gallantly fell in the moment of victory, grievously
wounded.

A GREAT TRIUMPH AT SMALL COST

By nightfall the crests of La Folie Farm Ridge
and Telegraph Hill were won and the Canadians
were gazing down the steep eastern slopes at the

"Time's Up. Over You Go."

A Canadian battalion going over the top to new triumphs. At the appointed hour the attacking force climbs out of the trench in three or more lines or "waves" and moves forward against the enemy's trenches across "No Man's Land."

PERILS OF WIRING WORK.

Frozen by the cold glare of a star-shell. Erecting barbed wire entanglements was work that could only be done at night. Even then the wiring parties were liable to discovery by enemy star-shells soaring up and revealing them to enemy machine gunners waiting to fire at any suspicious objects. When a shell burst every man "froze" hard in the position in which he was surprised, absolute

villages of Farbus, Vimy, and Petit Vimy and beyond to Bailleul, Willerval, Oppy, Arleux, and Mericourt. All their objectives had been won on schedule time excepting at one point. At the extreme north of the ridge lay Hill 145. Here a heroic band of Germans were stationed and although almost completely isolated kept up a strong resistance with machine guns. The lines won were at once consolidated and preparations made for further victories on the morrow. In this day of battle the Canadians had suffered about 2,000 casualties, and the night was spent by stretcher-bearers searching the battlefield for wounded men and rushing them back to the receiving stations. Fortunately the great majority of the wounded were "walking casualties," so that the price paid for this most striking triumph so far won in the war was insignificant.

COLD STEEL WINS "THE PIMPLE"

The morning of April 10th broke under atrocious weather conditions. During the battle of the previous day the rain of the early morning had changed to sleet and flurries of snow, but on the second morning of the fight a snowstorm was sweeping the ridge. However it in no way interfered with the work of the Canadians. Hill 145 was brought under fire at daylight and in a short time the left of the Canadian army was sweeping through the shell-splintered trees that lined its slopes. There was still another hill that needed attention. In their front was an elevation which they had christened "The Pimple." This hill was strongly held by a body of the Prussian

Guard. On the 12th the task of capturing this menacing point was allotted to the battalions that had carried Hill 145. A blinding snowstorm was raging, the slopes of "The Pimple" were a sea of mud, but at 5 A. M. the Canadians dashed forward in the face of a destructive fire and won their way to the German trenches. Now ensued a fierce hand to hand contest with the German guards. It was butt, bayonets, and boots for nearly an hour, but at length "The Pimple" was won and the garrison dead or prisoners.

SMASHING THE COUNTER ATTACK

The attack of the 10th, that placed Hill 145 in the possession of the Canadians, was followed by a counter attack by troops hurried up from Lens, but the British guns on the ridge smashed the attacking columns and the Germans retreated in disorder. On the 11th the battle continued, but for the Canadians it was largely a matter of patrol actions. Bodies of troops pushed down the eastern slopes of the ridge and gained much ground at practically no cost. On the 12th, as we have seen, the Germans were driven from their last stronghold in this quarter, "The Pimple." This was a crushing blow. They had now lost the whole ridge from the Souchez to the Scarpe and had taken from them their last hope of being able to regain the lost ground by a counter attack from the northeast. According to the Canadian War Records Office report of the engagement, it was not until the 13th that "the full fruits of victory took shape and form." Patrols could now be pushed eastward freely, only small rearguards being encountered. By nightfall the Canadian line had been extended to beyond the Vimy-Arras railway, and the villages of Willerval, Farbus, Vimy, Petit Vimy, La Chaudière, and Givenchy had been entered. In this movement the Canadian cavalry played an essential part, riding far in advance of the infantry capturing villages and gun positions—the first time in many months that cavalry had taken an active, part in battle. By no stretch of the imagination could the Germans call the retreat from Vimy Ridge and the villages on its eastern slope a strategic movement. It was a disorderly retreat and the enemy had no time to remove their guns. Thousands of rounds of ammunition were left behind and a number of uninjured guns. These were turned on the retreating foe or on batteries still holding out. In one instance the Canadian gunners using two captured guns engaged a hostile four-gun battery and "succeeded in completely silencing it with the enemy's own gas shells."

THE FALL OF ARLEUX COMPLETES THE VICTORY

On Saturday the 14th, the Battle of Vimy Ridge may be said to have ended with the dashing capture of Arleux by the Canadians. The enemy was in full retreat and he did not stop until he had reached positions beyond the range of immediate observation from the ridge. The victory was undoubtedly the most important so far won by the Allies in the war— according to Belloc "the greatest operation in the military history of England." The hinge of the Hindenburg line was captured and there was in its place an open door to the plains surrounding Douai. The British now dominated Lens, the important coal region surrounding it, and the valley of the Scarpe. The Canadians were still fighting and were forcing their way into the suburbs of Lens. But that city could be taken by assault only at a heavy price and Sir Douglas Haig was unwilling to pay the price. It could wait,—another point on the German western front was chosen for a smashing victory and the work of methodical preparation which preceded the Battle of Arras began in front of the next cluster of hills held by the Germans to the north. In this week of battle the Canadians alone captured 4,081 prisoners including 87 officers, 63 guns of all calibres, 124 machine guns, and 104 trench mortars, while their casualties barely equalled the number of prisoners taken.

CHAPTER VI

THE WORLD'S GREATEST NAVAL BATTLE

ARMAGEDDON ON THE SEA—ADMIRAL BEATTY SIGHTS
THE ENEMY—DESTROYERS OPEN ACTION—AN OLD
ENEMY ENCOUNTERED — SUPERDREADNAUGHTS
COME UP—NOTABLE DEED OF BRAVERY—FLIGHT
OF THE GERMANS—DARKNESS SAVED THE GER-
MANS—PLAYED GALLANTLY FOR HIGH STAKES.

IN THE ten years since the first "Dreadnaught" was
launched hundreds of millions of dollars have been put
into this new type of battleship, which was tried out for
the first time between the Skagerak and Kiel. Here,
on the last day of May, 1916, the greatest naval battle
in all history was fought.

The battle was fought along virtually the entire
west coast of Denmark, reaching the maximum intensity off the Horn Reef, near the southwestern extremity
of Denmark.

The German fleet, commanded by Vice Admiral
Reinhard Scheer and including at least five dreadnaughts, eight cruisers and twenty torpedo-boats and
destroyers, left the Skagerak Wednesday morning,
May 31st.

Vice Admiral Sir David Beatty, who commanded
the British cruiser squadron, had cruised many times
in the vicinity of the battlefield without succeeding in
luring the Germans from their mined waters, but on

this occasion the British seamen had an inkling that something important was about to happen.

ADMIRAL BEATTY SIGHTS THE ENEMY

Just before the conflict the battle-cruiser squadron was shoving through the water at a good twenty-five

MAP SHOWING THE SCENE OF THE WORLD'S GREATEST NAVAL BATTLE.

knots, the destroyers and light cruisers in their appointed places. The sea was smooth as a millpond. The day was warm and a slight haze hung over the water. As the official announcement put it, the visibility was low. For nearly sixteen hours the squadron steamed steadily on. Then the destroyer screen reported the presence of enemy craft, small craft, but significant perhaps of the presence of bigger ones.

DESTROYERS OPEN ACTION

A smart little destroyer action was begun, a light cruiser dashed up to assist, and soon the first phase of the battle was in full swing.

Having succeeded at length in drawing the whole German fleet out of its safe quarters, Vice Admiral Beatty, although greatly outnumbered and running heavy risks, determined to hang on grimly in order to detain the Germans in full strength. It was a daring maneuver, but the British fought doggedly and with great pertinacity, despite all disadvantages, confident that reinforcements were on the way.

For the first time since the war began the Germans stood up to Beatty and his indomitable ships, and from impressions gathered from Beatty's men who came through the fight the Germans suffered heavily during that phase. Their gunnery was good, but it was not so good as the British. It was a running fight, fought at a speed which gave the advantage to the British ships. The Lion, as on the memorable day of the Dogger Bank battle, led the line, followed by the mighty Tiger. Both performed marvels of speed, and there should be further honors for the engine-room staffs.

63

AN OLD ENEMY ENCOUNTERED

Opposite them at long range was, among others, an old enemy in the Derfflinger. In the Dogger Bank fight the Derfflinger sent a shell into the wardroom of the Tiger, and no report has been more industriously circulated among neutrals by the Germans than that the Tiger had been sent to the bottom. It was therefore with peculiar relish that the crew of the Tiger proceeded to demonstrate to their old enemy that they were very much alive.

From the Tiger there went a shell which got one of the Derfflinger's turrets and wiped out a whole gun crew. Others were planted with equally deadly effect.

The battle raged with tremendous violence. The air was filled with white-hot steel, dust and slivers, and ears were deafened with the tremendous crash and clatter of it all. Had the opposing forces remained as they were, the result was inevitable. Beatty's squadron was adding to its battle honors. Smart maneuvering, seamanship and fine gunnery were telling their tale, when another factor intervened which would have sealed the fate of the German squadrons.

SUPERDREADNAUGHTS COME UP

With the battle-cruiser squadron there had gone out from a Scottish port what in the official announcements are called fast battleships. The Warspite was one. Sister ships of the Queen Elizabeth class, the Barham Malaya and Valiant, were the others.

The battle-cruiser action was fought with the enemy lying close to neutral Danish waters, off Jutland.

Everything was going well with Admiral Beatty when the four superdreadnaughts came up, and rushed in to cut off the enemy from his southern base. Beatty was then to drive in from the northeast, and either force the Germans to shelter in neutral waters or compel them to accept the challenge of the heavy battleships. The strategy was excellent, but it was applied too late. From the south came reinforcements which provided an explanation of the reason for the Germans accepting Beatty's challenge. From the south came the major portion of the German Grand Fleet.

The Warspite got the brunt of the first attack. It is said she became isolated from her consorts, became surrounded by a half dozen ships, made a brilliant fight against impossible odds, disposed of more than one of them and by clever maneuvering showed a clean pair of heels.

NOTABLE DEED OF BRAVERY

It is this phase of the fight which will go down as one of the most gallant deeds in British naval history.

Beatty knew the risks he had to run, but he had to hold the enemy at all costs. He knew the Grand Fleet was not far behind, and he knew what it meant if he could hold on until Jellicoe arrived. What Beatty and his men went through during those hours of inferno no one but themselves can ever realize. Strong men, physically strong and strong of nerves, men who had looked death in the face in naval actions before, shuddered as they thought of it. "It was like forty thunderstorms rolled into one," said one of them. "It was as if all the ammunition in Britain and Germany had been let off in one-half an hour," said another. "It was hell," was the commonest description.

The Queen Mary was the first to go under. A great shell punched through her over her thinner armor plate. Her magazine exploded and the gallant ship, almost the latest British battle-cruiser, buckled up and sank like a stone. The Indefatigable went next. It was not war, it was murder. German shells with poisonous gas exploded, filling the ships with their fumes and doing great havoc among the crews at their stations. Annihilating blasts from twelve-inch guns took the vessels like a tornado, wiping away men like flies.

The Lion and the Tiger, maneuvering with marvelous skill and speed, kept their heads up and their face to the enemy. Then Admiral Hood, with the Invincible, Inflexible and Indomitable, arrived from another station. With them came armored cruisers of the second cruiser squadron, including the Warrior, Defence and Black Prince, three gallant ships resting from their labors. The gallant and brilliant admiral put up a great fight against heavy odds, but fate was against him, and the Invincible, with a deadly torpedo in her hull, followed her sister ships to the bottom.

FLIGHT OF THE GERMANS

From four o'clock in the afternoon for something like four or five hours the battle-cruisers, with the four battleships, had engaged and held the enemy. Their part was finished, and never was more welcome the aid which came in the shape of the Grand Fleet. With its arrival the balance of strength passed from the Germans. For a time they fought a running-away fight. They turned heel and made the shortest possible road for home. After them went the whole might of the British fleet and chased them home in the darkness to their lair, and adding in the process to the already heavy losses they incurred in the earlier phase of the battle.

DARKNESS SAVED THE GERMANS

The difficulties of the pursuers were increased by the growing darkness, and only eleven of all the British battleships managed to get a shot at the enemy before he had reached a place where Admiral Jellicoe deemed it would be foolhardy to attempt to dig him out. Admiral Jellicoe remained in the immediate neighborhood for twenty-four hours afterwards, waiting to give the Germans an opportunity of renewing the action on a grand scale, but nothing of the kind was attempted.

Under cover of night the German torpedo flotilla made an attack on the British fleet, but only succeeded in increasing their total of torpedo-boat losses.

The loss of life was very heavy, as dreadnaughts of the Warspite, Queen Mary, Kaiser and Lutzow classes have each a complement of upward of one thousand men, and most of the other warships, excluding destroyers, reported sunk carried each about seven hundred men. On the cruisers and destroyers whose loss was admitted in London there were all together about six thousand men. On the German vessels admitted lost there were probably two thousand two hundred men. Parts of the crews of the British ships were rescued by the Germans but, according to Berlin, of the seven hundred and ninety men aboard the Indefatigable all but two lost their lives. Fishing craft made their way into Dutch ports laden with dead and wounded.

A British official statement showed that with a few exceptions all the officers on the Invincible, Queen Mary, Indefatigable, Defense and Black Prince were lost. All officers of the Warrior except one were saved.

On the German side the only definite statements as to loss of life were that three hundred and forty-two of the three hundred and sixty-one men in the crew of the cruiser Frauenlob perished; and that ninety-nine out of one hundred and two lost their lives on the torpedo-boat V-28. There were no estimates of the number of wounded, although these soon began to pour into London and were to be found on practically every vessel putting into Dutch and Danish ports.

The outstanding impression gained from a visit to east coast ports, to which some of the ships engaged in the Jutland battle returned, was that the result was much more satisfactory than the first official announcement led one to expect. It was an interesting experience to get into touch with men who had been through the fight. There was no pessimism there. They were firmly convinced the British warships gave as good and better than they got. They said that if the full tale of the German losses were told by Berlin the battle would be hailed as one of the finest actions of the British fleet.

Whatever the German mission in the daring enterprise directed northward—whether to break out into the Atlantic or to carry out another raid on the British coast—it failed. The British battle-cruisers met them,

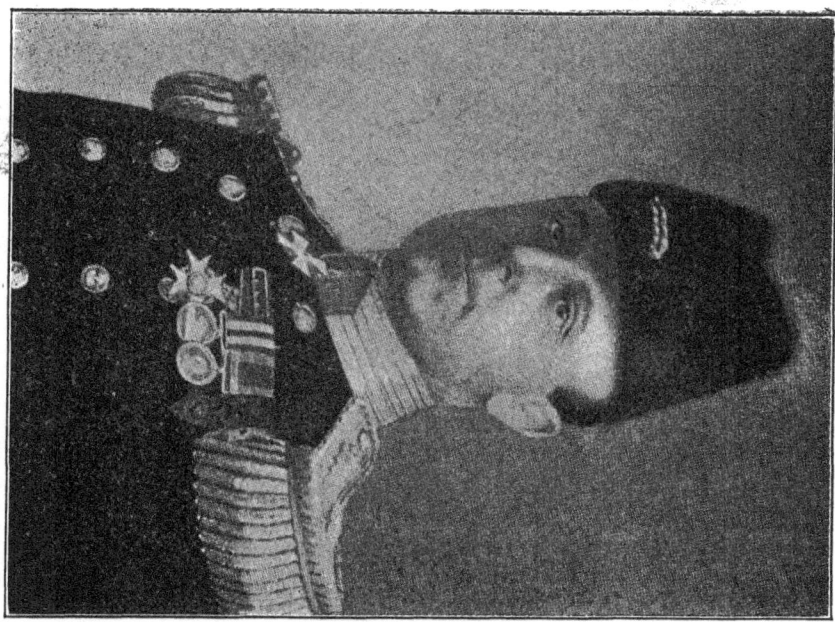

ADMIRAL SIR JOHN RUSHWORTH JELLICOE
First Sea Lord of the Admiralty.

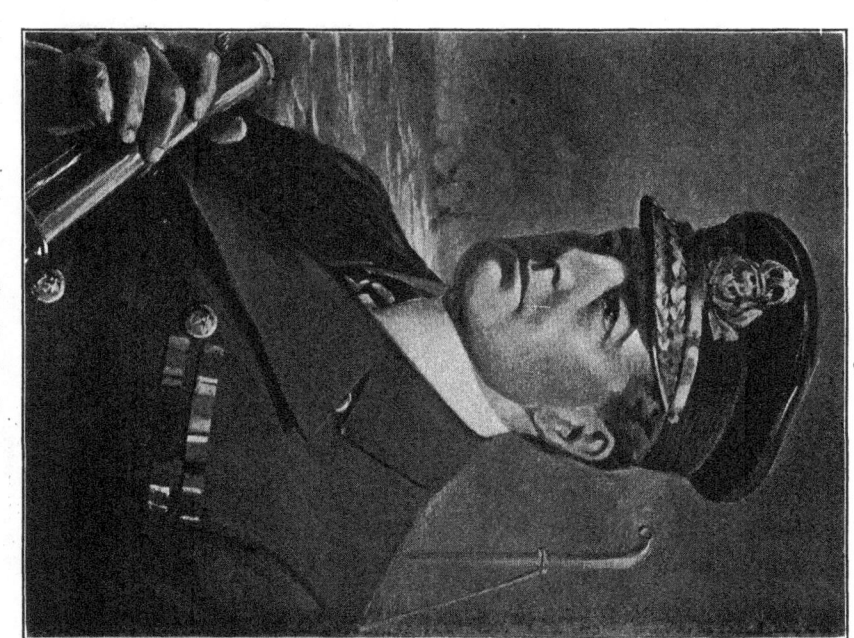

ADMIRAL SIR DAVID BEATTY
Commander-in-chief of the British grand fleet.

Photo by Brown Bros.

THE GREAT NORTH SEA BATTLE.

This picture shows the sinking of a German light cruiser during the great battle off the coast of Jutland In the back-

encountered the first of their battle-cruiser squadrons, gave them a merciless pounding and then when enemy reinforcements came held up the German battle fleet in a gallant but hopeless fight until the Grand Fleet arrived. Then the Germans, having bravely engaged a weaker force, bolted for home.

PLAYED GALLANTLY FOR HIGH STAKES

Vice Admiral Beatty could have avoided the fight, but it is not the British way. He knew the Grand Fleet was speeding to his aid. He knew that to engage the whole might of the German fleet was to sacrifice ships and men; but he knew also the high stakes he played for, and right gallantly did he do his part. Three of his battle-cruisers went to the bottom with their intrepid crews. Others came in bearing their battle scars, but Beatty's reputation stands untarnished.

CHAPTER VII

BRITAIN'S NAVY SAVES CIVILIZATION

TASKS OF THE NAVY—SUBSIDIARY DUTIES—COM-
MERCE PROTECTION — SAFEGUARDING THE FOOD
SUPPLY—PATROLS—CLOSING THE ENEMY'S PORTS—
TRANSPORT OF AN EXPEDITIONARY FORCE—MAIN
OBJECT DESTRUCTION OF THE ENEMY'S FLEETS—
GENERAL CONSIDERATIONS—CONDITIONS OF A GER-
MAN INITIATIVE.

THE THREE principal duties that the British Navy
was called upon to perform at the outbreak of the war
were, first, the securing of the seas for the passage of
British ships, especially the safeguarding of the food
supply and the transport of troops; secondly, the
destruction by capture of hostile shipping with the
object of depriving the enemy of his supplies and
rendering futile all projects of invasion; thirdly, the
destruction of the hostile fleets and naval bases.
It was obvious that the last, for practical purposes,
would comprehend the other two; but it was not so
certain that opportunities would offer for its accomplishment. In the meantime it was to be hoped
that the British fleet, by reason of its superior battle
strength, would be able either to force the enemy to
fight or to retire to his ports, and so afford an opportunity for its numerous cruisers to carry out the
all-important work of safeguarding their own and
destroying the enemy's commerce.

SUBSIDIARY DUTIES

The wide development of the closely-knit system of commercial protection, and the effect of the offensive action of British cruisers upon the enemy's shipping, were perhaps not quite adequately realized by the British public at the commencement of the war. A few days after the beginning of hostilities nearly every street corner in London displayed a placard bearing the legend, "Olympic saved by British cruiser." The suggestion was that this was an isolated occurrence deserving of special and emphatic notice. As a matter of fact, this was merely one of many such accidents; or, to speak more correctly, it was an incident of the general situation at sea that the Olympic should have come under the direct convoy of the particular cruiser which saved her. What really saved her, what rendered her practically safe from one end of the voyage to the other, was the fact that the British and French cruisers guarding that particular line of communication were numerous, vigilant, and well-nigh ubiquitous; whereas, the enemy's cruisers seeking to assail that line were few and for the most part fugitive.

COMMERCE PROTECTION

This incident has been used to illustrate the true nature and the immense significance of what our forefathers called "the sea affair." From the moment when war became imminent the main British Fleet melted into space. Nothing was seen of any part of it, except of the flotillas patrolling British coasts. Nevertheless, although it was invisible, there was never in the world's history a more sudden, overwhelming, and

71

all-pervading manifestation of the power of the sea than that given by the British Fleet, admirably seconded by that of France, in the first fortnight of the war. The rarity of properly-called naval incidents might have left a different impression. It might well have seemed that the Fleets of France and England had done nothing. As a matter of fact, they had done all in their power, and that all was stupendous. Those weeks saw German maritime commerce paralyzed; British maritime commerce fast returning to normal conditions in all the outer seas of the world, and not even wholly suspended in the area of immediate conflict. Nay, more, it was already seeking new realms to conquer—realms left derelict by the collapse of the maritime commerce of the enemy. That is, in a few words, the long and short of it. Prize Court notices of German and Austrian merchantmen captured on the seas or seized in British ports appeared daily in increasing numbers. Side by side with them appeared the familiar notices of the regular sailings of British liners for nearly all the ports of the outer seas. The newspapers published daily accounts of the new avenues of trade, manufacture, and transport opened up by the collapse of the enemy's commerce, and of the enterprise with which British merchants and manufacturers were preparing to exploit them.

CLOSING THE ENEMY'S PORTS

How it stood with Germany on the other hand there is unimpeachable German authority to show. At the outbreak of the war the *Vorwärts*, the German Socialist organ, said:

72

DESTRUCTION OF THE SEA-RAIDER "EMDEN"

The Australian cruiser "Sydney" came up with the German cruiser "Emden," off the Cocos Keeling Island on November 9, 1914. After the "Sydney" had fired six hundred rounds of ammunition and covered fifty-six miles in maneuvering, she forced the "Emden" to run ashore owing to the breaking of her steering gear. The German vessel ran at a speed of nineteen knots upon the beach, the shock killing the man at the wheel. (From a dired camera picture

SINKING OF THE GERMAN CRUISER "BLUECHER."

This most dramatic photograph of the Great North Sea Battle, in which the British fleet was victor, January 24, 1915, shows the death agony of the German cruiser "Bluecher" just as she turned turtle and sank. The ship is shown lying on her side, with her machinery and armament shot into masses of twisted iron and steel, great fires raging forward, amidship and aft. The officers and men can be seen ranged along the side of the vessel; many of them have slipped into the water and may be seen swimming about. (*Copyright by the International News Service.*)

"If the British blockade took place, imports into Germany of roughly six thousand million marks ($1,500,000,000) and exports of about eight thousand million marks ($2,000,000,000) would be interrupted—together, an oversea trade of 14,000 millions of marks ($3,500,000,000) This is assuming that Germany's trade relations with Austria-Hungary, Switzerland, Italy, Belgium, Holland, Denmark, Norway, and Sweden, remained entirely uninfluenced by the war—an assumption the optimism of which is self-evident. A glance at the figures of the imports shows the frightful seriousness of the situation. What is the position, for example, of the German textile industry if it must forego the imports of oversea cotton, jute, and wool? If it must forego the 462 millions ($115,000,000) of cotton from the United States, the seventy-three millions ($18,250,000) of cotton from Egypt, the fifty-eight millions ($14,500,000) of cotton from British India, the one hundred millions ($25,000,000) of jute from the same countries, and further, the 121 millions ($30,250,000) of merino wool from Australia, and the twenty-three millions ($5,750,000) of the same material from the Argentine? What could she do in the event of a war of longer duration without these raw materials which in one year amount in value to 839 millions ($207,500,000)?

"It may also be mentioned that Germany received in 1913 alone from the United States about 300 millions ($75,000,000) of copper, and further that the petroleum import would be as good as completely shut down. The German leather industry is largely dependent on imports of hides from oversea. The Argentine alone sent seventy-one millions ($17,750,000) worth of hides. Agriculture would be sensibly injured by the interruption of the exports of saltpetre from Chile, which in 1913 were of the value of not less than 131 millions ($32,750,000).

"The significance of an effecuve blockade of German foodstuffs is to be seen in the few following figures: The value in marks of wheat from the United States is 165 millions ($41,250,000), from Russia eighty-one millions ($20,250,000), from Canada fifty-one millions ($12,750,000), from the Argentine seventy-five millions ($18,750,000)—372 millions ($93,000,000) from these four countries. There will also be a discontinuance of the importation from Russia of the following foodstuffs: eggs worth eighty millions ($20,000,000), milk and butter sixty-three millions ($15,750,000), hay thirty-two millions ($8,000,000), lard from the United States worth one hundred and twelve millions ($28,-000,000), rice from British India worth forty-six millions ($21,500,000), and coffee from Brazil worth one hundred and fifty-one millions ($37,750,000) should be added to the foregoing. No one who contemplates without prejudice these few facts, to which many others could be added, will be able lightly to estimate the economic consequences of a war of long duration.

"If the British blockade took place," said the *Vorwärts*, and it dwelt on the consequences of a war of long duration. The British blockade was actually taking place at the moment these words were written, though it was not called by that name for reasons which need not here be examined. Acting together with the hostility of Russia, which closed the whole of the

Russian frontier of Germany to the transit of merchandise either way, the control of sea communication established by the fleets of Britain and France had already secured the first fruits of those consequences of a war of long duration on which the *Vorwärts* dwelt with such pathetic significance. Those consequences were bound to be continuous and cumulative so long as the control of sea communications remained unrelaxed. The menace of the few German cruisers which were still at large was already abated. Already its bite had been found to be far less formidable than its bark. War premiums on British ships at sea were falling fast. German maritime commerce was uninsurable, and in fact there was none to insure. Its remains were stranded and derelict in many a neutral port. One of the greatest dangers, in the opinion of some eminent authorities the most serious danger, that Britain had to guard against in war was already averted, or would remain so as long as the control Britain had established over her sea communications continued to be effective. This was the first result of British naval preparations, the first great manifestation of sea power.

TRANSPORT OF AN EXPEDITIONARY FORCE

But there was a second result far more dramatic than the first, and not less significant in its implications, nor in its concrete manifestation of the overwhelming power of the sea. The whole of the Expeditionary Force, with all its manifold equipment for taking and keeping the field, had been silently, secretly, swiftly, and safely transported to the continent without the slightest show of opposition from the Power which thought itself strong enough to challenge the unaggressive mistress of the seas. "Germany," says the Preamble to the Navy Law of 1900, "must possess a battle fleet of such strength that even for the most powerful naval adversary a war would involve such risks as to make that Power's own supremacy doubtful." Such a war had now been forced upon Britain, and one of its first accomplished results had been the entirely successful completion of an operation which, if the enemy had deemed British naval suprem- acy even so much as doubtful, he might have been expected to put forth his uttermost efforts to impeach. That Germany declined the challenge was a proof even more striking of the power of superior force at sea than the action of the British Navy upon the trade routes of the world.

MAIN OBJECT DESTRUCTION OF ENEMY'S FLEET

The third task of the Navy was the destruction of the hostile fleet. However great might be the imme- diate consequences of command of the sea, these advantages did not constitute the final and paramount end at which Britain should aim. That end was the overthrow of the enemy's fleets at sea. Britain could only wait until the enemy gave her the opportunity, but then Britain must make the best of it. The essential thing is always that if and when the enemy comes out in force he may be encountered as soon as may be in superior force, and forthwith brought to decisive action in a life-and-death struggle for the supreme prize of all naval warfare. Nothing can be further from the purpose of a superior navy than to keep the enemy's fleet penned up in his ports. "I beg to inform your Lordship," wrote Nelson in 1804, "that the port of Toulon has never been blockaded by me; quite the reverse—every opportunity has been offered to the enemy to put to sea, for it is there that we hope to realize the hopes and expectations of our country and I trust they will not be disappointed." But how if the enemy will not put to sea with his battle fleet? Then Britain could only wait, and in the meanwhile use her best endeavors to parry his sporadic acts of aggression and to give him as much more than he gets as she could manage. The *rationale* of this type of naval warfare—the type most likely to prevail between two belligerents, one of whom is appreciably stronger in all the elements of naval force than the other—is expounded as follows in Thursfield's book on "Naval Warfare":

"The weaker belligerent will at the outset keep his battle fleet in his fortified ports. The stronger may do the same, but he will be under no such paramount inducement to do so. Both sides will, however, send out their torpedo craft and supporting cruisers with intent to do as much harm as they can to the armed forces of the enemy. If one belligerent can get his torpedo craft to sea before the enemy is ready, he will, if he is the stronger of the two, forthwith attempt to establish as close and sustained a watch of the ports sheltering the enemy's armed forces as may be practicable; if he is the weaker he will attempt sporadic attacks on the ports of his adversary and on such of his warships as may be found in the open. . . . Such attacks may be very effective and may even go so far to redress the balance of naval strength as to encourage the originally weaker belligerent to seek a decision in the open. But the forces of the stronger belligerent must be very badly handled and disposed for anything of the kind to take place. The advantage of superior force is a tremendous one. If it is associated with energy, determination, initiative, and skill of disposition no more than equal to those of the assailant, it is overwhelming. The sea-keeping capacity, or what has been called the enduring mobility, of torpedo craft is comparatively small. Their coal supply is limited, especially when they are steaming at full speed, and they carry no very large reserve of torpedoes. They must, therefore, very frequently return to a base to replenish their supplies. The superior enemy is, it is true, subject to the same disabilities, but being superior he has more torpedo craft to spare and more cruisers to attack the torpedo craft of the enemy and their own escort of cruisers. When the raiding torpedo craft return to their base, he will make it very difficult for them to get in and just as difficult for them to get out again. He will suffer losses, of course, for there is no superiority of force that will confer immunity in that respect in war. But even between equal forces, equally well led and handled, there is no reason to suppose that the losses of one side will be more than equal to those of the other; whereas if one side is superior to the other it is reasonable to suppose that it will inflict greater losses on the enemy than it suffers itself, while even if the losses are equal the residue of the stronger force will still be greater than that of the weaker."

GENERAL CONSIDERATIONS

One must not assume, when the enemy does not come out, that the menace and display of superior force in every direction have acted as a deterrent and quelled initiative to the point of paralysis. No such hypothesis can be entertained on the merely negative evidence of a situation still obscure and undeveloped. It is far more likely that the enemy is preparing some great *coup* requiring him to keep all his available forces in hand and to use them when the time comes with the utmost vigor and determination. At any rate, that is what the British Fleet had to be prepared for. It must stand at all times in full readiness to parry the blow, whensoever and wheresoever it is delivered; to anticipate it, if it may be, and in any case to meet the enemy with a vigor, determination, and skill not inferior to his own, and with a force so superior as to crown the British arms with victory. No nation which wages war on the seas can hope for anything more or better than a decision sought and obtained on terms such as these.

CONDITIONS OF A GERMAN INITIATIVE

In the circumstances which prevailed in the war in 1914, it was peculiarly probable that the German Navy would, at the outset, show an apparent feebleness of initiative. In connection with the first great German Navy Bill of 1900 it was laid down that the German Navy need not be as strong as that of the greatest naval Power "for, as a rule, a great naval power will not be in a position to concentrate all its forces against us." Actually it was the German Navy that was at the outset least able "to concentrate all its forces" against "the greatest naval Power." The German Fleet was compelled at first to be a two-fold containing force—against a formidable military adversary in the Baltic and against an overwhelmingly superior naval adversary in the North Sea. To go out to fight in the North Sea might be to uncover the Baltic coasts of Germany to the assaults of Russia from the sea and thereby greatly to facilitate the military operations of Russia in that region.

CHAPTER VIII

VERDUN: THE GREATEST BATTLE IN HISTORY

STRATEGIC SITUATION OF VERDUN—AN UNEX-
AMPLED HUMAN FLOOD—A HALF-MILLION MEN IN
HIDING—A GLIMPSE OF THE GERMAN FRONT—
GATHERING FOR THE DEFENSE—A BURIED FORT-
RESS—A FRENCH CHARGE—DESPERATE HAND-TO-
HAND FIGHTING—BUILDING FORTIFICATIONS UNDER
FIRE—THE HEROIC BLASTING CORPS—ADVANCING
LIKE MOLES—FIGHTING WITH UNFIXED BAYONETS
—THE COURSE OF THE BATTLE—THE TURN OF
THE STRUGGLE.

THE CITY OF VERDUN itself, in spite of its high, encircling walls and citadel covering an immense subterranean town, has no longer any military significance; it owes its importance to the belt of detached forts which, spreading over a circuit of forty-eight kilometers (thirty miles), was intended to render stationary an entire army, to insure the investment of the city in view of a regular siege. General Séré de Rivières, the creator of the intrenched camp, estimated that it would take four army corps (160,000 men) to besiege it. But the attack had forces of a very different character and means of action which Séré de Rivières could not have guessed at, and was made at first on a sector of about seven kilometers (four and a half miles), that is to say, on one-seventh of the line of forts.

Séré de Rivières held that an offensive against Verdun must of necessity be directed against the works on the left (west) bank of the Meuse, which makes a curve from Dugny, down stream, to Charny, up stream; he thought that the line of the ridges of the Meuse was too strong to be the object of an attack, and considered hazardous any operations on the central sector. Yet this sector was the one attacked.

AN UNEXAMPLED HUMAN FLOOD

The enormous human flood, rushing upon a narrow stream, is without example in history. It explains the successive withdrawals of the Allies' troops up to the limits fixed by Séré de Rivières for the advanced defenses toward Douaumont, limits which the enemy did not quite reach.

The vast scale on which the battle of Verdun was fought requires perspective to be understood. It will be useful at this juncture to place on record some of the most vivid and stirring descriptions by eye witnesses. And first it may be well to get a panoramic view of the whole battleground as seen by a British correspondent with the French Army.

"Throughout the vast amphitheater, he writes, "twenty miles wide and ten miles deep, not a single human being was visible aside from the little group of officers around me. Over there to the northwest lies the broad dark bank of Malancourt Woods, which we know to be a busy hive of Bavarian and Württemberg grenadiers, sharpshooters, flame-squirters and gunners.

Beyond them on the horizon the queer cone of Mont-faucon, long the Crown Prince's headquarters, is plainly visible. Passing eastward the two French bulwarks of Hill 304 and Dead Man's Hill block the view northward. Then across the wide and still flooded valley of the Meuse we scan a higher and more deeply indented plateau directly north of Verdun.

"Through field-glasses we can follow every rise and fall of these forever famous slopes—the long shoulder of Talou in the bend of the river and behind in the Caures Woods, where the first avalanche fell, the Poivre-Louvemont block, which runs back north-eastward, and then to our right the Haudromont Woods, Douaumont Plateau, and Vaux Woods of bloody memories, and in the whole panorama there is not visible a single human being. In the hollow behind us lies the ancient City of Verdun under a cloud of purple smoke that tells the old tale of Teutonic vengeance.

A HALF-MILLION MEN IN HIDING

"Overhead several aeroplanes are soaring, and west-ward I can count five of the anchored observation balloons called sausages. Before us a network of communication trenches climbs up the open slopes, and, although invisible, we know it continues through coppices and forest patches toward the summits where geyser-like eruptions of earth mark the main stress of the artillery duel. The crest of Douaumont, in par-ticular, is continually shattered into a crown of cloud and around it the succession of gun flashes might be mis-

83

taken for heliograph signals were it not for the accompanying muffled roar of explosions.

"It is what they call a calm day on the front, but the sunshine deceives us when it gilds this scene into a semblance of peace. Before and around and behind us, hidden away underground and in less elaborate cover, half a million men armed with every deadly device modern science can suggest lie in wait, each host watching for any sign of weakness on the part of the other. The preparations for a tomorrow, wrapped in mystery save to a few chiefs themselves, never for a moment cease.

"Under its empty and smiling surface the bastion of Verdun is a vast human ant-hill seething with multifarious labor. The war has gone underground again in this sector, and that is the mark that the French victory is definitive."

A GLIMPSE OF THE GERMAN FRONT

A glimpse from the German front is given by an American:

"The important village of Esnes, lying south of Hill 304, is already suffering under the hail of German shells. There is something awe-inspiring, even stupefying, about this battle, raging from Fort de Belleville to Hill 304, particularly when one remembers that this is only one of three sectors of the battle for Verdun.

"The unequivocal emptiness and loneliness of vast battlefields give you a creepy sensation as of phantom armies fighting. Their presence, as I gazed today, was betrayed only by frequent fitful flashes of flame like fireflies on a summer night. One could see miles of these fireflies, despite the bright sunlight, each marking the mouth of a gun. They made one realize more vividly than figures possibly could how thickly the iron girdle tightening about Verdun is studded with German batteries. Not a man, horse, wagon, or motor could be seen moving about that fire-swept zone bounded by the rival artilleries.

"The only human touch was a giant yellow Cyclop's eye, blinking at us—a German heliograph in action. Turning about, we saw its mate winking back, but the theme of its luminous dialogue was not for publication.

"Even more fascinating than the unique bird's-eye view of the Verdun panorama was the grandeur of the battle symphony, surpassing anything ever heard before on any front. A deep, low, and unchanging basic leitmotif was played by the distant guns from as far away as the Argonne at the right and from Douaumont and the east and south fronts of Verdun to the left. Varying melodies, rising and falling in pitch, intensity and volume, were played by the nearby guns."

GATHERING FOR THE DEFENSE

That same night a writer on the French side witnessed the silent gathering of forces to defend Avocourt Wood, and between dawn and noon the fierce engagement in which the German attack was defeated. Mark how his words bring the stirring picture before the mind's eye:

"At midnight the concentration is completed and the reserves are in their appointed places. Is the cannonade fiercer or less fierce? I cannot say. The noise is so deafening that I have lost the power of

85

judging its intensity. I cannot even distinguish the explosion of the shells that fall near the listening post where we are sheltered. Only when they burst, the post and the earth around it shudder like a ship at full speed. Their explosion is but a minor note in the hurricane of sound. The French artillery is 'preparing' Avocourt Wood, where the German infantry is massed in force.

"The searchlights throw patch after patch of trees into bright relief, like the swiftly changing scenes of a cinematograph. Through binoculars one has a frightful vision. Not a yard of ground fails to receive the shock of a projectile. The solid earth bubbles before my eyes. Trees split and spring into the air. It is a surface earthquake with nothing spared, nothing stable. The Germans have abandoned the outlying brushwood and are huddled in the inmost recesses of the woods, but the French artillery pursues them pitilessly.

A BURIED FORTRESS

"Nearly three hundred yards from the rim of brushwood the defenders—Prussians and Bavarians—have constructed a kind of redoubt which they expect to be the rock on which all attacks will break. The searchlights reveal their fortress; it is a wall of earth and tree trunks and seems half buried in the ground. Now and again in the patches of brightness one sees tiny shadows running, falling, rolling over or flitting from trunk to trunk, like frightened night creatures surprised by sudden daylight. It is the soldiers of the Kaiser trying vainly to escape from the rain of death.

"Dawn breaks, and the searchlight beams vanish as the first grayness of morning rolls away night's curtain from the battlefield. We shiver in our blockhouse; is it cold, or nervousness? The officers around me say the moment has come. It is an agony of expectation; the attack is about to break.

"A shrill ringing startles every one. The Captain springs to the telephone, listens for an instant, and then cries: 'All goes well!' in a firm voice. He hangs up the receiver, murmuring, 'They're off.'

"Our guns still thunder, but they have lengthened their range, and the line of smoke-blobs opposite leaps forward toward the horizon. Suddenly the mitrailleuses set up a rattle right in front of us. They are firing from our front-line trenches in a concave around the eastern corner of Avocourt Wood.

A FRENCH CHARGE

"Some one grabs my arms and points northward. Down the slopes of Hill 304 a multitude of nimble figures are rushing westward. Their numbers increase; armed warriors spring from the ground, as in the old Greek legend. 'Our men,' says the officer beside me. It is the soldiers of France at the charge.

"For a while they are sheltered from the German fire by a swelling billow of ground. They mount its crest and pour headlong downward. Now the pace is slower; they advance singly or in scattered groups— crawling, leaping, running, each man taking advantage of every atom of cover. The leaders have reached the first trench that lies across the path; but, see! they pass it without hesitating, as though it were a tiny brook.

"I learned afterward that a hundred tree trunks had been arranged like bridges all along the trench.

"Now the whole mass is across and we can see what cunning brain has planned the attack. For the charging men go straight forward like runners between strings, leaving open lanes along which their comrades can still fire upon the defenders.

DESPERATE HAND-TO-HAND FIGHTING

"At last the edge of the woods is reached, and the rattle of the mitrailleuses ceases. It is hand-to-hand now in that chaos of storm-tossed earth and tortured trees. Rifles are useless there; it is work for bayonet or revolver, for butt and club, or even for fists and teeth. Corpses are everywhere; the men fall over them at each step—some to rise no more—until the bodies form veritable heaps, among which the living fight and wrestle."

The fiercest struggle on the sector between Douaumont and Vaux was that which raged around Caillette Wood. Eye witnesses describe it as one of the most thrilling episodes in the whole great series of battles. The importance of the position lay in the fact that if the Germans could keep it they could force the French to abandon the entire ridge. The heroic deeds on both sides in the French recapture of this ground are narrated by a staff correspondent in the following remarkable story:

"The Germans had taken Caillette after twelve hours' bombardment, which seemed even to beat the Verdun record for intensity. The French curtain fire had checked their further advance, and a savage

AMERICAN TROOPS MARCHING TO THEIR CAMP IN FRANCE.

A long column of "Sammees" just off the transport marching through a historic town "Somewhere in France" on their way to a training camp preparatory to taking their places in the front line trenches.

GERMAN PRISONERS IN AN AMERICAN CAMP IN FRANCE.

American soldiers keeping a watchful eye on their captives. The "Boches" are useful as laborers in American Training Camps behind the lines and as a rule are very glad to exchange the life of the trenches for the safe, if monotonous life, of a prisoner.

countercharge in the early afternoon had gained for the defenders a corpse-strewn welter of splintered trees and shell-shattered ground that had been the southern corner of the wood. Further charges had broken against a massive barricade, the value of which as a defense paid good interest on the expenditure of German lives which its construction demanded.

"A wonderful work had been accomplished that Sunday forenoon in the livid, London-like fog and twilight produced by the lowering clouds and battle smoke. While the German assault columns in the van fought the French hand to hand, picked corps of workers behind them formed an amazing human chain from the woods to the east over the shoulder of the center of the Douaumont slope to the crossroads of a network of communication trenches, six hundred yards in the rear.

BUILDING FORTIFICATIONS UNDER FIRE

"Four deep was this chain, and along its line of nearly three thousand men passed an unending stream of wooden billets, sandbags, chevaux-de-frise, steel shelters, and light mitrailleuses, in a word, all the material for defensive fortifications, like buckets at a country fire.

"Despite the hurricane of French artillery fire, the German commander had adopted the only possible means of rapid transport over the shell-torn ground, covered with débris, over which neither horse nor cart could go. Every moment counted. Unless barriers rose swiftly the French counter-attacks, already massing, would sweep the assailants back into the wood.

"Cover was disdained. The workers stood at full height, and the chain stretched openly across the hollows and hillocks, a fair target for the French gunners. The latter missed no chance. Again and again great rents were torn in the line by the bursting melinite, but as coolly as at maneuvers the iron-disciplined soldiers of Germany sprang forward from shelters to take the places of the fallen, and the work went apace.

"Gradually another line doubled the chain of the workers, as the upheaved corpses formed a continuous embankment, each additional dead man giving greater protection to his comrades, until the barrier began to form shape along the diameter of the wood. There others were digging and burying logs deep into the earth, installing shelters and mitrailleuses, or feverishly building fortifications.

"At last the work was ended at fearful cost, but as the vanguard sullenly withdrew behind it, from the whole length burst a havoc of flame upon the advancing Frenchmen. Vainly the latter dashed forward. They could not pass, and as the evening fell the barrier still held, covering the German working parties, burrowing like moles in the maze of trenches and boyaux.

THE HEROIC BLASTING CORPS

"So solid was the barricade, padded with sand bags and earthworks, that the artillery fire fell practically unavailing, and the French General realized that the barrier must be breached by explosives as in Napoleon's battles.

"It was eight o'clock, and already pitch dark in that blighted atmosphere, as a special blasting corps, as devoted as the German chain workers, crept forward toward the German position. The rest of the French waited, sheltered in the ravine east of Douaumont, until an explosion should signal the assault.

"In Indian file, to give the least possible sign of their presence to the hostile sentinels, the blasting corps advanced in a long line, at first with comparative rapidity, only stiffening into the grotesque rigidity of simulated death when the searchlights played upon them, and resuming progress when the beam shifted; then as they approached the barrier they moved slowly and more slowly.

"When they arrived within fifty yards the movement of the crawling men became imperceptible; the German starshells and sentinels surpassed the searchlights in vigilance.

"The blasting corps lay at full length, just like hundreds of other motionless forms about them, but all were working busily. With a short trowel each file leader scuffled the earth from under the body, taking care not to raise his arms, and gradually making a shallow trench deep enough to hide him. The others followed his example until the whole line had sunk below the surface. Then the leader began scooping gently forward while his followers deepened the furrow already made.

ADVANCING LIKE MOLES

"Thus literally, inch by inch, the files stole forward, sheltered in a narrow ditch from the gusts of German mitrailleuse fire that constantly swept the terrain. Here and there the sentinel's eye caught a suspicious movement and an incautiously raised head sank down, pierced by a bullet. But the stealthy mole-like advance continued.

"Hours passed. It was nearly dawn when the remnant of the blasting corps reached the barricade at last, and hurriedly put their explosives in position. Back they wriggled breathlessly. An over-hasty movement meant death, yet they must needs hurry lest the imminent explosions overwhelm them.

"Suddenly there comes a roar that dwarfs the cannonade, and along the barrier fountains of fire rise skyward, hurling a rain of fragments upon what was left of the blasting party.

"The barricade was breached, but seventy-five per cent of the devoted corps had given their lives to do it.

"As the survivors lay exhausted, the attackers charged over them, cheering. In the mêlée that followed there was no room to shoot or wield the rifle.

FIGHTING WITH UNFIXED BAYONETS

"Some of the French fought with unfixed bayonets like the stabbing swords of the Roman legions. Others had knives or clubs. All were battle-frenzied, as only Frenchmen can be.

"The Germans broke, and as the first rays of dawn streaked the sky, only a small northern section of the wood was still in their hands. There a similar barrier stopped progress, and it was evident that the night's work must be repeated. But the hearts of the French

A GIGANTIC FRENCH HOWITZER.

One of the mammoth guns built by France to batter the German positions. It is mounted on a specially built railway car and may be readily moved from one firing position to another.

AN ATTACK ON THE GERMAN TRENCHES

Under cover of artillery fire and a storm of bullets from rifles and machine guns in the woods forming the background the charge is made on the angle of the trench.

soldiers were leaping with victory as they dug furiously to consolidate the ground they had gained, strewn with German bodies as thick as leaves.

"Over six thousand Germans were counted in a section a quarter of a mile square, and the conquerors saw why their cannonade had been so ineffective. The enemy had piled a second barrier of corpses close behind the first, so that the soft human flesh would act as a buffer to neutralize the force of the shells."

THE COURSE OF THE BATTLE

Enough has been said to indicate the overwhelming fierceness of the struggle. Never before in history have men fought one another with greater ferocity. It remains now only to chronicle the course of the battle. This can be done briefly, for names and dates incidental to the struggle as a whole count for little.

The French Staff reckoned that Verdun would be attacked when the ground had dried somewhat in the March winds. It was thought that the first enemy movement would take place against the British front in some of the sectors of which there were chalk undulations, through which the rains of winter quickly drained. The Germans skilfully encouraged this idea by making an apparent preliminary attack at Lihons, on a five-mile front, with rolling gas-clouds and successive waves of infantry. During this feint the veritable offensive movement softly began on Saturday, February 19, 1916, when the enormous masses of hostile artillery west, east, and north of the Verdun salient started registering on the French positions. Only in small numbers did the German guns fire, in order not to alarm their opponents. But even this trial bombardment by shifts was a terrible display of power, calling forth all the energies of the outnumbered French gunners to maintain the artillery duels that continued day and night until Monday morning, February 21st.

THE TURN OF THE STRUGGLE

The attack continued unabated until midsummer without the loss of the main objective point. Gradually the offensive weakened in the face of one of the most determined defenses in history, and then came a lull. On October 24, 1916, a sudden and brilliant French attack took the Germans completely by surprise. At no one point did they succeed in stopping the impetuous rush, and in three hours the French regained territory that had cost the Germans many months of patient effort to capture, including such positions as Douaumont Fort and Thiaumont Work, which in the past had been won and lost repeatedly. They smashed the German line north and northeast of Verdun over a front of four and one-third miles, penetrating it along its entire length, in the center gaining a distance of nearly two miles. The French rapidly consolidated their gains and it became more than ever clear to the world that the Germans could never take Verdun.

CHAPTER IX

FIGHTING THE SUBMARINE

SECRET METHODS OF DESTROYING SUBMARINES—
THE FISHERMEN'S IMPORTANT PART — SPOTTING
THE SUBMARINE WAVE—USING THE MICROPHONE—
LIEUTENANT WENNINGER'S ADVENTURES—CAUGHT
IN A STEEL NET — EXPLOITS OF BRITISH SUBMA-
RINES—HUNTING SUBMARINES WITH SEAPLANES—
—A BOUT WITH A ZEPPELIN.

IT IS DOUBTFUL whether the principal secret means used by the British for combating submarines will ever be revealed. What they purchased by long, arduous, and terrible experience will not be discussed for the enlightenment of foes, but will remain rather a hidden fund of working knowledge to be handed down in training with other valuable traditions of the Senior Service.

The new art of submarine hunting was developed with deadly passion after the sinking of the Lusitania. With their wide experience in delivering submarine attacks in the Heligoland Bight, the Dardanelles, and the Baltic, the British officers knew so fully what the submarine could do, that they were able to devise ways of combating the class of vessels they used so well. These Sea Lords also called men of science to their aid, with the result that strange devices of many kinds were constructed. Many hundreds of small, fast, handy vessels were added to the Grand Fleet in order to extend and accelerate the operations against U-boats. It was during this great increase in the number of British warships that one grand and happy discovery was made. The long-trained officers and men could be relied on to carry out their varied tasks with fine skill and flexibility of mind. But long-service naval men were not sufficient in number to man the immense number of small craft added to the Home Fleet. Even the Royal Naval Reserve was not large enough to supplement the ordinary ratings; for ships were increasing in number, with swarms of new light cruisers, destroyers, and little motor-vessels of terrific speed. Many fishermen, therefore, were called up for service.

THE FISHERMEN'S IMPORTANT PART

The fishermen were the least experienced of all the British fighting seamen. They began on the humble but dangerous job of trawling for mines and keeping clear the fairways to England's ports. The noble courage of these men was displayed in the Dardanelles and on the Belgian coast, where they coolly fished up enemy mines under heavy fire from hostile land-batteries. This is only what one would expect from the best deep-sea fishermen in the world. After years of perilous endurance, by which they won food for the nation at the risk of their lives, they were not the men to flinch from the work of saving the Fleet. At first, however, their labor was rather of a passive kind. Few of them could take part in the active work of sinking enemy ships. Yet by an extraordinary vicissitude of circumstances, these quiet, steady drudges of the

Grand Fleet became the most deadly active fighters of the modern scientific school. They it was who developed submarine killing into a science that staggered and daunted the most adventurous spirits of the German Navy.

SPOTTING THE SUBMARINE WAVE

The most important beat along the English shores was held by a band of fishermen, with a naval officer partly directing them and partly learning from them. Manning a small squadron of fishing boats, they watched for German submarines as they used to watch for a school of mackerel. There was a certain wave for which the look-outs always searched. No matter at what depth an 800-ton submarine traveled, it produced a curious wave on the surface of the water, and the trained eyes of the fishermen were able to discern this wave with exceptional quickness. Men with a naval rating knew how to handle guns, and intricate machinery, but deep-sea fishermen, who had searched the waters since boyhood for schools of fish, had a quicker knack of spotting a submarine wave. This disturbance was often very small, especially when the water was broken or choppy; but the fishermen on Beat 1 did not let many underwater craft go unperceived and unattacked. There was that in their hearts that quickened their eyesight. One of them said that almost every time when he was watching the water he seemed to see the floating hands and drifting hair of the women and children who were drowned in the Lusitania, A cold, sustained Berserker rage against the assassins of the sea nerved the fishermen to their unending, weary, deadly task. Men of slow minds, patient and quiet in trouble, and hammered by a hard seafaring life into a sort of mild endurance, it took much to rouse them into lasting passion; but their ordinary quality of patience became terrible when it was bent by the hands of dead women and children to the work of retribution. But it may be said that any U-boat they perceived far under the water seldom rose again. It was trapped—the great, steel-built, mechanical fish—before it could rise and use its weapons; and as the trap closed round it, something came down through the waves and cut the great steel fish in two. There was no fight, though the German Marine Office often complained that British fighting vessels caught their unsuspecting submarines on the surface and shattered them with quick-firing guns. This was not how the work was carried out, though there may have been some artillery duels in the opening phase of the campaign. The main work of destruction was done by "fishing," with fishermen in fishing boats matched against an unseen submarine that did not even show its periscope.

USING THE MICROPHONE

One of the methods by which the U-boats were hunted down was devised by Mr. William Dudilier, who invented a mechanism for the Allies by means of which a submarine traveling fully submerged could be located within a radius of twenty miles. The mechanism consisted of a microphone which picked up the hum of the electric motors used in a submerged submarine. There was a sound-sieve which kept out all other noises coming through the water—the vibration of engines, and beating of propellers in passing vessels—so that only the whine of electric motors used in submarines was picked up.

Two detectors were submerged at a considerable distance apart, and made so that they could be turned to get in direct line with the submarine. An increase in the volume of sound received told when the detector was being turned in the right direction; and when both detectors were fully responding, a rapid and simple trigonometrical calculation gave the position of the submarine. The tract of water covered by the detector had been mapped out beforehand in numbered squares, known to all the guardships. At the signal, they steamed to the square the submarine was approaching, and there began their trapping and killing operation, while the detectors and the detecting officers kept them informed of all further movements by the hidden German war-shark.

There is no special information concerning the methods by which the enormous transport of troops and war material across the Channel was protected against the German submarines. All that we know is that this protection became stronger as the war went on, the mining of the hospital-ship Anglia being a disaster of a rare kind. According to an enemy source, the "Vossische Zeitung," the French and British naval authorities closed the narrow seas by huge steel nets, sometimes forty miles long, in which hostile submarines were entangled until their crews were suffocated. The enemy's account, which we give for what it is worth, is as follows:

A net has been drawn from Dover to the French coast opposite, and another from Portland Bill, near Weymouth, to Cape La Hague. Between these two nets there is a space of over one hundred and fifty miles, sufficient for all transport service. Further, a net extends from the Mull of Kintyre in Scotland to Ireland, and another from Carnsore Point in Ireland to St. David's Head in South Wales, in order to protect the Irish Sea.

To allow the passage of trading vessels and the warships of the Allies, these nets have been fitted with gates which can be shut and opened, like pontoons. These passages are known only to the British Admiralty, and are often changed. Since submarines can descend to three hundred feet under water, these nets reach to sea-bottom, as the Channel is never deeper than two hundred and sixty-five feet.

The upper edge of the net is fastened to buoys, and both upper and lower edges are anchored so that storms and ebb and flood tides cannot change the position of the net or damage it in any way. The anchor chains are also so shortened that the buoys are a few feet below the level of the water, consequently the submarines cannot see the nets either above or below the water. If one of them plunges into the net, it becomes entangled and so damaged that it is an easy prey to the enemy.

LIEUTENANT WENNINGER'S ADVENTURES

Small nets were largely employed by both British and German surface vessels engaged in hunting underwater craft. From Lieutenant Wenninger, commander of the German submarine U17, we have a lively account of his escape from the British net throwers off the East Coast. He left his base early one morning, and passed into the North Sea with hull submerged and periscope awash. On looking through the periscope he could see a red buoy behind his boat. He looked again ten minutes later, and saw the buoy still at the same distance behind him. He steered to the right,

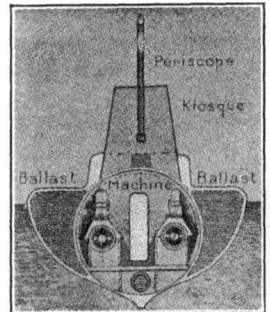

THE GERMAN SUBMARINE AND HOW IT WORKS.

Upper left picture shows a section at center of the vessel. Upper
right view shows the submarine at the surface with two torpedo tubes
visible at the stern. The large picture illustrates how this monster attacks
a vessel like the Lusitania by launching a torpedo beneath the water while
securing its observation through the periscope, just above the waves.

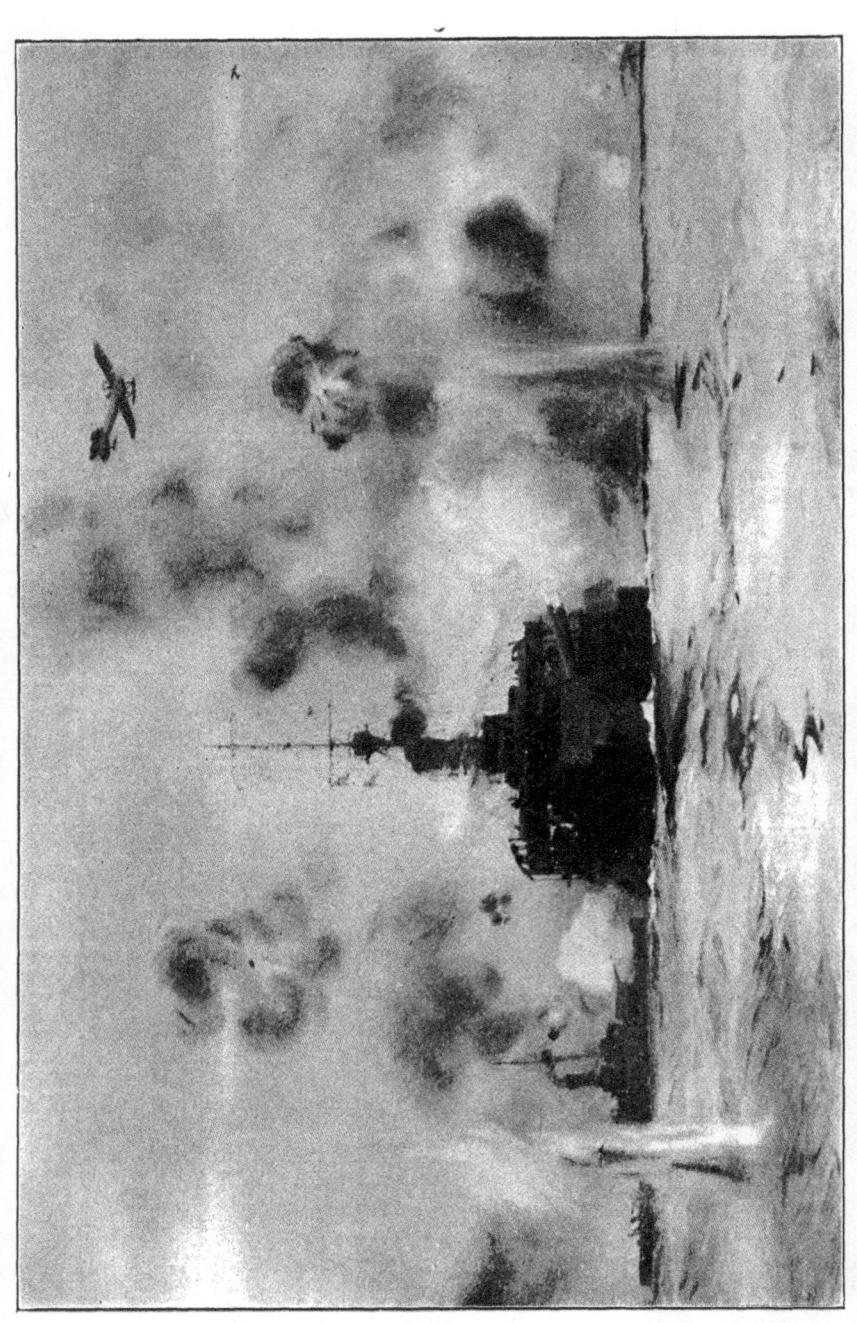

A Battle of Four Elements.

British monitors shelling the German land batteries near Nieuport. German submarines were actively engaged in trying to torpedo these monitors and the British monoplane was useful for giving the range to the ship and reporting the accuracy

he steered to the left, but the buoy followed him. He descended deep into the water, and then rose until his periscope was again awash, but still saw the buoy floating on the surface above him. He had caught the chain of the buoy and was dragging it along with him, and a small British patrol-boat had observed the strange voyage of the buoy, and was intently following it, and calling with her wireless.

Wenninger then revealed the fact that the German submarines hunted down British ships by means of microphone detectors, which have a longer range than the periscopes; for he said that his sounding apparatus indicated that two steamers were approaching, and soon afterwards he saw five British torpedo-boats coming from the north. The German officer first increased the speed of his vessel with the intention of attacking the foremost torpedo craft. But he noticed that they were ranging themselves around him in a menacing semicircle; and, giving up the idea of an attack, he dived as deep as possible, and began to crawl away. Suddenly it seemed that an accident had happened to his boat. It rolled in a most alarming manner, and rose and sank uncontrollably, as though the steering-gear was out of order.

CAUGHT IN A STEEL NET

But Wenninger discovered that it was not his steering-gear which was wrong, but his boat. One of the hunting torpedo-boats had steamed in front of him and had dropped a steel net. The U-boat had driven into it, and had got entangled in an almost hopeless manner. For an hour and a half the netting carried

101

the submarine with it, and though Wenninger made every effort to get clear, pumping up and down, and trying to work under the net, it was all in vain. His boat was always dragged back. He then resolved to increase the weight of the submarine as much as possible, and attempt to tear through the netting. He was fortunate in having pumped in about six tons of water when he started. He now filled all the tanks to their limit, and drove clear of the netting. He then descended as low as he could; and with his menometer marking thirty meters, he stayed under for eighteen hours, but when at last he rose, his menometer still showed thirty meters, and his compass and rudder also refused to work. Moreover, the torpedo-boats were still watching close above him. Down he went again to the bottom of the sea for another six hours, by the end of which time he had repaired his steering-gear, and had got his compass to work. Once more he lifted his periscope, only to bring a vigilant torpedo-boat charging straight at him. So he went again to the bottom for two hours, and at night managed to crawl away unobserved.

Lieutenant von Hersing had a somewhat similar adventure in a British net on his way to the Mediterranean and his victories over the Triumph and the Majestic.

EXPLOITS OF BRITISH SUBMARINES

British submarine boats also had some horrible escapes from German nets. The Germans used aircraft to spot submerged boats. One of these was seen from above when she was lying in the mouth of a German river. There was only five feet of water over her conning-tower, so that even a torpedo-boat would strike her while steaming over. The British commander thought that all was lost, for he heard the rasp of a wire trawl sweeping over his hull. But to save the nerves of his men he turned on a gramophone, which made a noise covering the deadly outside sound. Happily the wire trawl did not catch on the boat, and after conducting the search in a most thorough but fruitless manner, the Germans went away and in due course the submarine got home.

In another case a British submarine ran her nose into a German net, and rose to the surface so that the entanglement could be cut away. But as soon as she rose, down fell an aerial bomb. A Zeppelin was waiting above the net, while calling with her wireless for destroyers to come and finish the British vessel. Escaping the bombs, the entangled submarine descended very carefully and slowly, in order that the net should not get more closely wrapped around her. The British commander wriggled and maneuvered his vessel, listening for the scrape of the steel links on his hull, and guessing blindly at the results of all his workings. At last he drew quite clear of the web of death, and sat his boat on the bottom of the sea and thought out the next move. His problem was to decide whether it would be better to push away under water and warn other British submarines of the snare, or wait until the German destroyers arrived in answer to the call of the Zeppelin, and attack them when they thought they had an easy victim still tangled up in the net. He resolved to try for the double event. When his sound detectors told him that there were four destroyers searching above him, he rose, and going towards the sound of the nearest screw, got a torpedo home on one of his enemies and crumbled her up. He then dived and waited, following the sound of the next destroyer that came to take the damaged vessel in tow. Again the British submarine rose, and with her last torpedo she smashed up the second destroyer. Then she went on to the rendezvous, and reached it in time to warn other British underwater craft.

HUNTING SUBMARINES WITH SEAPLANES

A good deal of the submarine hunting was done by British seaplanes and German Zeppelins. British naval airmen who flew above the water seeking for U-boats running awash or partly submerged, had two striking successes.

On August 26th, 1915, Squadron-Commander Bigsworth, who had previously distinguished himself by bombing a Zeppelin that raided Ramsgate, swooped down on a German submarine which he had spotted off Ostend.

The U-boat turned her gun on him while he was maneuvering for position, and the German shore batteries tried to bring him down by a tempest of shrapnel. But with great coolness and skill, Squadron-Commander Bigsworth descended to 500 feet, and after several attempts to get a good line over the zigzagging enemy boat, he mastered her movements and dropped his bombs with shattering effects.

Then, on November 28th, 1915, Flight-Lieutenant Viney, accompanied by a brilliant French lieutenant,

104

SUBMARINE HUNTING.

A small naval dirigible used for scouting by the British Navy. Under the cigar-shaped balloon is swung an aeroplane chassis equipped with powerful motors and steering apparatus, together with a light gun.

Hide and Seek in the Baltic.

A Zeppelin flying over a British submarine in the stormy sea.

the Comte de Sinçay, attacked another enemy submarine off the Belgian coast.

Lieutenant Viney, as pilot, maneuvered the machine and got it in line over the U-boat, and the Comte de Sinçay, as bomb-dropper, launched the missiles which destroyed the hostile vessel.

A BOUT WITH A ZEPPELIN

On the other hand, a British submarine submerged near the German coast, came up for air and found a Zeppelin waiting for her.

The monster airship was hovering so low down that her immense shining belly shut out the sky when the astonished British officer looked up. She launched her bombs at high speed, but by happy chance the E-boat had come to the surface beneath the harmless end of the aerial leviathan. Moreover, the airship had to work against a strong wind, and could not therefore quickly get her stinging end over the British submarine, which was widely dancing about on a rough sea. Meanwhile, the gun was manned by a sailor, who, though half-drowned in the breaking seas and washed about like a rag, clung on to his gun and got in a few shots between the walls of water that broke over him. He ripped a large patch out of the Zeppelin, and she made away with a list on her; but turned up a fortnight later with a new bright piece of covering on her port side. The shells supplied at that time to British submarines were apparently not powerful enough to smash a Zeppelin.

CHAPTER X

HOW THE CONQUEST OF THE AIR REVOLUTIONIZED WARFARE

THOSE WHO less than half a dozen years ago, crowded to the flying meetings and watched with fascination those gallant pioneers of aviation—the Wrights, Bléroit, Hubert Latham, Bertram Dickson, Colonel Cody, and the rest—disporting themselves in space, little guessed that they were assisting at the development of a science which was calculated to affect war more deeply than any invention since the magazine rifle. For the aeroplane has revolutionized warfare. Its effect has been more far-reaching than even the most sanguine supporter of the new arm ever dared to prophesy. Future wars can never be carried on without aeroplanes.

Curiously enough, however, its usefulness has not laid along the lines foretold by its disciples in the past. The areoplane has not taken the place of troops as a weapon of attack. Its enormous importance lies in its functions as a scout. It has done away forever with "the fog of war." It has become the eyes of the army. By means of it the commanders, working undisturbed with their maps and telephones and wireless at the headquarters far in the rear, are able to spy out the enemy's movements, to see deep back into the enemy's country

BEFORE A GREAT ATTACK

When military operations are in progress, the activity in the air increases. At such a time it is essential for the army command to be kept exactly and promptly informed of the precise strength of the enemy at given points, and of the location and disposition of his reserves. Every move is preceded by days of incessant flying on the part of the airmen reconnoitring or raiding strategic points in the enemy lines. Once the move has started, in addition to the aeroplanes which are out from dawn to dusk "spotting" for the guns, others are despatched on bombing expeditions against the enemy lines of communication, to destroy the railway, to blow up trains and bridges—in short, to do everything possible to delay the bringing up of reinforcements.

Finally, the aeroplane has come to be regarded as the most efficient defense against hostile aircraft. Therefore, aeroplanes are employed day after day to chase off the enemy airmen who sally forth over the lines on reconnaissances or bombing raids. In 1915, London awakened to the fact that the aeroplane, properly utilized, is a more effective source of protection

107

against Zeppelin raiders than any number of anti-aircraft guns, and on the rare occasions that hostile airships ventured forth over the towns and villages in the British zone of operations in France and Belgium, the British aeroplanes drove the invader off before he had time to inflict any great damage.

It was the British military airmen who discovered Von Kluck's famous swing-round from his march on Paris to the southeast, and by their timely intimation of this change of direction enabled the Allies to make in season those dispositions which inflicted on the Germans the great decisive defeat of the war.

MASTERY FROM THE BEGINNING

These were the early days of the war, but, though the British airmen were almost in the learning stage, they showed themselves the possessors of all that infinite resource and glorious courage which still distinguish them now that they have perfected and mastered the whole theory of aviation in war. Thus in September, 1914, a pilot and observer of the Royal Flying Corps were forced by engine trouble to land in the enemy lines. They sprang out of their machine and bolted for cover to a small wood. The Germans lost no time in possessing themselves of the British aeroplane, but failed to find the prisoners, who eventually managed to creep away under cover of darkness to the steep banks of the Aisne. Here they cast away their Flying Corps field-boots, and, descending to the water, swam across in the dark, and reached their aerodrome in safety, but barefoot.

A little later one of the most successful British airmen

108

was out scouting in a single-seater monoplane when he came across a German machine. Being alone he had no rifle, so promptly maneuvered his monoplane so as to get in a revolver shot at the enemy. As he was mounting above the German, the German observer winged him with a well-aimed rifle shot. The Briton never lost his presence of mind, but turned and flew for home, landing in the British lines, close to a motor-ambulance, which carried him off to the nearest dressing station.

A THRILLING AERIAL COMBAT

The importance of the position of the propeller in an enemy machine is seen in the following account of a thrilling aerial combat which took place between a British and a German airman on the Aisne. A British airman, who was flying a speedy scout, caught up with a German biplane of the "pusher" type (*i. e.* with the propeller behind the driving seat), which he recognized to be an Otto machine. At first sight, therefore, he was able to make two important observations—namely, that he had the advantage of speed, and that his adversary, owing to the position of his propeller, could not fire from behind. The Briton had two rifles clamped down one on either side of his engine, and at once started out after the enemy, taking good care to keep well in the latter's wake. At sixty yards' range he opened fire without any apparent result; then, as his speed was bearing him past his opponent, he turned and came back and gave the Boche the contents of the other rifle. The German wavered and began to descend. The British airman's rifles were empty.

He was alone. He had no one to reload. Depressing the elevating plane, he planed down at a dizzy angle, and was thus able to take his hands off his steering wheel for a moment and recharge his weapons. The rifles jammed, but the airman managed to cram four cartridges home, and loosed them off at the stern of his adversary, who a minute later disappeared in a swelling cloud-bank. The Briton instantly dropped speedily down through the sky after him, but in the clear azure below could see no trace of his enemy, who must have come to earth in the French lines over which they had been maneuvering.

FRIGHTFULNESS PREFERRED BY GERMANS

At Bailleul on October 21st, 1914, a German airman dropped a bomb on the hospital. The projectile had a so-called "sensitive" fuse—that is to say, a fuse that would make it explode on impact. The shell burst accordingly as it went through the roof, and the greater part of the force was expanded in mid-air in one of the wards which forty patients had just left. A solitary patient remained, and he was wounded.

On the same day two German airmen who were brought down with their aeroplanes in the British lines were made to cut a very sorry figure. Their machine fell into a part of the line held by the Indian troops. On searching the machine the British officers found large numbers of circulars, written in very faulty Hindi, inciting the Indians to mutiny, and announcing that the Caliph had proclaimed the Jehad, or Holy war. The German airmen watched with amazement the British officers distributing these circulars to the Indian troops who, to the further stupefaction of the discomfited Boches, laughed with childish glee at the clumsy grammatical mistakes of the German Orientalist who had composed the proclamation. For a time the Germans were extremely uncomfortable, for they were apprehensive as to the penalty for their violation of The Hague Convention by inciting belligerent troops to mutiny. However they suffered no harm, but they undoubtedly received an unforgetable lesson on Great Britain's method of Imperial administration.

On November 1st the German Emperor was given an ocular demonstration of the prowess of the British airman, which he is not likely to forget to the end of his days. The Emperor had been visiting Thielt, in Belgium, where the German General Headquarters were then established. There is every reason to believe that his Majesty was in the General Staff building, when a British airman created something like a panic by suddenly appearing from the clouds and dropping bombs into the middle of a knot of motor-cars assembled outside. By way of retaliation the Germans bombarded Furnes from the air on the following day, in the belief that President Poincare was in the place on a visit to the Belgian lines.

The British success at Neuve Chapelle was largely due to the invaluable co-operation of the military air service with the Staff. It was the British airmen who were in the main responsible for the selection of the slope running from the village of Neuve Chapelle to the Aubers-Fromelles ridge as the most suitable spot for a thrust at the enemy line. They ascertained the weakness of the Germans at that point and were able moreover, to undertake that a series of carefully-prepared and daringly-executed air raids on important places on the German lines of communication would give the British sixty-six hours in which to make good any advantage they might gain before the enemy could bring up reinforcements.

THREE WEEKS OF SUCCESS

During the fighting that took place in the spring and summer, the Second Battle of Ypres, the British offensive on May 9th against the Fromelles ridge, the operations in the Festubert region and about the ruined Château of Hooge, the aeroplanes continued to play their part quietly, modestly, usefully. But it was in the great Franco-British advance on September 25th that the airmen on the British front again had a great opportunity for showing what they had learned in thirteen months' active service. They availed themselves of the opportunity to the full, and once more earned the admiration of their enemy and the warm eulogy of their commanders.

Probably all records for air mileage per day were eclipsed by the Royal Flying Corps in the three weeks or so preceding the advance against Loos on September 25th, 1915. The weather was by no means invariably favorable, but, notwithstanding this, the British airmen were out daily on reconnaissances of the enemy trenches, watching for any indication of the Boches being aware of the great events taking place, or of taking measures to meet the "big push." On more than one occasion British aeroplanes remained for two hours at a stretch over the German lines, sometimes

112

hovering at no greater altitude than seven thousand feet, the low-lying clouds preventing reconnaissance from anything like a safe distance above the enemy anti-aircraft batteries.

The great offensive was preceded by air attacks on the German railway communications south of Lille, the routes by which they would naturally bring reinforcements from Belgium. Events subsequently showed that these systematic air raids materially delayed the arrival of reinforcements to stem the collapse of the German front line under the sledge-hammer blows struck by the British First and Fourth Corps. On September 23d, two days before the day fixed for the attack, a German goods train was wrecked on the railway near Lille, and the line torn up in several places by bombs dropped from our aeroplanes. On the following day the railway was damaged in three places, while on the morning of the attack, despite hazy weather, the British airmen sallied forth once more and bombed a train rushing up troops to the Loos region, damaging three coaches, and afterwards derailing a goods train and tearing up the railway line at three points.

On the day after the attack, when the British troops were well through the German front line, and looked as though they would get to Lens, one of the British airmen appeared over the station of Loffre, east of Douai, two most important German military centers, and dropped a bomb on a troop train there. As the airman sped away he noticed that the German soldiers were swarming out of the train, and were gathering with a number of railway officials about the wrecked carriages. This airman must have remembered the feat of his comrade-in-arms at Courtrai during the Neuve Chapelle affair, for he turned back, and, gliding down to only about five hundred feet above the ground, unloosed a 110-pound bomb, which he carried slung beneath his machine, into the midst of the group.

TWENTY-SIX BRITISH WINS

On the same day the engine and six coaches of a troop train were derailed by aerial bombs dropped on the railway at Rosult, near St. Amand, on the line from Valenciennes to Orchies. Probably the most destructive raid of the British flying men, however, was the air attack on the new railway station at Valenciennes, a railway junction of vital military importance to the enemy, as here the lines from Brussels and Maubeuge meet with the lines going out to Lille, Cambria, Tournai, and Douai, the great military supply depôts in the northern part of the German western front. That the Britons were not permitted to accomplish these fine feats unopposed is shown by the circumstance that in the single week preceding the British offensive there were no less than twenty-seven fights in the air between British and German machines, all of which save one, terminated in favor of the British. One German machine was definitely known to have been wrecked.

Every time an aeroplane went out on duty over the British lines on the western front its occupants braved death in half a dozen forms. The one thought inspiring every member of the Royal Flying Corps was to make his report—that is to say, to accomplish his mission successfully and return home to submit the results to headquarters. As the aeroplane hovered out over the German lines the German anti-aircraft batteries spat out their pear-shaped globes of pure white smoke with the characteristic "pom—pom—pom," a sound which will haunt forever the memory of every man who has served in the trenches on the western front. The German firing-line machine-guns and rifles poured their stream of lead upwards against the invader in the sky, but the pilot kept his aeroplane steadily on its course with one thought uppermost—to make that report.

MODESTY OF THE BRAVE

There are dangers in flying quite remote from war, those defects of the engine or in construction which no amount of care can guard against with absolute certainty. To these must be added the ever-present risk that a rifle bullet or the merest splinter of shell may, all unknown to the pilot, inflict irreparable injury on a vital part of the machine which will reveal itself at a critical moment in his flight, perhaps when he is assailed in the air by two or three hostile aeroplanes. Death from machine-gun, rifle, or shell fire in the air, death on the cruel earth many thousand feet below, wounds, capture—these are the risks which confront every member of the Royal Flying Corps as he fares forth on his frail bark of canvas, wood, and metal over the tortuous scars in the earth's surface marking the belligerent trench lines. But such was the spirit of the Royal Flying Corps—part and parcel, be it said, of the spirit of the British Army in the field—that the British airmen counted these risks as nought, so be it they might "make their report."

Thus it is that the annals of the Royal Flying Corps in this war may be said to be the most amazing record of thrilling adventures which the world has ever known. The rules of the corps prevent the names of the heroes of some of the most fantastic of these experiences from being given, but this rule may be relaxed in the case of three gallant airmen who made the supreme sacrifice of their lives in the country's service. They are Rhodes-Moorehouse, V.C.; Mapplebeck, D.S.O.; and J. Aidan Liddell, V.C.; all of whom were killed flying.

"Eye-Witness" made Briton ring with the heroism of Rhodes-Moorehouse. While on reconnaissance work he sustained a terrible wound from a shrapnel which burst close beside his machine and maimed him in an appalling way. Nevertheless, he fulfilled his mission, and then turned his machine for home, and landed at his point of departure with a grim jest on his lips at the expense of himself for the horrifying nature of his injuries. Before he would consent to be attended by the doctor, he insisted that he must "make his report." That was his honorable epitaph: "He made his report," for when the doctors came to him he was past human aid.

Captain Aidan Liddell, a comparative newcomer to flying, came from a famous Highland regiment. At the beginning of August, 1915, he was piloting his machine on a strategical reconnaissance in Belgium in the heart of the enemy's country when a high-explosive
116

shrapnel from a German anti-aircraft gun burst right over his machine. His leg was simply riddled with bullets, and all but severed. The pilot lost consciousness on the spot and collapsed over his steering-wheel, while, to the horror of the observer, the machine dived nose foremost earthwards. The jerk jammed Liddell hard between the steering-wheel and the sides of the driving-seat, while it flung the observer between the machine-gun and the struts, fortunately enough, as it proved, for the aeroplane proceeded to turn a complete somersault. Luckily it was at a great height when the mishap occurred, and it thus had time to right itself.

Liddell regained consciousness as the machine regained a horizontal position, Faint as he was with the loss of blood—he had some fifty separate wounds in his leg—he turned the machine round and made off straight across country for a Belgian aerodrome which he knew to be his nearest haven. He knew that he could not last very long, so would not waste time by climbing out of range of the enemy guns, but headed straight for the Belgian lines. He made a good landing at the flying ground, and said to those who ran forward to greet him: "You must lift me out. If I move I am afraid that my leg will drop off."

This brave man died in hospital a week or so afterwards without living to receive the Victoria Cross which was laid on his bier in recompense for his deathless endurance.

MAPPLEBECK'S MEMORABLE EXPLOIT

Lieutenant Mapplebeck, who was killed while flying a new machine in England, was the hero of one of the most remarkable adventures of the war. He was shot down on a reconnaissance flight one day in the neighborhood of a large town in the German lines. He was able to make a landing, but as his engine was so badly damaged he could not hope to get away, he concealed himself, abandoning his aeroplane to the enemy. Presently German troops arrived, and started with loud hallo to search for the enemy airman, whom they knew must be somewhere in the vicinity.

They searched in vain. This remarkable young man, who spoke English, French, Flemish, German, and Dutch with equal fluency, managed to procure civilian clothing, and for about a week actually mixed with the German soldiers in the town, and even went so far as to attend their sports. The town was covered with placards announcing the flight of a British airman, and threatening dire penalties on whomsoever should venture to harbor him. Mapplebeck eventually succeeded in making his way through Belgium into Holland, doing thirty miles a day, a noteworthy performance, seeing that, as the result of an accident, one of his legs was shorter than the other. In a month he was flying at the front again.

EFFECTS OF BRITISH ASCENDANCY

The tenacity and fearlessness wherewith British airmen engaged and pursued any hostile machine they encountered gave the Germans a very healthy respect for their aerial prowess. For many months the ascendancy established by British fliers over the enemy was so complete that the German airman seldom waited to engage battle in the air, but made for home as soon as it appeared that the advantage was not immediately and obviously on his side. The British airman on the contrary, was not only always ready for a fight, but looking for a chance to close with the enemy, and destroy him in the air or drive him to a forced landing.

One day in October, 1915, a British aeroplane with pilot and observer sighted on patrol duty two German machines approaching from the eastward—that is to say, from the enemy's country. They let the first German machine come within fifteen yards, and then opened with their machine-gun. The German did not wait to reply. He hurriedly dived for the earth at a very steep angle. The Briton did the same, the pilot firing at the enemy as long as he had a clear field of vision, and then passing the light automatic gun, with which British aeroplanes were fitted, to the observer, who gave the Boche the rest of the "drum" (or charger containing forty-seven cartridges).

The German machine, which was obviously quite out of hand, crashed heavily to earth in the British lines. The British troops found the pilot stone dead in his seat, with a bullet through his heart, and the observer wounded. The British airman characteristically disdained to do any gloating over his prize, but without even troubling to look at it, clambered aloft again, without landing, and went after the second German machine. Unfortunately the engine of the British aeroplane began to miss fire, so the chase had to be abandoned, and the airmen were compelled to content themselves with a single prize.

A few days after this a British machine, while patrolling—*i.e.* looking out for German machines on reconnaissances—saw a British aeroplane hotly pursued by a German. The British patroller, who was at a very great height, dipped downwards to attack the Boche. The latter seemed to lose his head for the moment, for he turned and flew directly beneath his two assailants, who "let him have it" from their machine-guns as he passed. The British machine which the German had been pursuing went away, leaving the field to the patroller and the foe, who circled round each other, firing rapidly, drawing ever nearer to the earth. Suddenly the German dived for his lines under a steady stream of fire from the British machine, turned, "banked" steeply, lost his equilibrium, and flopped up-side-down to earth. Pilot and observer were killed.

No modern battle picture would be complete without the aeroplane, glittering up very high aloft, ringed about with tiny white balls of shrapnel smoke gleaming dead white against the background of clouds or clear sky. The airmen were highly popular figures with the men in the firing-line. The man in the trenches knew that the aeroplane was, so to speak, the periscope of the Army. Every aeroplane he saw he knew to be out guarding against any form of "frightfulness" that the ingenious German might be preparing for him—the man in the fire-trench—the man who was first to get the knocks. If a well-concealed battery made itself a nuisance by shelling the British trenches, smashing up the dug-outs, and knocking down the parapet, word was sent back post-haste by telephone for an aeroplane to locate the hidden nuisance and reveal its emplacement to British guns. If the British patrols ascertained that undue activity was going on in the trenches

SCENE AT AN AVIATION CAMP SOMEWHERE IN FRANCE

On the right is a sergeant of the R. F. C., wearing the new badge of a propeller on his arm. He is saluting two aviation officers, one dressed for flying, the other wearing the flying certificate badge. On the right is an army B. E. biplane, with its four-bladed propeller and two seats for pilot and observer. This type, it is stated, is becoming more and more the standard

FALLING TO EARTH LIKE A BLAZING METEOR.

This stirring picture represents a German aeroplane of the type called Aviatik, beaten in a fight high up in the air by the famous French Aviator Garros, plunging to earth in flames, turning and turning like a falling star.

opposite them, if they heard the clink of entrenching tools night after night, and by day caught glimpses of fresh earth accumulating behind the enemy trenches, an aeroplane was despatched for a "look-see."

WORK OF THE NAVAL WING

A word should be said of the splendid work accomplished by the Naval Wing of the Royal Flying Corps, which for long had its headquarters at Dunkirk, and distinguished itself by a number of daring and successful raids into Belgium and Germany, principally against the sheds in which the Germans harbored their Zeppelins with a view to air raids on England. On September 22d, 1914, Flight-Lieutenant Collet flew to Düsseldorf—a distance of some two hundred miles from his point of departure—and, descending to a height of only four hundred feet, dropped his bombs upon the Zeppelin shed there. Though the airman had his machine hit, he managed to return in safety. About the same time a similar raid was executed on Cologne, but the aeroplanes returned without dropping their bombs, having been prevented by the haze from locating the airship sheds. In the following month— on October 8th—two parties of aeroplanes repeated these performances. At Düsseldorf, Lieutenant Marix literally flattened out the Zeppelin shed and the Zeppelin harbored there, and though the raiders' machines were damaged, they all managed to get back safely. At Cologne the great military railway-station was badly damaged.

CHAPTER XI

THE HEROIC STRUGGLE ON THE GALLI-POLI PENINSULA

LEADERS WORTHY OF THEIR MEN—EVERYTHING AGAINST THE ALLIES—COMBINED OPERATION HELD UP—GREAT CHARGE AT KRITHIA—FOOTING GAINED BELOW ACHI BABA—GERMAN SUBMARINES INTERVENE — MEETING THE NEW MENACE — HUNTER-WESTON'S RUSE — NAVAL DIVISION'S BRILLIANT WORK — TURKS' DEADLY COUNTER-ATTACK—MANCHESTER'S GREAT EXPLOIT.

APPARENTLY we have to go back to the Walcheren Expedition to find a parallel to the circumstances in which the Dardanelles campaign was conceived. For, though the Crimean War was sadly muddled, the mistakes there do not seem to have been so serious as were those which the British, Australasian, and Indian troops were asked to retrieve along the gateway between the Mediterranean and the Black Sea. Sir Ian Hamilton was a commander of experience, and he was admirably served by subordinate officers like Generals Sir W. R. Birdwood and Hunter-Weston, of whom it is sufficient to say that they were worthy of the men they led into action. The heroism of the troops was marvelous, and solely by their indomitable tenacity they won a narrow footing along the cliffs below the mountain fortresses, from which the Germans

122

and Turks continued to sweep every landing-place with shell fire.

But after a footing had been won below Krithia and north of Gaba Tepe, the attacking forces could make no further progress of importance. There mustered at first scarcely two army corps of them, including the 29th Division, the Australian and New Zealand Expeditionary Force, the Naval Division, an Indian Brigade, and a French division composed of Zouaves, African troops, and some white battalions. After the losses of the landing battles, Sir Ian Hamilton must have had less than 35,000 bayonets immediately at hand for the desperate work of a thrusting attack at the seat of power of the Ottoman Empire, which could draw upon half a million or more men for the defense of the road to Constantinople. As a matter of fact, the Turco-German commanders concentrated all their principal armies on the defense of the Dardanelles. The campaign against Egypt was discontinued, and the attack on Russia across the Caucasus was reduced to an unimportant defensive battle. Even the comparatively small Indo-British army advancing along the Euphrates up towards Bagdad was only opposed by a single weak Turkish army corps. All the main military resources of one of the greatest warrior races in the world were organized by capable German officers and set in a series of almost impregnable mountain defenses, in order to safeguard the channel forts, which prevented the allied fleet from forcing the waterway to victory.

EVERYTHING AGAINST THE ALLIES

There were never less than 150,000 Turkish soldiers, with thousands of German engineers and artillerymen, holding the entrenched heights between Achi Baba and Sari Bair. It mattered little if the Allies put more than their number of foes out of action. New Turkish armies poured down the mainland track to Gallipoli, or were carried across the Sea of Marmora in transports. No wonder the Allies' advance was slow and their casualty lists terribly heavy. Everything was against them. The enemy was deeply entrenched on one of the finest lines of natural fortifications in the world, with guns and howitzers commanding every site occupied by the allied troops. The enemy could bring most of his provisions and supplies up by road at night, with little or no interference from the fire of the Allies' ships, and a flotilla of small sailing vessels, plying across the Sea of Marmora greatly assisted in the provisioning of the defending army. There was scarcely any water in that part of the mountainous Peninsula occupied by the attacking troops. Even their machine-guns at times became unworkable through want of water in the jackets to keep the barrels cool. Everything necessary for existence had also to brought to the bombarded beaches, and thence carried laboriously by hand through narrow communication trenches to the men in the firing-line. As summer came on, the white troops were almost prostrated by the tropical heat, and plagued by a monstrous number of flies. It became at last a feat of great ingenuity to swallow food without eating live flies also. The Anzacs, as the men of the Australian and New Zealand Army Corps were called, reverted to a state of picturesque savagery. They left off all their clothes, except for one garment around their loins, and

The Historic Landing from the "River Clyde" at Seddul Bahr, Gallipoli, April 25, 1915

The Loss of the "Irresistible" in the Dardanelles

During a bombardment of the Turkish forts in the narrows of the Dardanelles, the "Irresistible" quit the line of the French and English fleet and sank in deep water. The whole ship was lifted up in the explosion, and to increase the horror of the situation the Turks commenced bombarding the vessel with their big guns.

their bare bodies were baked to a Red Indian color, so that they looked at last, by reason of their state of nature and their magnificent physique, more terrifying barbarians than the Turks opposed to them.

At the end of April, 1915, the allied troops in the southern end of the Peninsula had forced their way forward for some five hundred yards from their landing-places. By this time both sides showed signs of exhaustion, but Sir Ian Hamilton resolutely judged that the troops who could first summon up spirit to make another attack would win some hundreds of yards of ground. And as his own force was crowded together under gun fire in a very narrow space, he determined to be the first to strike out. He therefore brought the 2d Australian and New Zealand Infantry Brigades down from the Sari Bair region, and rearranged the 29th Division into four brigades, composed of the 87th and 88th Brigades, the Lancashire Territorial Brigade, and the 29th Indian Infantry Brigade. Then with the remnant of his forces he formed a new composite division, which he used as a general reserve, after reinforcing the French division with the 2d Naval Brigade.

GREAT CHARGE AT KRITHIA—COMBINED OPERATION
HELD UP

The 29th Division went into action at 11 A. M. on May 6th, when it moved out leftward, on the southeast side of Krithia. Half an hour afterwards the French force on the right also advanced along the lower slopes of the river ridge of the Kereves Dere. The combined operation, however, made little progress.

125

The British troops were held up outside a pine wood, which the enemy had transformed into a machine-gun redoubt; and the French also were checked by a terrible fire from a strong fieldwork after reaching the crest of the ridge. The following morning the Lancashire Territorials charged gallantly up the slope towards Krithia. They were caught by the German machine-guns; but as they retired, another Territorial force, the Queen's Edinburgh Rifles, took the pine wood by a magnificent rush. Besides dislodging the machine-gun parties, they brought down Turkish snipers working from wooden platforms on the trees, and thus cleared the way for the general advance. But just as all seemed to be going well, and the Inniskilling Fusiliers came up to maintain the hold on the pine wood, the Turks, by a gallant charge, won back this clump of trees in the center. Nevertheless, the Inniskillings went on and captured three enemy trenches, till in the afternoon all the advance was again held up by an enfilading fire from hostile machine-guns hidden on a ridge between the gully running towards Krithia and the sea. The operation looked like ending in a stalemate; but neither General Hunter-Weston, one of the greatest thrusters in the army, nor Sir Ian Hamilton, a man with all the fighting temperament of the Highlander, would submit to the check. The commander threw in all his reserves, and ordered a general advance; and despite their weariness and their heavy losses, the men rose with a will, and in a great bayonet charge recaptured the pine wood and advanced nearly all their line some three hundred yards.

The troops were quite worn out, but Sir Ian

Hamilton kept most of them working when darkness fell at the task of consolidating their new position. His airmen had told him that the enemy were receiving reinforcements, and he was resolved to make one more push before the new hostile forces got into position. At half-past ten the next morning (May 7th) he flung out the New Zealand Brigade, and won another two hundred yards in front of the pine trees. Then, at half-past four in the afternoon, he threw the 2d Australian Brigade into his front, and sent his whole line forward against Krithia. The sparkle of the bayonets could be seen through the smoke of shells from the ships' guns and heavy artillery, as the attacking troops went forward in a long line stretching right across the Peninsula. The Senegalese sharpshooters were broken by the storm of heavy shells from the ridge by Kereves Dere. But the black troops were rallied by their officers, and sent forward in another rush, supported by a small column of French soldiers. Their figures were seen outlined against the sky on the crest of their ridge just as darkness fell and veiled all the battlefield.

FOOTING GAINED BELOW ACHI BABA

When morning came, Sir Ian Hamilton found that the French had captured the machine-gun redoubt on the ridge, and had entrenched in front of Zimmerman Farm. On the right of the British line the 87th Brigade, fighting in the darkness, had taken another two hundred yards of ground; while the Australian Brigade, though swept by shrapnel, machine-gun, and rifle fire, extended the Allies' front for another four hundred yards.

127

The gain of ground in the three days' battle was only six hundred yards on the right, and four hundred yards on the left-center. It does not look much on the map, but in practice it meant life instead of death, for it gave the allied troops just living room on the tip of the Peninsula, enabling them to scatter sufficiently in bivouacs in a network of narrow ditches, to avoid annihilation from the high-placed enemy batteries. Sir Ian Hamilton confessed that it was only on May 10, 1915, that he felt that his footing below Achi Baba was fairly secure.

Meanwhile the officer commanding the 6th Gurkhas had begun on his own initiative the new method of advancing by local efforts. Between Krithia and the open sea there was a deep, picturesque river bed, known on the map as the Saghir Dere, and known in the camp as Gully Ravine, and crowned seaward by a steep bluff. Below the bluff was Y Beach, where some of the troops had fought their first landing battle. Since then the enemy had transformed the bluff into a powerful fortress, from which a number of machine-guns had continually broken up the left wing of our attacks. To assail the fortified cliff across the gully was madness, but the mountaineers of Nepal worked their way along the shore, and then started in the darkness to crawl up the steep height on their hands and knees. They reached the top, but failed to surprise the enemy, who beat them back with a sweeping fire. The enterprising Gurkhas, however, had shown the way in which the bluff could be captured, and the next day Major-General H. V. Fox, commanding the 29th Indian Infantry Brigade, devised plans for a

128

concerted attack. This was carried out in the evening of May 12th, when the Manchester Brigade made a feint of a storming attack on the right of the enemy's position. The guns of H.M.S. Dublin and H.M.S. Talbot opened fire seaward on the Turkish trenches, while the guns and howitzers of one of the British divisions kept up a heavy shell fire from the land. Evening deepened into night, and the great bluff flamed with bursting shells that kept the Turks below their parapets. Then again in the darkness a double company of Gurkhas crept along the shore, and, scaling the cliff, carried the position with a rush. They were followed by their machine-gun section, and another double company of their battalion, and when dawn broke the conquered position had been connected with our main line, advancing our left flank by nearly five hundred yards.

GERMAN SUBMARINES INTERVENE—MEETING THE NEW MENACE

Nothing of much importance was done for another fortnight. During this time the hardest work fell on the sappers, who tried to work up within rushing distance of the enemy's second line by means of winding saps from which the troops could debouch. On May 25th the Royal Naval Division and the 42d Division were able to entrench a hundred yards nearer the Turks, and four days afterwards the entire British line was helped onward by means of engineers' work. At the same time the French force also progressed and captured a machine-gun redoubt on the ridge going down to the Kereves Ravine. But all this slow movement of approach against the hostile mountain fortress was suddenly complicated by a series of terrifying naval disasters. Some German submarines worked down to the Dardanelles in the third week in May, and all our naval dispositions and transport work were abruptly checked.

We had already lost the Goliath, a useful old battleship, by a destroyer attack delivered by a very enterprising German naval officer. This disaster only entailed greater watchfulness on the part of our scouts; but the torpedoing of H.M.S. Triumph on May 26th, and the torpedoing of H.M.S. Majestic on May 27th, were blows so serious that even some of the British thought that the Dardanelles campaign was suddenly about to end in collapse. The outlook was indeed very serious. The large steamers which had been supplying the troops with food and ammunition could no longer be safely used, and it seemed at first as if the Germans and Austrians had only to send half a dozen more large underwater craft to the Dardanelles in order to maroon the troops that had landed on the Gallipoli Peninsula. It was a situation to test to the uttermost the ability of the British sailor; but by fine ingenuity and inventiveness he saved the army which he had put ashore with such remarkable skill. All the transports were sent into Mudros Bay, where there was only a narrow channel to guard. Men, stores, guns, and horses were henceforth conveyed across forty miles of water from Mudros to the Peninsula in minesweepers and other small, shallow vessels, which did not lie deep enough in the water for a torpedo to strike them at the ordinary depth. Then the large warships, whose guns were very useful and sometimes of vital value in the military operations, were sheltered near the shore by means of submarine defenses, while the destroyers and patrol boats tracked the hostile underwater craft and assailed them in various ways.

Almost every night the Turks assailed the Allied line, hoping, no doubt, to find that the attacking troops were weakening under the submarine menace. But the Allies' positions remained intact, and Sir Ian Hamilton, on June 3d, made his first deliberate assault on the Achi Baba fortifications. For his line of battle he deployed the 29th Division on his left, the42d (East Lancashire) Division in his center, with the Naval Division linking on with the French Army Corps. General Hunter-Weston, directing the British troops on a front of four thousand yards, had about 17,000 men on the firing-line, with 7,000 men in reserve. The action began on the morning of June 4th with a preliminary bombardment which lasted for more than three hours, after which the allied troops moved to attack, and then scurried back to their trenches. This was a little stratagem on the part of General Hunter-Weston to draw the fire of the enemy's artillery and machine-guns. The device was successful, and amid a heavy fire from the enemy's batteries and trenches, the Allies renewed their bombardment with increasing intensity, being able to mark more exactly the hostile targets. Precisely at noon the Allies lengthened their fire, and the entire British line charged with fixed bayonets. Both the French divisions stormed

131

forward at the same time, so that the glittering line of bayonets sparkled right across the Peninsula from the open sea to the closed Strait.

NAVAL DIVISION'S BRILLIANT WORK

The Lancashire Territorials and the new recruits of the Anson, Howe, and Hood Battalions of the Naval Division did extremely well. They captured the first Turkish line in front of them in from five to fifteen minutes, and then burst through the second Turkish line in another fierce, swift spurt. In less than half an hour from the time when they leaped from the trenches, the men of the East Lancashire Division and the Naval Division had penetrated a third of a mile in the enemy's front, and were consolidating the conquered ground in a cool, workmanlike way. The 29th Division was less fortunate, as its left wing was held up by a wire entanglement, so placed as to have escaped damage from our shells. It was an Indian brigade that was checked in this manner, and though a company of the 6th Gurkhas, the heroes of Gurkha Bluff, battered their way into the Turkish works, they had to be withdrawn with the rest of the brigade in order to avoid being cut off.

TURKS' DEADLY COUNTER-ATTACK

While a fresh attack was being organized the French corps on the right got also into difficulties. The 1st French Division carried the opposing enemy trench, while the 2d Division stormed in a magnificent charge the strong Turkish redoubt on the Kereves Ridge, known as the Haricot. But the French left wing, acting on the right flank of the Royal Naval

132

Division, was unable to gain any ground, and this led to a disaster. In the afternoon the Turks, pouring out through the series of communication trenches, delivered a massed counter-attack on the Haricot Redoubt, while their guns prepared the way for them with a storm of shrapnel and high-explosive shells. The French lost the redoubt and fell back, and in so doing completely uncovered the right flank of the Naval Division. The men of the 2d Naval Brigade were enfiladed and forced to retire with heavy losses from the postion they had captured, and the Collingwood Battalion, which had gone forward in support, was almost completely destroyed.

It looked as though the Turks were about to roll up the whole allied line, for when the Naval Brigade was compelled to retreat across the open, sloping fields under a terrible fire, the exposed flank of the Manchester Brigade was in turn caught by Turkish and German machine-guns, and swept by volleys of rifle fire, and then hammered by hostile bombing-parties. But the Manchester men—nearly all of them Territorials—fought with bulldog courage to hold what they had won. There were places in which one Lancashire man resisted every force that the enemy could bring to bear upon him. Company-Sergeant-Major Hay, having captured single-handed a redoubt near Krithia, held it for ten hours with four men until he was relieved. Company-Sergeant-Major Alister killed eight Turks and cleared a trench. But probably the best fighter of all was Private Richardson, who fought on alone in a trench south of Krithia for nearly twenty-four hours, and beat back every hostile assault.

133

THE HEROIC STRUGGLE

The fighting around Krithia in the afternoon of June 4, 1915, was a matter upon which every Territorial can look back with deep pride. The Manchester Brigade equaled the finest exploits of the old Regular Army. They answered the attack on their flank by throwing back their right wing; and such was their desperate courage that Sir Ian Hamilton could not bear to let them retire. Their position was one of extreme peril, for they were surrounded on two sides, and the Turks were making a sustained and furious effort to drive across the salient and cut off the brigade. So the British Commander-in-Chief formed up the Naval Division, and asked General Gouraud to co-operate in making an attack that should advance the right of the line, and connect and protect the flank of the Manchester men. But the French corps itself was still in great difficulties. Twice the attack was postponed at the request of General Gouraud, and at half-past six in the evening he reported that the pressure of the Turkish masses against him was so heavy that he could not advance.

Nothing remained but to withdraw the Manchester men from the second Turkish line which they were holding to the first Turkish line. The troops were very angry, and some of them desired to stay on and die rather than give up any of the ground they had won. But after much persuasion all the East Lancashire Division was extricated from the second line of captured trenches, and placed back in the Turkish first line, which they had won in five minutes at the beginning of their attack. The net result of the day's

134

operations was an advance on a depth of two hundred to four hundred yards, along a front of nearly three miles. It was less than had been hoped for, but it was still a very considerable gain. Not only was there a substantial and very useful extension of ground, but the Turks were so severely punished that, though flushed with the victory of regaining their second line, they had not enough spirit left to attempt a counter-attack to recover their firing-trenches and forward machine-gun redoubts. Four hundred prisoners were taken, including five German officers, who were the remnant of a machine-gun party from the Goeben. Most of the captures were made by the Lancashire Territorials, whose capable divisional commander was Major-General W. Douglas.

CHAPTER XII

THE VALIANT DEFENSE OF SERBIA AND MONTENEGRO

BRIGHT SPOTS IN SERBIA'S DARK SKY—VASSITCH ROBBED OF SUCCESS—SARRAIL ASSAULTS MOUNT ARKANGEL—BULGARIANS TAKE THE OFFENSIVE— SARRAIL'S LACK OF MEN—BATTLE OF KATSHANIK PASS—SERBIAN ROUT AT PRISREND—HORRORS OF THE FLIGHT—SARRAIL'S FIGHTING RETREAT—TENTH DIVISION'S MEMORABLE STAND — FATE DECIDES AGAINST MONTENEGRO.

THE DISASTROUS week which saw the fall of Nish on November 5, 1915, and the enemy in occupation of the greater part of Serbia, did not, however, close without witnessing a splendid vindication of the fighting qualities of the Serbians. If by this time the general situation of the little kingdom was becoming gloomy, the dark sky was not entirely destitute of gleams of light. The soldiers of Bojovitch and of Vassitch respectively had repelled all assaults of the Bulgarians on the Katshanik Pass, northwest of Uskub, and the Babuna Pass, southwest of Veles, two places of extreme strategic importance, as subsequent events clearly showed. The heroic Vassitch did far better than merely hold the Babuna Pass against repeated attacks, for he was victorious there in a battle which, had circumstances been more propitious, might have favorably
136

SERBIAN GUNNERS DEFENDING THEIR FRONTIER AGAINST THE AUSTRO-GERMAN INVADERS.

The passage of the Danube and the conquest of the hills behind Semendria was only achieved after a desperate resistance on the part of the heroic Serbs. The Serbian artillery in particular made a brilliant memorable stand

165

A New Weapon in Warfare.

One of the Belgian armored motor cars surprising a party of Uhlans. Several of the enemy were killed by the rapid fire from swivel machine gun and rifle, but the car driven at a furious pace was wrecked on a fallen horse.

influenced the whole course of the later phases of the struggle for his country's existence.

During that first week of November, 1915, Vassitch, in and around the Babuna Pass, had only 5,000 men to pit against over 20,000 Bulgarians, who besides had much heavier artillery. Day after day, night after night, his small force of Serbians, often without food, always under fire, but cheered by their commander, and singing their plaintive national airs, fought dauntlessly on, repulsing with serious loss to the invader all his most stubborn and persistent efforts to force the pass. They did more. From November 4th to November 6th an incessant and sanguinary hand-to-hand fight, in which the combatants made free use of their knives, raged in the deep and narrow gorges of the defile, ending in the complete rout of the Bulgarians, who were driven through Izvor pell-mell into Veles.

And on the other side of the hills the French, under General Sarrail, were only a few miles away—almost in touch. It looked as if the Allies might effect a junction, and telegrams were despatched from Greece which actually asserted that not only French but also British troops had united with the Serbians. The truth, unfortunately, was altogether otherwise.

A thoroughly capable soldier, who had already proved his merit in France, General Sarrail did wonders considering the shortness of the time at his disposal and the inferiority of the facilities at his command, but the numbers of his men were utterly insufficient for their task, and he could not achieve the impossible. He made a great, an even desperate, attempt to join up with Vassitch, and so nearly accomplished it that nothing but the absence of reinforcements at a critical moment robbed him of success. In this effort his troops were entirely French, the British, lying around Lake Doiran, being well to the south and east on his right flank.

As soon as possible after his arrival at Salonika, he railed all his available forces up the Valley of the Vardar, towards Veles. He had only a single-tracked and indifferent railway for the transportation of both men and supplies, yet he pressed on with surprising speed. The line followed the snaky twistings of the river, and parts of it, built on shelves cut out of the solid rock, passed through deep gorges, the longest of which, known as the Demir Kapu Ravine, extended for ten miles. As possession of this defile by the enemy would have been a fatal bar to his advance, his first business was to get it into his own hands, and after some fighting at Strumnitza station, a few miles to the south, he secured it without further opposition. Then he pushed on north of it to Krivolak, about 110 miles from Salonika. He reached Krivolak on October 19th, but at first he had only a handful of troops, and could do little till more had come up.

VASSITCH ROBBED OF SUCCESS

By a magnificent thrust Vassitch recaptured Veles from the Bulgarians on October 22d, and managed to hold it for a week. This town lay along the railway some thirty-five miles northwest of Krivolak, but the French were not sufficiently strong to push their way up the line to it, and they had to fight hard, as it was, to maintain themselves. It was not till after they had gained possession of a steep and forbidding height,

138

called Kara Hodjali, three miles north of Krivolak on the road to Ishtip, that they established their position, and, defeating furious assaults of the enemy on October 30th and November 4th and 5th, made an effective bridge-head on the east side of the Vardar. In the meantime Vassitch, far outnumbered and outgunned, had been compelled to evacuate Veles again and withdraw to the Babuna Pass.

SARRAIL ASSAULTS MOUNT ARKANGEL

Krivolak was twenty-five miles almost due east of the pass, and Sarrail's problem now was to bridge the distance which intervened between himself and Vassitch. The first part of the way was easy, fifteen miles across an undulating plain to the Tserna, a tributary of the Vardar; but the remaining ten miles, on the west side of the former river, were over very difficult country, consisting of rugged hills and mountains, interspersed with water-courses, the whole of this terrain, on which the Bulgarians had erected fortifications, lending itself readily to a powerful defense.

Having secured Kara Hodjali, which the French soldiers renamed Kara Rosalie, after the pet word of their bayonets, Sarrail, for whom reinforcements had all the while been arriving at Krivolak, marched southwest across the plain through Negotin and Kavarda to the Tserna, an unfordable stream of considerable width, with but one bridge over it, and that of wood at a place called Vozartzi. On November 5th the French moved over the bridge, and occupied the adjacent crests of the precipitous slopes which, often rising above 1,000 feet in height, line for miles that

139

side of the river. Here they were so near the Babuna Pass that they could hear the thundrous rumble of the artillery taking part in the fierce battle in which Vassitch was victorious. Advancing northwards along the west bank of the Tserna, Sarrail next day began an assault of Mount Arkangel, ten miles down stream from Vozartzi, and the center of the Bulgarian position, which had to be stormed if a junction was to be made with the Serbians.

Mount Arkangel, however, was an extremely hard nut to crack. The Bulgarians had strongly fortified it, were numerically much superior to the French, and, moreover, were constantly being reinforced by Teodoroff from his main army. In war, "L'audace!" typified the spirit of the French, and on this occasion, with their precarious communications and relatively small numbers, it needed all their boldness and courage to make the attempt. After skirmishes with outposts at the base of the mountain, they drove the Bulgarians out of the villages of Sirkovo and Krushevitza, and on November the 10th they carried, by an encircling movement, with great dash, the village of Sirkovo, situated some distance up the side of the eminence. But they did not get far above this point. By the close of the second week of November the Bulgarians concentrated upwards of 60,000 men, with a corresponding strength in guns, on Mount Arkangel and along the west bank of the Tserna, and on the 12th they took the offensive.

BULGARIANS TAKE THE OFFENSIVE

Their obviously best course was to cut the French off from the Vozartzi bridge, the latter's sole line of supply and retreat, and then hem them in against the impassable river in the rear. For three days, in fighting of the most violent description, they made the most determined efforts to carry out this purpose, but the French, combining higher skill with equal determination, held their ground, and in a grim conflict, which took place on Mount Arkangel itself, inflicted a severe defeat on the enemy, who was forced to retire in great disorder, leaving 3,500 dead on the field. In this battle the Bulgarians charged to within twenty yards of the French trenches, but, faltering under a withering fire and then counter-charged by the French with the bayonet, broke, turned, and ran. Mr. G. Ward Price, the authorized representative of the London *Press* with the allies in the Balkins, reported that if only there had been enough French troops to throw into the struggle at the moment, the retreat of the Bulgars would have been made a rout.

SARRAIL'S LACK OF MEN

Vassitch held out in the Babuna Pass, ten miles away all the next day, November 15th, but the French could not get across the hills, and as he was compelled to retire, in order to escape envelopment, on Prilep on November 16th, the opportunity passed. The French, still hoping to assist the Serbians in some way, retained their positions. It was November 20th, nearly a week after the battle of Mount Arkangel, before the Bulgarians, freshly strengthened, renewed the attack, and they were again heavily checked, but Sarrail was unable to advance, the plain fact being that he neither had nor could get men in adequate force.

And, meanwhile, in other parts of the country the progress of events, moving from disaster to disaster for the brave but unfortunate Serbians, had rendered it evident that the enemy's overrunning of the rest of Serbia was a question of but a very short time, on which the venture of the Allies would exercise little or no influence.

BATTLE OF KATSHANIK PASS

About November 10th Bojovitch's slender army of 5,000 men was reinforced by three regiments, including one from the Shumadia and one from the Morava Divisions, which were sent by the railway—the only bit remaining to Serbia—from Pristina to Ferizovitch, some ten miles from the Katshanik Pass. The weather was intensely cold, and the roads were indescribably bad. The Serbians, though exhausted by much marching, and weak from want of food, pressed on to the pass, and Bojovitch began the attack without a moment's delay. According to one account he had a hundred guns, mostly of the French 75 and 155 type (3-in. and 6-in.), which rained thousands of shrapnel and high-explosive shells on the trenches of the Bulgarians, who, under this terrible fire, retreated south for four miles. Then the Serbian infantry drove on, falling wave after wave on the reeling Bulgarian ranks, which, however, rallied as their supports came up. One Serbian regiment charged desperately seven times, each time capturing and then losing six Bulgarian guns. In several parts of the field there was a savage hand-to-hand mêlée, in which the combatants, throwing down their rifles, fought with daggers, knives, fists, and even

142

teeth, the wildest, fiercest scenes in the envenomed fighting on the Timok being far outdone. For some time the Serbians on the whole made progress, the enemy's center being pierced by a prodigious effort of the Shumadia and Morava troops, and it seemed as if Serbian valor would prevail. But here, once more, the Serbians had no reserves to ensure success. The Bulgarians were all the time being strengthened by large numbers of fresh men railed up from Uskub, and in the end this superiority was the deciding factor. On the 15th the battle was lost, and the Serbians were forced out of the pass, retiring by the passes of the Jatzovitza Hills on Prisrend.

SERBIAN ROUT AT PRISREND

From Mitrovitza a part of the Serbian Army, accompanied by multitudes of civilian fugitives, retreated to Ipek in Montenegro, and some proportion of them eventually arrived at Scutari, by way of Podgoritza, after suffering the cruelest hardships and privations— the rest perished miserably from cold and starvation. Retiring from the same town, another part of the force which had opposed Kövess stood and fought him again at Vutshitrin, but was beaten and pursued across the Sitnitza. But the main line of retreat of the Serbians was along the high road from Pristina to Prisrend, and the Bulgarians pressed on quickly behind in this direction, took the heights west of Ferizovitch, and also advanced northerly towards Ipek, against which town Kövess had sent a detachment. The retreat to Prisrend was covered by the Shumadia Division. On November 27th upwards of 80,000

Serbians stood at bay in front of this town, but next day, after a most sanguinary conflict, and having fired their last shell, they spiked their guns, and fled across the frontier into Albania, making along the White Drin for Kula Liuma, sometimes called Lum Kulus, while several thousand prisoners fell into the hands of the enemy.

HORRORS OF THE FLIGHT

Marked by horrors unspeakable, the retreat of the Serbian Army will remain one of the most terrible in history. Day by day thousands of men, ill-clad, ill-shod, or with bare and bleeding feet, and, crazed with famine, eating raw horse-flesh with avidity, stumbled painfully and wretchedly along the two available roads, and these no better than mule-tracks, from Kula Liuma, one going west to Scutari, and the other south through Dibra to Elbasan. Saddest of all, with these wearied and war-worn soldiers there traveled long, mournful processions of the aged of both sexes, of the women and children, of Serbia, exhausted and starving, but preferring to face anything than to fall into the hands of the Austro-German and Bulgarian conquerors. Each *via dolorosa* was strewn thickly with bodies of these unfortunate people. It was estimated that out of half a million civilians, who sought refuge in flight into the Albanian mountains, more than 200,000 died.

SARRAIL'S FLYING RETREAT

The French bore the brunt of the struggle on the Tserna—perhaps because they were more numerous than the British, who were not actively engaged in force until the first week of December. Their trenches lay north and west of Lake Doiran, among bleak hills covered with snow, spreading out fanwise in the direction of Strumnitza, and they had taken them over from the French when the latter had gone up the Vardar to Krivolak. One of the difficulties of Sarrail's retreat was that while it was going on he was unable, owing to the nature of the country, to maintain close communication with the British prior to the 10th.

On the east side of the Vardar Teodoroff had massed four divisions—or roughly 100,000 men—and he made his first great assault on the British in the grey of early morning, and under cover of a fog, which permitted him to get close up to the British trenches, without being clearly perceived, on December 6th. The British force opposed to this Bulgarian army—for it was nothing less—consisted of the 10th Division, which had come from Suvla Bay, and could hardly have been in anything like full strength, and supports drawn from the Salonika base. The enemy first of all poured a rain of high-explosive shells on the British trenches, which were held mainly by the Inniskillings, the Connaughts, the Munsters, and the Dublin Fusiliers—the pick of Ireland—and the Hampshires. After very heavy fighting, often hand-to-hand, with the advantage now on the one side and now on the other, the overwhelming strength of the Bulgarians told, and the British were driven out of their first line. The battle had raged all day, with hardly a pause, and it was renewed next morning with equal or even fiercer intensity.

TENTH DIVISION'S MEMORABLE STAND

As on the 6th, the conflict commenced with a tremendous bombardment by the Bulgarians of the British lines, and then the enemy came on, hurrahing and cheering, and threw himself in successive waves on the 10th Division, which, resisting stoutly, gave ground slowly, its rate of retirement being about two miles a day, which was wonderfully little considering the enormous pressure exerted by Teodoroff's four divisions. More than once the British looked as though they would be annihilated, but a free use of the bayonet, added to Irish and English pluck, succeeded in extricating them from the most dangerous situations.

Without much further fighting, the Franco-British troops on December 12th gained the other side of the frontier, having torn up the railway behind them, and fired Gevgheli and other points on the Macedonian side, so as to delay the Bulgarian advance. By a fortunate coincidence Greece had on the previous day agreed to accept the proposals of the Allies by which their forces were to have free and unimpeded liberty of action. Considering the difficulty of the operations in face of the immense strength of the enemy, the whole retirement, which reflected the greatest credit on General Sarrail, had been carried out most successfully. Although his men had at their disposal only one line of railway and no roads, their retreat was executed in such an orderly manner that they were able to save and withdraw all their stores, while the total of their casualties did not exceed 3,500, a very moderate figure in the circumstances.

VALIANT DEFENSE OF SERBIA

When Serbia was overrun, Mackensen redistributed his forces, various German and Austrian divisions being sent north to watch the Russians who, at that juncture, were rumored to be about to make a diversion in the Balkans, either through Rumania or by a descent on the Bulgar shore of the Black Sea. German troops were transferred to Bulgaria, and even to Turkey, both of which countries were now openly "run" from Berlin. But troops were not withdrawn from the Montenegrin front; on the contrary, they were greatly increased. Just as Austria hated Serbia with a deadly hatred, so she hated this still smaller Slav State which, with a population of less than half a million, had been long independent of her as of Turkey. Austria determined to destroy it. The undertaking was difficult, because of the almost inaccessibly mountainous character of the country and the bravery of its inhabitants, who were inured to war and every kind of hardship, like the Serbians; but it was not impossible, if men and guns were provided in adequate strength. What could be done in Serbia could be done in Montenegro.

Although the Austrians advanced during December some distance on the east side, or Sanjak front, capturing Plevlie, Ipek and Bielopolie, their great offensive did not start till January, 1916. In the interval the Montenegrins had at least one considerable victory, at Lepenatz, but in general they were driven steadily back. In the last days of the year Mount Lovtchen was heavily shelled, and then attacked in some force, but the Montenegrins were successful in repelling this assault on their stronghold. It was not till January

6th that Kövess began decisive operations by a series of concerted violent attacks on the Montenegrin east front, on the Tara, the Lim and the Ibar, while at the same time warships in the Gulf of Cattaro opened a terrible fire on Mount Lovtchen.

Desperate fighting continued for four days. Berane, on the Lim, was captured by the Austrians on the 10th; and, far more important, Lovtchen succumbed on the same day to infantry assaults prepared by the fire from the warships. Some surprise was expressed among the other Allies that the fortress should have fallen in such a short time, but the feeling changed when it became known that the place was defended by less than 6,000 men—starving, with insufficient clothing, and lamentably short of guns and munitions. With Lovtchen gone, Cetinje could not be held by the Montenegrins, and it was occupied by the Austrians on the 13th. Four days later the announcement was made in the Hungarian Parliament that Montenegro had "surrendered unconditionally."

CHAPTER XIII

THE TERRIBLE MESOPOTAMIAN CAMPAIGN

WHY NEITHER BRITON NOR TURK VENTURED FAR
INTO BABYLONIA—INSECTS VS. MAN—BATTLE OF
NORFOLK HILL—FIGHTING THE HEAT—AN AWFUL
MARCH—THE ADVANCE ON BAGDAD—BATTLE OF
NASIRIYEH—MAGNIFICENT WEST KENTS—ROUT OF
THE TURKS—NUREDIN PASHA OUT-MANEUVERED—
THE SECOND BRITISH MESOPOTAMIAN EXPEDITION
—THE FALL OF BAGDAD.

THERE IS nothing of the romantic atmosphere
of the "Arabian Nights' Entertainments" remaining
in the region between Bagdad and the Persian Gulf.
In ancient times, it is said, a cock could hop from house
to house from Basra, the city of Sindbad, past Babylon
and Seleucia, to the capital of Haroun Al-Raschid.
But since the Mongol, the Turk, and the nomads of
Arabia swept over the most fertile country on earth,
the tract between the Tigris and the Euphrates has
lapsed into desert sand and riverside jungles of cane-
brakes, where the Mesopotamian lion ranges. Instead
of being a land of vines, orange groves, and rose
gardens, Babylonia has become one of the most desolate
wastes in Asia, and the reason why neither the Turk
at Mosul nor the Briton at Koweit succeeded in
occupying the wilderness was apparent in the spring
of 1915. In April the commander of the Indian
Expeditionary Force, Sir Arthur Barrett, fell so
seriously ill that Sir John Eccles Nixon had to take

149

over his command. The following month many men of the British regiments began to feel unwell, and when the full heat of the summer smote the Indo-British force the sufferings of the white men were extreme.

The heat was not much worse than that of the Punjab, yet the Indian troops suffered almost as much as the British troops. This was due to the fact that the steaming marshlands of the great rivers not only gave a trying, humid quality to the burning tropical sunlight, but also the vast stretches of stagnant water, full of rotting refuse, formed the breeding places of an absolutely incomparable swarm of mosquitoes, biting flies, and vermin. These biting and blood-sucking insects were the main defenders of the legendary site of Eden, of the river-lands of Ur, where Abraham pastured his cattle, and the desolate yellow mounds representing all that remained of the hanging gardens by the Euphrates, where Alexander the Great died. Alexander had been able to conquer all emperors, kings, and chieftains between the Mediterranean and the Indian Ocean, but at the height of his power and glory he had been stung by a gnat, and infected with a deadly fever.

INSECTS *vs.* MAN

Many of the troops at last went through the campaign in a state of absolute nudity, protected by mosquito-nets, with mats of woven reeds over their heads, as a slight shade against the flame-like sunshine. But they could not get away from the flies; a man could not eat his food without eating flies. A piece of white bread became black before it reached one's mouth, and the inevitable result was some kind of dysentery. And such was the effect of the heat that a body of vigorous troops in the prime of life, marching at the top of their powers, seldom did more than eight miles a day. . . By this time they lost so much of the fluid of their blood that, though they emptied their water-flasks, they were tortured by thirst, and suffered like men in the last stages of kidney disease.

Sir John Nixon began his part of the campaign by turning his soldiers into sailors. For some weeks in the spring the whole brigade stationed at Kurna was engaged in learning the art of navigation in bellums. This type of boat has a length of about thirty-five feet and a beam of two and a half feet; it is propelled in shallow water by poles, and in deep water by paddles. Two men were required to work it, and as it was likely they would both be shot down when the action opened, all the men in the flat-bottomed craft had to learn how to punt and paddle, so as to be able to look after themselves if their boatmen fell. It was also at this time that a considerable part of our field artillery was put on the water, and, by great feats of carpentry and smith work, mounted on rafts, sailing-boats, tugs, and launches. Machine-guns were also mounted in large numbers, and at dawn on May 31st the extraordinary new Indo-British navy moved out to attack.

BATTLE OF NORFOLK HILL

In front of hundreds of river-boats were the three sloops Clio, Odin, and Espiègel, each with six four-inch guns, and the Royal Indian Marine steamer Lawrence, with rafts and boats containing field-

151

guns. This remarkable squadron had to steam through something that was neither land nor water, but a tract of mud thinning into a liquid form, while retaining the appearance of land by reason of the reeds growing out of it. The progress of the boats was much impeded by the reeds, and the Turks, with their Kurdish levies and German officers, entrenched on the low hills to the north, had a magnificent target. But their 6-in. field-guns used only the old segment shells, sold by the English government to the Ottoman Empire soon after the South African War. These shells made a noise, but did very little damage. What was more important, the Turks had no machine-guns, and their musketry fire was not good. After the steamer squadron had bombarded the enemy trenches, the newly-made sailor-soldiers of the bellum brigade—2d Norfolks, 110th Mahratta Light Infantry, and 120th Rajputana Infantry—beached their boats among the reeds, then squelched through the marsh and charged with the bayonet up the high, dry ground. The entrenched Turks, on the hill now known as Norfolk Hill, put up a good fight, but they were rushed and shattered, and the enemy troops in the other six positions fled in disorder up the Tigris to Amara.

FIGHTING THE HEAT

The garrison work, though unexciting, was almost a relief after a skirmish in the desert. In the desert at times the temperature was up to 130 degrees in the small tents, and on very sultry days the sandstorms came. A dense khaki-colored cloud rose on the horizon, and then rolled towards the encampment.

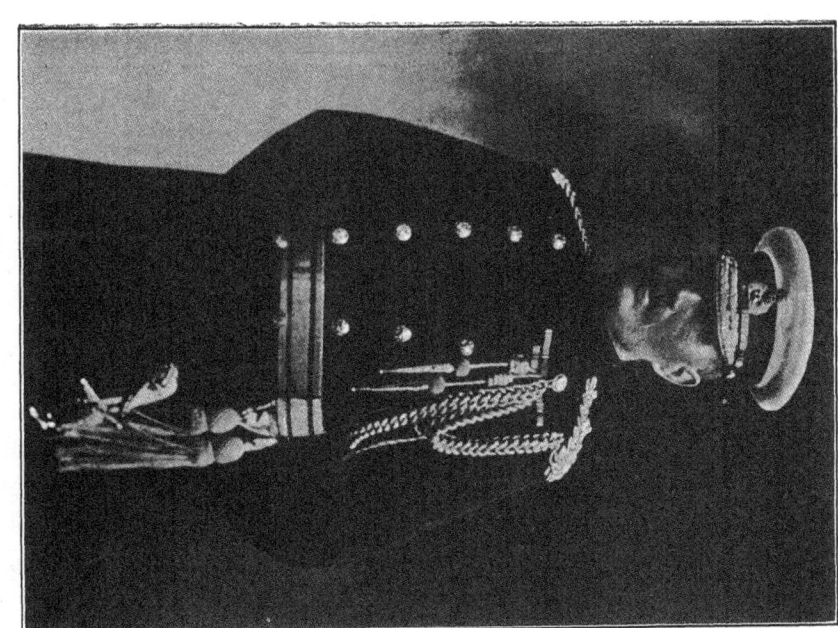

General Sir William R. Robertson
Chief of the Imperial General Staff.

General Sir Douglas Haig
Commander-in-chief of the British forces in France.

THE BRITISH CRUISER "HIGHFLYER" RIDS THE SEAS OF A GERMAN PEST

The sinking of the German commerce-destroyer "Kaiser Wilhelm der Grosse" by a light British cruiser off the West coast of Africa. The German commerce-destroyer, which had previously been a fast trans-Atlantic passenger vessel, was in the very act of capturing a British steamer when the cruiser came up and speedily sent her to the bottom of the sea.

The men rushed about strengthening their tent-pegs and ropes, and collecting all the loose kit; but often no preparation was adequate to meet the storm. The tents were blown down like packs of cards, and all had to hide their heads under tent-flaps, bedding, or boxes, as it was impossible to face the blasts of cutting sand. In violent tempests the sand made a black darkness which lasted for hours. When the storm passed, and the troops emerged, shaking themselves like dogs coming out of water, their eyes were bloodshot, their mouths and nostrils coated thick and black with sand and mud, and all their bodies were a mass of sand.

It was in these circumstances that the work of chasing down hostile Arab tribes and burning their camps had to be carried out. The actual conflicts with mounted bands of Bedouin guerrillas were not much of a trial. As the Bedouins usually had no guns, they scattered among the dunes when our men offered battle, and our reconnoitring aeroplanes were hard put to it to trace the lines along which they were going to again concentrate. The Indian cavalry, with a section of horse artillery concealed behind them, managed at first by feigning a flight and leading the unsuspecting Bedouins towards the British guns, to ambush some of the more daring Bedouin parties. But the Bedouin, being a born guerrilla fighter, mounted on a fine desert horse, soon learned all the tricks of the British cavalry, and had to be hunted down by converging columns of infantry. Infantry, however, had been hunting down the Bedouin for some ten thousand years; and when the Indo-British troops took up the work which Turk, Mongol, Persian, Assyrian, Babylonian and Sumerian had been unable to accomplish, the son of the desert resorted to his ancient tactics.

He retired deep into the sandy waste, where he could water by springs known only to himself. There he tried to outfight his foes by his last and most terrible weapon of defense—thirst. The British pursuers had some narrow escapes from the most awful of deaths. On one occasion a strong column of their troops was set the apparently easy task of rounding up some Bedouins whom the British airmen had discovered camping only ten miles away. The men marched all night through the hot desert, charged the Arabs early in the morning, burned their tents, and hunted them over the sand-ridges for miles, and then returned to the captured camp for food and water. By this time the sun was terribly fierce, and the men, having emptied their water-bottles while marching in the hot night, were exhausted. And no water had been brought for them. It had apparently been thought that, as the river was only ten miles away the column was in no danger of dying from thirst.

AN AWFUL MARCH

At seven o'clock in the morning the troops began their march back to the river. But after covering only two miles the situation became desperate. The men began to stagger out and drop with exhaustion, and every hundred yards they went things looked blacker and blacker. At the end of four miles, when the sun was high and all the air was aflame, the column had to stop. The men—mostly Indians, and accustomed to tropical heat—could not get any farther.

154

Some of the British officers, who had been very careful with their water-bottles, gave their last drop to Indian officers and other bad cases. Then the general ordered tents to be pitched, and sent his Staff and cavalry to bring water from the river. Meanwhile, the column was in an awful condition, the agony of many of the men being dreadful to witness. One British infantry officer, feeling he was about to die, thought he would make a struggle for it. He strung water-bottles round his neck and around the camp mules, mounted one of the chargers, and made for the river. He could not afterwards tell how he reached it. He was half unconscious. But the animals found the water, and the officer rolled in it on his charger, drank up something that was more mud than water, and filled the bottles. With his refreshed pack of mules he regained the camp before the cavalry arrived, and saved many lives.

THE ADVANCE ON BAGDAD

About the beginning of July, 1915, the Mesopotamian campaign against the Turkish forces guarding Bagdad was undertaken.

At the Dardanelles the British had first thrown at the Ottoman Empire—which had six hundred thousand men under arms—a single army corps, shipped in disorder, and unprovided with the heavy howitzers needed in the siege battles of modern times. When this operation had failed, and the Ottoman Government was reported to be waiting only for equipment in order to arm a million men, the British Cabinet sent General Townshend to operate on the other side of the Ottoman Empire and capture Bagdad, in a zone where the Turks were believed to have large forces.

After fighting through the enemy's advanced position below Hamar Lake, the wonderfully-mixed British flotilla arrived, at the end of the third week in July, at a distance of about seven miles from Nasiriyeh. The division was then split up. Two brigades were landed on the right or westerly bank, while to the other brigade was assigned the task of working through the groves of date-palms on the left bank. As a reserve, a fourth brigade was brought down from Amara, and held ready for action in river-boats. Each of these boats had four guns, and pushing slowly up the river it covered with its fire the British troops on either bank, and silenced some of the enemy's guns that tried to shell the flotilla. The reserve brigade did not come into action, so complete and rapid was the success of the division.

The battle began about half-past four on the morning of July 24, 1915. For half an hour the brigades had been moving forward; but before the infantry charged, all the British howitzers, field and mountain guns bombarded the enemy's foremost trenches with high-explosive shells. For a full hour the batteries continued to smash up the enemy's entrenchments and gun positions; and then the 2d West Kents advanced through the date groves, while eight machine-guns, with the supporting battalions, covered the advance by rapid fire on the opposing trenches. Despite this covering fire, however, the West Kents were met by a terrible fusillade that swept their front lines. An officer in one of the regiments that was maintaining a covering musketry fire said the most magnificent sight he had ever seen was the West Kents going on under the enemy's terrific fusillade, and maneuvering as if they were on parade. As soon as they got up to the Turkish trenches, they wheeled round to the right, and, while their comrades stopped firing for fear of hitting them, they leapt into the trenches and were lost to view.

As they disappeared they get to work with the bayonet, and in a short time the spectators watching the game of life and death saw the Turks running as if the devil himself were after them. So the brigade opened fire again at the fugitives.

ROUT OF THE TURKS

The Turks lost many men, for they fought with matting over their trenches to keep the sun out, and the Kents and the Sikhs stuck them with the bayonet through the matting while they were firing up rather wildly, without being able to see clearly what was happening over their covering. After capturing the towers and a considerable number of prisoners, the Sikhs and the handful of white men had ten minutes' rest, which they spent in binding up their wounded and putting them in the shade of the towers. Then the small force fought the Turks out of another long line of trench, running down to the edge of a creek which formed the extreme left of the Turkish position. Here there was a village with another

157

couple of towers, and these were also stormed after long, terrible bayonet work above the last mat-covered trench. By this time the division had won the battle. The Turks could be seen running away on the left, and the Sikhs and the West Kents were signaled to hold the ground they had won, and not to advance any farther. So, posting guards, they slept by the last two captured towers that night.

General Townshend continued to perform miracles with a force that never consisted of more than four brigades. Towards the end of October the Turks were so strongly established in their new fortifications near Bagdad that they left only a single brigade in their advanced position near Azizie. This rear-guard had a large number of guns, by means of which it held the river against the British gunboats, and pestered the British camp with occasional shells. The British force preserved a grim silence, with the object of lulling the Turk, and making him forget his danger. On one very dark night two British brigades made a long roundabout march in Kut-el-Amara fashion, with a view to getting on the enemy's rear and encircling him, while a third Indo-British brigade undertook a frontal attack at dawn. But the Turk showed himself capable of learning by experience. On this occasion his outposts were flung far into the desert, apparently with a portable wireless instrument well out on their flank. Long before the wide British turning movement threatened their main position, the Turks were in full retreat, taking with them all their guns and most of their stores. Their movement looked like a headlong flight, but it was really a well-executed

158

retirement in face of superior forces, which had carried out so well-planned a maneuver that instant retreat was the only answer to it.

The Indo-British division at once embarked in pursuit upon its picturesque flotilla of bellums, launches, paddle-steamers, horse-barges and gunboats. An unending series of uncharted mud-banks continually interrupted the progress of the extraordinary river armada, boats sticking sometimes for a day on a shoal, and having to wait till the large steamers arrived and dragged them off. A couple of gun-launches scouted ahead for possible ambushes which British aviators might have missed, and airmen in seaplanes and aeroplanes circled over Bagdad, and watched the enemy's lines of communication running across the desert towards Syria, and up the river towards the Caucasus heights. By November 9th General Townshend's officers knew that the great adventure was about to be undertaken. The small British force was set the task of breaking through to Bagdad with a view to linking on with the advanced columns of the Russian army in the Caucasus. One of these columns was rapidly working down the Persian border by Lake Urmia, and another was advancing much farther south towards the city of Hamadan. From Bagdad to Hamadan the distance was 250 miles, across difficult and mountainous country. But it seems to have been thought that, with the Turks beaten at Bagdad, and the German-Persian force routed at Hamadan, the task of connecting the troops of Sir John Nixon and the army of the Grand Duke Nicholas would be fairly easy. On November 19th General Townshend's division having captured the village of Zeur marched against Nuredin Pasha's main system of defenses. These works had been constructed eighteen miles from Bagdad, near the gaunt and imposing ruins of Ctesiphon, which loomed against the sky, at the edge of a reed-grown marsh, half a mile from the Tigris.

NUREDIN PASHA OUT-MANEUVERED

Nuredin Pasha's army was greatly increased. He had four divisions strongly entrenched against four British brigades at Ctesiphon, with a large reserve of good troops encamped a little farther up the river near Bagdad, and composed probably of forces detached from the Caucasian front during midwinter. Yet, in spite of his overwhelming number of troops, his strong and well-planned lines, and his increased batteries of both heavy and light artillery, the Turkish pasha entered the battle a half-beaten man. He had been so continually outmaneuvered by British commanders with inferior forces that he could not trust his own judgment, and the truth is that the British needed only one division of the new armies that had been training for ten months in India in order to conquer Mesopotamia and capture Bagdad and Mosul. On the military authority, or on the politician, who did not send General Townshend—a man of proved genius—the twelve thousand more bayonets he needed, rests the responsibility for all that afterwards happened.

On the morning of November 22d the single Indo-British division attacked the four Turkish divisions, stormed their fortress lines, wiped out an entire army division, taking eight hundred prisoners and a large quantity of arms, and bivouacked victoriously in the captured works of defense. The Turkish report of the battle, spread through the world from the German wireless stations, estimated the number of British troops at 170,000. As a matter of fact, General Townshend, at an extreme estimate, could not have had more than 25,000 men all told, and his striking force could not have exceeded 16,000 Indian and British infantrymen. In spite of heavy counter-attacks by the reinforced Turkish army, the British troops held on to the Turkish position at Ctesiphon till the night of November 24th, when want of water again robbed them of their full victory, and they had to retire four miles to the Tigris. Their position by the river, however, was too weak to be held, and as their small force had incurred heavy losses, many battalions being reduced to less than half their strength, a withdrawal was necessary. They removed their wounded to the boats, and embarked their prisoners, numbering 1,600, and then, after a rearguard action near Azizie, on the night of November 30th, their troops retired in perfect order on Kut-el-Amara. Two of the river-boats, which had been disabled by the enemy's shell fire, had to be abandoned after their guns and engines had been made useless, and the pursuing Turkish army arrived within two hours' march of Kut on December 3d.

Our losses around Ctesiphon were 643 killed, 3,330 wounded, and 594 men not accounted for, bringing the total of 4,567. Having regard to the fine achievement of the British, the list of their casualties was light, and if the British Government had given General Townshend and Sir John Nixon the comparatively small reinforcement of another division, Bagdad would certainly have been won at Ctesiphon.

THE SECOND BRITISH MESOPOTAMIAN EXPEDITION

On December 13 and 14, 1916, the British offensive was launched which resulted in the capture of Kut-el-Amara in February, 1917. The British force which resumed operations in this sector was unofficially reported to consist of 120,000 men under the command of General Frederick Stanley Maude. The advance was made from the Babylonian plains while a second force moved up the Tigris. The new force was supported by artillery much superior to that of the Turks, who were operating far from their base of supplies. The main advance was made along the southern bank of the Tigris where the British were reported to have built a narrow gauge railway to supply their troops. After clearing away all obstacles on this bank the north bank became the scene of operations, and the British lines were drawn close around the town, which fell on February 26th for the second time. The British captured several thousand Turks and pursued the fleeing remnants of the garrison toward Bagdad. The British forces were prompt in pursuit, and although the Turks attempted stands, and high winds and sandstorms harassed the pursuers at frequent intervals, yet the troops swept on, capturing many prisoners and much war material. They found Ctesiphon, where the British surrender of 1915 took place, undefended and, passing on, engaged the Turks on the Diala line, southeast of Bagdad. The British troops effected a surprise, crossing of the Diala on

March 7th and, having bridged the Tigris, a detachment marched up the right bank and drove the enemy from his positions.

THE FALL OF BAGDAD

On March 11th, Bagdad, "the magnificent" famed city of the Arabian Nights and the chief Turkish city in Mesopotamia, fell into British hands.

After consolidating this new conquest the British forces were divided into two columns, one moving north and the other northeast. The first having as an object the capture of the remaining Turkish strongholds above Bagdad, and the second a junction with the strong Russian column which had been operating in western Persia with great success. The Russian forces crossed the Turkish frontier on March 21st and continued the pursuit of the retreating Turks in the direction of Mosul, the powerful Turkish base northwest of Bagdad.

CHAPTER XIV

THE FRENCH ATTACK IN THE CHAMPAGNE DISTRICT

EXTRAORDINARY GERMAN FORTRESS—KETTLE-DRUMS OF DEATH—OPENING OF THE ASSAULT—GENERAL DE CASTELNAU'S SCHEME—MIRACULOUS ADVANCES—FRENCH TROOPS ROUND MASSIGES—AWFUL SLAUGHTER AT TROU BRICOT—CHECK AT BOIS SABOT.

THERE IS an ancient Roman road running from Rheims to the Argonne Forest. About twenty miles east of Rheims this Roman way crosses the Suippes River near the small town of Auberive; thence it runs for about fifteen miles to the outskirts of the forest, some distance south of the hamlet of Massiges. The country through which the old road runs is a barren table-land of chalk that continually swells into low, rounded hills, many of which have been planted with pine-trees. The land is part of the Champagne district, but to mark it from the fertile region of famous vineyards the French themselves call the unfruitful waste of chalk Lousy Champagne. This coarse term is indeed quite an official geographical expression among the French.

Immediately south of the Roman road is a vast circle of earthworks, known as the Camp de Chalons. Old tradition has it that the earthworks were made by Attila, king of the Huns, whose forces were for the first time broken in a great battle on the plateau, whereby Paris was saved and the Huns chased from France. A few miles due west of Attila's camp is the hamlet of Valmy, where the Army of the French Revolution won its first victory over the Royal forces of Prussia and Austria, and thereby founded the democratic movement in modern Europe. For these reasons all the poor, mean country was holy ground to the French soldier, and despite the previous checks to the Army of Champagne, the general opinion in France was that over the stretch of chalk between the Argonne and Rheims the decisive advance against the German host would at last take place; for it was at this position that the breaking of the German front would be most disastrous to the enemy. All the invaders' lines, from Zeebrugge and the Yser to the northern heights of the Aisne, and the hills round Rheims would be taken in flank and the rear, and menaced by a cutting of all the lines of communication if a French army crossed the Dormoise and Py streams. But the Germans proudly boasted that their lines in Champagne were absolutely impregnable, and General von Kluck remarked to a German-American war correspondent that the position was that, if he could not take Paris, neither could the French capture Vouziers.

Between Vouziers and the French front there were four fortified lines, each a mile or more apart. All the downs, on and between these lines, were deeply excavated and transformed into underground fortresses, armed with quick-firing batteries, mortars for aerial torpedoes, piping for the emission of poison-gas clouds, and thousands of machine-guns. Of all their military engineering works the Germans most prided themselves upon their Champagne defenses. These defenses had been greatly strengthened and extended since the French made their first great thrust in February, 1915. The French had then captured the first German line, running close to the Roman road by the hamlet of Perthes. But the loss of this line had put the German engineers on their mettle, and in the intervening months they had brought up hundreds more guns and thousands more Maxims; they had fitted many of the sunken invisible forts with domes of armored steel, and had driven a series of tunnels through the chalk to allow of supports being moved to the fire trenches safely through the heaviest storm of shrapnel and melinite shell.

KETTLE-DRUMS OF DEATH

Despite the confused haste with which this large medley of forces was assembled, the German commander on the Champagne front, General von Einem, had so absolute an assurance of victory that on the eve of the struggle he invited German war correspondents to come and watch the spectacle of his triumph. It was from one of these correspondents, Dr. Max Osborn, of the "Vossische Zeitung," that we obtained the best description of the French bombardment. After telling how the French heavy artillery swept the German rear, seeking to explode hand-bomb depots and other magazines of ammunition, the German with the English name said: "The violence of the bombardment then reached its zenith. At first it had been a raging, searching fire; now it became a mad drumming, beyond all power of imagination. It is impossible to give any idea of the savagery of this hurricane of shells. Never has this old planet heard such an uproar. An officer who had witnessed in the summer the horrors of the Souchez and the Lorette heights, told me they could not in any way be compared with this inconceivably appalling artillery onslaught. Night and day for fifty hours, and in some places for seventy hours, the French guns vomited death and destruction against the German troops and the German batteries. Our strongly-built trenches were filled in, and ground to powder; their parapets and fire platforms were razed and turned into dustheaps; and the men in them were buried, crushed, and suffocated. One of our privates, a high-school young man who survived, amused himself by counting the shells that fell in his limited field of vision. He calculated that nearly a hundred thousand projectiles fell around him in fifty hours."

By September 24th the bombardment reached its sustained level of intensity, and a trifling event that happened in the evening told the soldiers that the advance was about to be made. They were given an extra ration of wine. They tried to sleep, with the kettle-drums of death roaring close behind them, and when réveillé sounded at half-past five on Saturday morning, September 25th, the men drank their coffee, and as the guns made talk impossible, they squatted in their shelters, as far out of the rain as they could get, and smoked their pipes.

At a quarter past nine, as the rain was falling more heavily, a long line of strange figures leaped from the fire-trenches, and charged across the grassy slopes, over which the gas cloud had rolled. Clad in their new invisible blue uniforms with steel helmets to protect them from shrapnel, the infantry looked more like medieval warriors than like modern soldiers. Their bayoneted rifles resembled the ancient spears, and the most novel weapon they carried, the hand-bomb, was but a deadlier form of the old-fashioned grenade. Most of the battalions seem to have been divided into two sections, bombers and bayoneters. On reaching the first German trenches, the men with the bayonets crossed them and charged farther into the German lines, while the men with the bombs stayed in the captured position until they had smashed the Germans out of it.

OPENING OF THE ASSAULT

The first waves of the assault broke over the entire German front, from Auberive to the Argonne Forest, for a length of fifteen miles. But this was only meant to test the general strength of the enemy and pin his men down to every yard of the Champagne position. The main series of thrusts were then delivered at four points, the men advancing in narrow but very long and loose masses which spread out behind the first hostile line of downs. On the extreme left, at the village of Auberive, where the Germans held most of the fortified houses and the French were deeply entrenched along the southern outskirts, little progress could be made. Here the force of the French attack was skilfully directed northwestward up the long slopes leading to the hamlet of L'Epine de Vedegrange. Another strong attacking force was directed from Souain through the Punch-bowl northward and against a line of fortified heights known as Hill 185, on which Navarin Farm lay, the Butte of Souain, and Tree Hill. Eastward of Tree Hill was the formidable height of Tahure Butte, with the village of Tahure south of it, and in the triangle of Tahure, Souain, and Perthes villages was the immense German fortress called the Trou Bricot, and nicknamed the Hollow of Death. East of this hollow was the fortressed escarpment of the Butte of Mesnil. Eastward of Mesnil was Bastion Crest, with the group of houses called Maisons de Champagne behind it, and still farther eastward, near the edge of the Argonne Forest, was a large hand-shaped down, known as the Hand of Massiges, with south of it a quarried hill, called from its curious appearance the Earhole.

GENERAL DE CASTELNAU'S SCHEME

General de Castelnau's main scheme was to penetrate between each principal German hill position, and then turn and encircle it with two flanking columns. But before this could be done, the first German line had to be captured, the strength of each hostile fortress tested, and then the columns had to advance along the valleys and the slopes with terrible enfilading fires sweeping them on both sides. It was afterwards calculated by observers of the conquered ground that along this front of fifteen miles, with a depth of two and a half miles, the German engineers had constructed nearly four hundred miles of trenches. And, despite the extraordinary duration and intensity of the French bombardment, in which millions of shells were used, this enormous system of human warrens was only damaged badly on the front slopes and in the southernmost hollows between the downs. The high ramparts of chalk protected from destruction far the greater part of the vast earthworks. The new French howitzers threw to a height of 12,000 feet a very heavy shell that descended almost vertically. Yet this wonderful projectile could not destroy the sheltered caverns and trenches in the downs on which the German sappers had been laboring for twelve months.

MIRACULOUS ADVANCES

Both the French and British leading divisions had made advances of a miraculous kind. In particular, the position of the Colonial troops at Maisons de Champagne resembled that of the Highland Brigade at the Cité St. Auguste at Lens. Pouring with sweat, the men had stormed through machine-gun fire, wire entanglements, rows of trenches, and gun positions, and after a rush of three miles they reached the last crest of chalk from which the valley of the Dormoise and the village of Ripont were dominated. Had supports quickly arrived, the road to Vouziers, Namur, and Liège would have been won. But, apparently, the single battalion that reached the Maisons, having lost all its officers and being commanded by a sergeant, had moved too quickly. The French Staff could not get more men up in time, and the half-shattered battalion, caught between two flanking fires from

170

Massiges and Beauséjour, and attacked in front from Ripont, had to leave the heavy German and Austrian batteries it had captured on the crest, and fall back at two o'clock on Saturday afternoon.

The French mountain-gun, first issued in small numbers to the Chasseurs in the mountains had become the supreme weapon for nearly all battlefields. It was a variation of the "75," lighter and shorter of range, but with a higher angle of fire. It was used close behind the troops, almost like a machine-gun, but while a machine-gun could not hit men behind a hill, the mountain-gun could shell or shrapnel enemy troops sheltering in a hollow or on the reverse slopes of a down. Under the cover of a bombardment of this kind the French bombers rushed to the German hill trenches, and flung in grenades, forcing the Germans to retreat.

FRENCH TROOPS ROUND MASSIGES

From September 25th to the 30th, the Germans round Massiges continually counter-attacked, with a view to winning back their lost line. It was then that they suffered quite as heavy losses as the French had done in their attacks. The last of the German counter-attacks came from Cernay, in the northeast. The troops deployed at the foot of the slopes of the little rounded down known as La Justice. But the French light guns shattered this counter-attack before it got under way, and the troops round La Justice broke and fled in a panic. This was quite an extraordinary feature of the conflict, for hitherto the German soldiers had fought with remarkable tenacity, and when defeated had either surrendered or been killed. The

171

spectacle of a large body of veteran enemy troops breaking and fleeing in panic under shell fire was regarded by the French command as highly significant.

AWFUL SLAUGHTER AT TROU BRICOT

Trou Bricot, seen first on the photographs taken by the reconnoitring French airmen, formed three round, pale blots, connected by a long white streak—the communication trench. Then there were six more whitish rounds, strung along the white line like balls on a string. It was on the white line that the French gunners began their work, and their heaviest shells fell in hundreds, at a range of five miles, on the main communication trench, cutting the telephone wires, destroying the shrapnel-proof passages, and choking the outlet. Then, at a signal from the watching airmen, a hurricane of shells fell on Trou Bricot and on the great Elberfeldt Camp behind it, and turned the gigantic fortress into a slaughter-house. The German divisions that garrisoned the extraordinary fortress were so staggered and dazed by the·bombardment that a single division of French-African troops sweeping up the road from Souain to Tahure cut them off in the rear from Tree Hill and the position of Baraque, where the Breton Division, advancing from the other side of the work, connected and formed a great net with the Savoy troops working forward from the Pocket in front.

CHECK AT BOIS SABOT

The Bois Sabot was a horse-shoe-shaped fortress, surrounding a pine-wood on the right of Navarin

Farm. The work spread along the foot and sides of a gently-sloping hill, and it was laid out with such skill by the German engineers that they regarded it as one of the strongest points in their entire line of defense. The heavy bombardment had done little damage to its network of wire entanglements and deep subterranean lines; and in the evening of September 25th the French troops could only lie flat on their stomachs near this work, with the rain pouring on them and asphyxiating shells from the German batteries along the Py River blinding and strangling them. It was then that the Foreign Legion advanced through a curtain of shrapnel and flung themselves down by the Colonials. The Colonials were relieved in the night by the Zouaves and Moroccan troops, and the Legion crawled the following day into a stretch of woods to prepare for an attack. But the weather was so foggy that the French guns on September 26th and September 27th could not do any useful work, and, much to the disadvantage of the Allies, the fighting had to be temporarily suspended, so that the enemy won forty-eight hours in which to bring down reinforcements, guns, and ammunition to the Champagne front.

At last, at half-past three in the afternoon of September 28th, the air cleared sufficiently for the attack to be launched. The Legion had lost more than half its force in the great drive on the Vimy Heights in Artois in the spring, when it penetrated farther than any French troops. But two thousand more foreign lovers of France had since joined the Legion, and brought it up to full strength.

In the advance from Souain, in the pine-wood near Navarin Farm, the Legionaries had again lost nearly a quarter of their men from shell and shrapnel before firing a shot. This made them very angry. They always disliked being in reserve when a charge was made, and they asked their colonel, in the evening of September 27th, to beg the general at Souain to let the Legion, as a special favor, lead the grand charge against the enemy's last line.

The request was allowed, and the famous corps, which has figured in so many romantic novels since Ouida wrote "Under Two Flags," went out to die. Every Legionary knew that he was doomed; for the plan of attack was that the Legion should fling itself straight on the front of the fortress of Bois Sabot, and there engage the enemy with such fury that 12,000 other men—Zouaves, Moors, and Colonials—could make a surprise attack on both flanks. The Legion gathered in the woods in two columns, and then, amid the cheers of the French troops occupying the trenches in front of them, they leapt across these trenches, over the heads of their comrades, and charged across the zone of death into the mouth of the Horse-shoe. First a rain of shrapnel smote them: then the stream of bullets from machine-guns and rifles caught them in the front and raked them on both sides. With a dense curtain of shrapnel behind it and torrents of lead pouring on its front and flanks, the Legion was mowed down as by a gigantic scythe. Platoons fell to a man, but the regiment went forward. At some points in the line the stream of lead was so thick that falling men were turned over and over, the dead bodies being rolled along the ground by more bullets, as withered leaves roll in the winds of autumn. Yet some men of the leading battalion lived through it, and, reaching the wire entanglements, pounded them aside with the butts of their rifles. But of that battalion only one man got through the wires, and he fell headlong into the first German trench with a bullet through his knee. Then the second battalion followed, and a few men lived to get into the first trench and began to clear it out. But the last battalions of the Legion came forward in a tiger-spring and bombed and bayoneted their way into the fortress.

There, in the maze of trenches, and the shattered pine-wood, the Legion fought to the last man, and when the other troops closed on the flanks there were very few Germans alive in Bois Sabot. The Foreign Legion had also perished; only a small handful of its men remained. But in its great death-struggle the regiment had done one of the most amazing things in war. And when the noise of its achievement spread through France and echoed over the earth, thousands of volunteers from neutral countries came to Paris to enlist. Thus out of its glorious ashes the most famous of all corps in the modern world was born again from the inspiration given by the men who died on Vimy Ridge in Artois and the slopes of Bois Sabot in Champagne. Such is the power of the heroism of the dead upon the minds of living men who have scarcely any call to fight; for it was the Swiss, the American, the Scandinavian, and the Spaniard and Portuguese who traveled at their own expense to France to join the new Foreign Legion. The heroism of the Legion firmly established the Army of Champagne in the region of Navarin Farm.

In all some 26,000 German prisoners were taken in Champagne, besides three hundred and fifty officers and one hundred and fifty cannon. And as the enemy suffered terribly in counter-attacks, the total French losses were at least balanced by those of Einem's, Heeringen's and the Crown Prince's troops. It is calculated that the killed, wounded and captured among the Germans were equivalent to the infantry of six army corps, or about 150,000 men. Fully twelve German army corps were shattered, and had to withdraw for large drafts. The general result of the French thrust in Champagne and the British thrust in Artois was that the enemy's entire strength was so diminished that the pressure against the Russian armies was greatly relaxed. This was the principal achievement of the western Allies. They obtained breathing space for Russia.

CHAPTER XV

ITALY'S PART IN THE WAR

HOW TEUTONIC CONSPIRACY DELAYED THE ATTACK
AGAINST AUSTRIA—ITALY'S BOLD INITIAL STROKE
—BATTLE OF MONTE CROCE—WESTERN TYROL
THREATENED—GALLANT ITALIAN SAPPERS—BATTLE
OF PLAVA—THE GREAT DRIVE OF 1916—GENERAL
CADORNA'S LAST VICTORY—THE ITALIAN ARTILLERY
—THE BATTLE OF SAN MICHELE—THE ATTACK
ON 121-METRE HILL.

IT WOULD be necessary to go back fifty years into
history to explain why it was that Bismarck's treachery
placed in Austrian hands every mountain pass through
which an Italian army could move against Austria.
Yet this was the condition which Italy faced upon her
entrance into the Great War. Even this fearful
handicap would have been less onerous if General
Cadorna had been able to make the surprise attack
against Austria which he had planned. By the
cunningness of plutocratic German interests in
Italy, Signor Giolitti, the chief representative of
Teutonism in Italy, intervened and overthrew the
War Cabinet, delaying hostilities for nineteen
days. But against these tremendous odds the
Italian troops started their campaign with a series
of brilliant successes, because the enemy reckoned
them too lightly.

ITALY'S BOLD INITIAL STROKE

Thus it befell that the Archduke Eugene, with General von Höfer as his Chief of Staff, and Dankl as army commander in the Tyrol, made the mistake of holding the first line on the Austrian frontier with a ridiculously small number of troops. The Alpini and the Bersaglieri, with some battalions of the line and some gendarmes, crossed the frontier soon after midnight of May 21, 1915, at all the strategical points, and by a hundred swift, fierce little skirmishes, began to reverse the positions of Austria and Italy.

Meanwhile the Alpine troops were climbing the mountain, by ways only known to themselves through many mountaineering excursions undertaken by their leaders in summer holidays. The officers led the men over the trackless screes and rocky falls, over glaciers and snowdrifts, and then descended the opposite slopes at some distance behind the enemy vanguards skirmishing near the entrance to the path.

By the evening of May 25th, all the passes of the Dolomite Alps were won, and good breaches were made at Tonale Pass along the northwest and in the Carnic and Julian Alps along the northeast front.

The gun trains began to move more rapidly towards the holes made in the great mountain rampart, and tens of thousands of Italian engineers went up by train and motor-vehicles, and started building trenches and making gun emplacements. Meanwhile, the main Italian Infantry force, consisting of the Third Army, moved with great speed across the Friuli Plain through Udine, Palmanova, and St. Georgio, where two railway lines ran into the Isonzo Valley and the Torre Valley.

178

Here the covering troops had moved forward over the frontier at midnight on May 24th, and in a single day they captured nearly all the towns and villages between the frontier and the Isonzo River, from Caporetto, nestling in the north below the precipices of Monte Nero, to the hamlet of Belvedere southward on the Gulf of Trieste.

The Italian Commander-in-Chief, having conquered practically all the enemy's first line along a front of three hundred miles, waited to see in what sector the Austrian pressure would be most strongly felt. The answering counter-thrust of the enemy came at Monte Croce Pass, in the Carnic Alps, on May 29th. It was a foggy day, and under cover of the mist the enemy massed a strong force through the railway from Villach and brought them to Mauthen, from which they made five stubborn attempts to regain the pass. The Alpini and Bersaglieri swept away each wave of assault by musketry and machine-gun fire at almost point-blank range; then, leaping up after the last attack, they drove the enemy down the valley at the point of the bayonet.

BATTLE OF MONTE CROCE

This was only the beginning of the Battle of Monte Croce. Each side had large forces within call, and fed the troops up the valleys as the fighting-lines wasted. So the struggle continued day and night, while the Italian commander pushed over the neighboring passes and strengthened himself for the great counter-attack. The height known as Freikofel, commanding the Plöcken Plateau, near Monte Croce Pass, was stormed on June 8th, and the Pass of Valentina and the Pass of Oregione, 7,590 feet high, overlooking the thickly-wooded Gail Valley, were taken. The last pass was won by the Alpini climbing over the white mass of Paralba and fighting their way down to the high saddle.

When war broke out, sand-bags, machine-guns, and quick-firers were hauled up to the eyrie, and in a few hours a governmentally-subsidized hotel on the road to Falzarego became a splendid fort, with quarters for a large garrison, and guns dominating the far-famed ravine. But the Alpini were led by men with ingenious minds and minute knowledge of the ground. Most of the fighting took place on the great northern mountain height, crowned by the glaciers and snow-fields of Tofana, and around the Cinque Torri, a line of apparently inaccessible peaks.

WESTERN TYROL THREATENED

At Falzarego and Sasso d'Istria the Italian troops were approaching the rear of the Col di Lana, and its neighboring mountain masses on which the fortress defending Cordevole Valley were constructed.

General Cadorna, having both the gift of strategy and ample fighting troops of fine quality, was able to impose his will on his adversary. The Austrians had only to advance some twenty miles across their Trentino frontier to reach Verona, that city of old romance still fragrant with the memories of Romeo and Juliet.

All the first striking successes by General Cadorna, between the last week in May, 1915, and the third

180

week in August, 1915, were accomplished with a total casualty list of less than 30,000 names. The Austro-Hungarian losses in the same period on the same front were 18,000 dead, 54,000 wounded, and 18,000 prisoners.

GALLANT ITALIAN SAPPERS

Along the Isonzo the retreating Austrians had broken down the high embankment used to carry off the snow-water, and had thereby inundated the plain in the manner of the Belgain Yser defenses. The gallant Italian sappers, working under a plunging fire from the enemy's batteries on the mountains, foothills, and Carso table-land, had rapidly thrown some light pontoon bridges over the flood. Along these frail temporary structures the first Italian contingents crossed in the darkness, took the first line of Austrian trenches near the waterside, and broke up the light artillery positions close to the river.

The Isonzo was forced by a smashing bayonet attack, and the Italian troops headed by motor-cyclists with machine-guns, cycling scouts, and aeroplane observers, flowed in two arms around every position at which the Austrians tried to make a stand. By this continual threat of an encircling movement they forced the Austrians into Monfalcone. The enemy then for the first time displayed a telling ingenuity in warfare. Like the Turk in the Suvla Bay battles, he set fire to some of the slopes which the Italians were attacking. But while the pine-wood near Monfalcone flared to the skies, the quick-maneuvering Italians, headed by a grenadier battalion, broke into the open town and occupied it, after storming the Rocca promontory.

181

All went well during the week following the capture of Monfalcone. General Cadorna had the keen joy of recapturing the Isonzo town of Gradisca, which his father had won from the same foe forty-nine years before. This capture completed the Italian control of the Lower Isonzo, and the general attack on all the fortresses guarding Trieste was then prepared.

THE BATTLE OF PLAVA

In the center of this long fortress-line was the railway town of Plava, lying on the eastern bank of the Isonzo, beneath the wooded heights of Ternovane Forest. It was a key position, and the general Italian offensive began by a night attack on Plava, from Mount Korada on the other side of the river. The Italian sappers, with great coolness and skill, built a pontoon bridge in the darkness; and the infantry crossed the water on June 17th, and by a violent bayonet attack carried the town and the surrounding heights. The Italian general, having breached the enemy's second line in this place, poured strong forces into the gap, and a great battle took place on the edge of the forested highland. The Italian heavy artillery across the river on Mount Korada was able to send a plunging fire on the lower table-land, and with this help the dashing Italian troops won the battle and drove the enemy back.

The first grand open-field battle began on June 22d, and it was not until the last days of July that the battle drew to a close. In this long and terrible conflict in the open field, the theatre of which included all the Carso front, the Vipacco River valley, and the southern part of the Ternovane Forest, the enemy suffered such heavy losses that his army was half shattered.

Yet his position had been found impregnable by the forces of the Italian commander, for the five hundred guns which the Italian general employed were quite inadequate. The ground was unassailable. There are innumerable caves from which quick-firing guns could be worked, and labyrinths of crags and scattered rocks, and foliage-hung cliffs behind which large reserves could safely be sheltered.

But General Boroevics lost all the tremendous natural advantages of this immense natural fortress when he sent his divisions charging across the open ground against the lines to which the Italians were clinging; for though the Italians only held on to the rim of the table-land, with a flooded river a third of a mile broad beneath them, yet their well-built sand-bag trenches gave them excellent cover against the enemy's artillery.

The first phase of the Battle of Gorizia ended in the repulse of the Austrian counter-attack in the middle of July. General Cadorna then delivered a fiercer assault, based on the knowledge he had obtained by his first reconnaissance in force. For three days and nights—July 18th, 19th and 20th—the troops of the Italian Second and Third Armies leaped forward with heroic energy all along the zone of the Isonzo, and broke through the wire entanglements and the armored trenches, taking 3,500 prisoners. As a rule, the Italians attacked by day, and then resisted in their newly-won positions the nocturnal counter-attacks by the enemy.

Owing to the fine work of their engineers, they retained all the ground they had won, and began to deliver night attacks on July 20th.

BOTH SIDES REINFORCED

But the next morning General Cadorna stayed the forward movement of the Duke of Aosta, and bringing reinforcements, ordered every man to help the engineers in strengthening and extending the trenches; for the commander, either through his aerial observers or his secret agents, had obtained knowledge that the enemy was about to make his supreme effort. July 21st passed quietly; then, on July 22d, a mightier concentration of heavy Austrian artillery opened a hurricane fire on the Italian lines.

SUPREME AUSTRIAN EFFORT

The main infantry attack was delivered towards Gradisca, where the Italians had built their chief bridges across the Isonzo. The first line of Italian troops could not kill the closely packed lines quickly enough, and it seemed as though the position would be lost. But the Italian gunnery officers, watching the operation from their observing-posts, had the situation well in hand, and at the critical moment a storm of shrapnel from five hundred guns and howitzers fell on the large target in front of the first Italian line, and made such holes in it that the garrison of the fire-trench beat back the remnant of the attacking masses with little difficulty.

The next day General Boroevics launched another strong attack on the Italian positions near the sea-edge of the Carso table-land, but it failed completely, though the rough ground did not permit the Italians to make another fierce pursuit. Finally two Austrian divisions, which advanced from the heights of San Michele and San Martino to storm Sagrado, were so smashed up that, on July 25th, the Italian troops were able to carry some of the entrenched slopes of San Martino, and to storm the hill of Sei Busi.

The crest of San Michele was very important, as it dominated a large part of the table-land, and the main tide of battle surged around and over it for many days. At last the Italian infantry, on July 27th, tearing forward with passionate ardor, bombed and bayoneted their way to the summit, along which they then tried to establish themselves. They also sand-bagged part of the lower slope facing the enemy; but under the torrent of high-explosive and asphyxiating shell the crest and the exposed slopes beneath it could not be garrisoned.

Like the grand drive of the Franco-British forces at Massiges and Loos, the Italian offensive on the Gorizia fortress chain failed to break the enemy's resistance. Yet, as in Artois and Champagne, so on the Isonzo, the heroism, endurance, and violence of effort of the attacking forces were tremendous.

When it is remembered that Gibraltar, with only a hundred guns, held out against the attacking forces of two kingdoms for more than three and a half years, it cannot be wondered that the Italian army found the great, peaked, rocky mass of the Carso a very difficult thing to conquer; for most of the advantages derived from the developments in modern artillery rested with the defending forces. In particular the Austrians had heavy mobile batteries, moving on newly-made railway tracks, and lighter motor-batteries working along many new branching roads. These could seldom be put out of action, and they came rapidly into the battlefield when a movement of the Italian infantry was signaled on the observation heights. All night the table-land was swept by search-lights, which quickly picked out any body of troops trying to steal an advance, and lighted them up for destruction by the artillery. All the wire entangle-ments were charged with deadly currents of electricity; and more formidable than all the guns, howitzers, poison-gas cylinders, aerial torpedoes and flame-pro-jectors which the enemy employed, was his ubiquitous and skilfully used secondary armament of machine-guns. The sea-mists, floating in from the Adriatic, often tempted the Italian sand-bag brigades to make a dash for the enemy trench, when the hostile artillery was blanketed with the fog. But even in these circum-stances the remarkably complete organization of the enemy enabled him to parry a stab through the fog. As soon as a trench was lost telephone reports reached the German and Austrian gunners, and these, knowing to an inch the range of the lost, invisible position, battered it with asphyxiating shell, by way of prepara-tion for a strong counter-attack by their bombing parties Such were the conditions under which the Third Italian Army wore down the opposing effectives, and very gradually yet continually worked forward to the Doberdo Plateau. The heroism displayed in this work will never be fully known.

THE GREAT DRIVE OF 1916

The Italian lines formed an immense semicircle, running from Monfalcone to Boschini. At the extreme right the enemy was, to the north and east of Monfalcone, in possession of a series of heights, the most important of which, the Debeli and Cosich, completely dominated the Italian works. At the extreme left, on the sides of St. Michael's Mount, the situation was identical. In the center there was nothing but an entanglement of trenches and approach works climbing up from the plain of the Isonzo along the steep slopes of Selz, Monte Sei Busi, and Bosco Capuccio.

The offensive of July, October and November had made it possible to rectify favorably the Italian front, but they had been able to climb only one stage of this Calvary, which led them up to the Doberdo Plateau. In spite of obstacles, the Italian troops were not discouraged. From the end of May battles succeeded each other at Monfalcone. On June 28th the 85-Meter Height was attacked. On July 3d and 4th progress continued; on August 4th a general attack was opened on the extreme right with such vigor that the Italians captured 85-Meter Hill.

GENERAL CADORNA'S LAST VICTORY

The Italian troops were commanded by an old General, ill with cancer, who followed the development of operations in an invalid chair. He had persistently refused the advice of his doctors to leave his troops and undergo treatment behind the lines. His malady grew worse; it had almost carried him away when the attack was decided. The Italian troops, with superb dash, went up to the assault, overthrew the defense works, and, with the bayonet, conquered the positions. Then the General, with tears in his eyes, gravely said to those who surrounded him: "You can take me away now to die in the hospital; the battle is won." He has just been gazetted Corps Commander.

The enemy, deceived by this activity of General Cadorna's troops to the east of Monfalcone, sent important reserves to that point. For two days the Italians were forced to abandon some advanced trenches. But this action was only a demonstration. The principal attack was planned against that part of the Carso which had been best defended by nature—San Michele and Monte Sei Busi.

The system of fortifications which our allies were to attack was composed of three lines:

The first, which was certainly the most solid, followed the crests of San Michele, descended before San Martino del Carso, ran between the burned woods and the Polazzo, traversed the heights of Sei Busi, overhung the Isonzo plain at the Selz caverns, ran around La Rocca, and descended to the sea on the east of Monfalcone.

The second line followed the first a slight distance further back as far as San Martino del Carso, passed behind Doberdo, climbed up the Crni Hrib hillock, and supported the first line of the Debeli.

The third line descended from the valley of the Vipacco, at the height of Rupa, and gained the heights to the east of Oppacchiasella, passed Novavas and 208-Meter and 114-Meter Hills, reached 77-Meter Hill, crossed the Lissert, and reached the sea at 21-Meter Hill.

THE ITALIAN ARTILLERY

Suddenly, on August 6th, a terrible bombardment was begun on the Italian side. While Podgora and Monte Sabatino were shaken, the attack began from San Michele to Monte Sei Busi and Selz, also with unaccustomed vigor. A hurricane of fire was poured down upon the stone trenches. On this Carso, where so many struggles had already been fought and where so many thousands of men had found their graves, a new phase of the war was developed—the entry on the scene of powerful Italian artillery. Once the way was opened for them, the Italian regiments went up to the assault with an indescribable ardor. For long months they had suffered, in the trenches of the Carso, all possible privations. They had had to accept the furtive struggle underground. Today they were taking their revenge.

THE BATTLE OF SAN MICHELE

Monte San Michele, which dominated all this region west of the Carso—the most arid of all—is composed of four summits, following each other from west to east, their heights varying from 810 to 902 feet. The battle there lasted two days. The Twentieth Division of Honveds (Hungarian Landwehr), which was defending the positions, multiplied counterattacks, sending clouds of asphyxiating gas against the assaulting columns. On both sides the losses were terrible, but the Italians continued their advance; one by one the summits were conquered, the trenches turned, in order to be able to meet the attacks of an enemy which felt that, once San Michele was lost, the

189

Doberdo Plateau would be invaded, the first line would be taken and the second hard hit. The innumerable machine guns hidden in the caverns spat out their fire incessantly, hand grenades flew on all sides. The attackers had to climb over heaps of dead in order to continue their advance.

When the last height had fallen the infantry, the grenadiers, and the Bersagleri (light infantry) rushed toward the high plateau. The Austrians suffered enormous losses. A Budapest regiment numbering 2,500 men ceased to exist.

On August 9th, the Italians captured San Martino del Carso, a little village completely ruined by shellfire, where the Carso cave dwellers, whom the Italians had driven forth from their grottoes, were putting up a last defense. Then the action continued with vigor; Cadorna's armies swept the whole Doberdo Plateau. One by one the positions were cleared. Doberdo, the bare peak of Cosich, Marcottini, and, to the north of San Michele, the village of Boschini were conquered by vigorous assault. The whole western part of the Carso was in the hands of the Italians; the Austrian troops withdrew to the east of Vallone.

They were not given time to fortify themselves there; the dash of the Bersaglieri and the Italian infantry was so impetuous that Oppacchiasella was soon in their hands. And, on the wooded slopes of Nad Logem, a violent action was begun.

THE ATTACK ON 121-METER HILL

To the south of the Carso, the forward march was more difficult; 85-Meter Hill definitely taken, the struggle began for the possession of 121-Meter Hill. The enemy had transformed that stony hill into a veritable fortress. Behind the trenches the troops had as shelters deep caverns which could contain several battalions. Confident that they would never be beaten back, the Austrians had fitted them out luxuriously; the walls were paneled, electricity was installed everywhere, ventilating ducts made it easy to change the air, water mains brought good drinking water. Along the Vallone ridge, every regiment had its numbered cavern. The officers' rooms were sumptuous; bed, chairs, sofas, tables, carpets, nothing was missing in them. The newspapers found there were dated August 3d, and reported the declarations of Premier Tisza, assuring his auditors that the Austrian Staff had taken all the necessary measures to keep the Italians forever out of Gorizia.

CHAPTER XVI

THE MARVELOUS WORK OF THE RED CROSS

VITAL NEED OF VOLUNTARY AID—A FAMOUS FOUN-
DATION — RED CROSS HOSPITALS IN ENGLAND —
TRACING WOUNDED AND MISSING—CANADIAN RED
CROSS WORK—THE GREAT HOSPITAL AT CLIVEDEN—
WORK IN BELGIUM—AMERICAN HELPERS IN FRANCE
—SERBIA'S PITIFUL PLIGHT.

IN TIMES of peace comparatively little is heard of
the great voluntary organizations whose business it is
to keep the machinery always going for dealing with
the wounded when war breaks out. Best known of
these is the Red Cross Society, taking its name from
the familiar symbol—the reversal of the colors of the
Swiss national flag—denoting everywhere throughout
the Christian world work for the sick and wounded.

Working with the Red Cross Society in the war
was another body, the Order of St. John of Jerusalem,
more generally known as the St. John's Ambulance
Brigade. This order claims descent from a famous
foundation which arose in the earliest days of the
twelfth century, with the object of giving shelter and
assistance to pilgrims to the Holy Land, who were at
that time suffering under the heel of the Turk.

Its task today is very different. From its home at
St. John's Gate, in Clerkenwell, it organized ambulance

brigades which soon became a familiar feature in most parts of England. It had, in the days before the war, some 30,000 members who had secured their certificates in first-aid, who worked under discipline, and many of whom had been given a certain amount of training each year in War Office and Admiralty hospitals on the understanding that they would offer themselves should war break out.

At the start of the war the .authorities appealed to the St. John's Ambulance Brigade for volunteers. There was an immediate response. The Ambulance volunteers enabled the members of the Royal Army Medical Corps to be released from home work and to go out with the Expeditionary Force. In addition, some six hundred and fifty St. John's Ambulance men were mobilized and sent out with the force. The services of these St. John's Ambulance workers and of other voluntary workers secured by the Order of St. John were of unquestioned value.

It became evident at the beginning of the war that these voluntary bodies would have to expand their activities to a degree undreamed of before, and would further have to raise money on a previously unknown scale. A joint War Committee was formed of the British Red Cross and the Order of St. John, and the task of raising the money was undertaken, at the request of Lord Rothschild, the President of the Joint Committee, by *The London Times*.

The first great task that fell to the Red Cross was the sudden improvisation of a fleet of motor-transports. Old horse-ambulances were still being used. Their slowness, jolting, and inadequacy were responsible for much needless suffering among the wounded. If it were possible, wounded men were taken down from the front in the motor-wagons which had brought up stores. These motor-wagons were almost springless, accentuating every jolt in the road, particularly on the paved roads of Northern France. They were trying enough for hardy and able-bodied men to travel in, but hideous for the wounded.

Money was asked for motor-ambulances. Within three weeks funds were raised to purchase over five hundred. Motor manufacturers went to work day and night, and by the end of January, 1915, over a thousand motor-ambulances and other motor-vehicles were at work. An army of trained drivers had been enlisted to handle them, and over 100,000 patients had been carried in them.

Then the societies established a number of hospitals of their own. In France six were opened immediately around Boulogne, and three in or near Calais. The voluntary hospitals offered by British donors to the French and Belgian Governments were inspected and supervised. The Red Cross established several hospitals in England itself. The largest of these was the King George's Hospital in Stamford Street, London

RED CROSS HOSPITALS IN ENGLAND

The British Red Cross had 2,300 Voluntary Aid Detachments, with a membership exceeding 67,000. With the aid of these some six hundred auxiliary hospitals were equipped, and rest stations were formed for attending to the wounded on the way to hospital. Convalescent homes were established. One department of the Red Cross which constituted a romance—often enough, alas! a very painful romance—was for tracing the wounded and missing. Its agents traveled throughout the battle-stricken regions of Northern France, searching everywhere for news which could relieve the anxiety of those at home.

TRACING WOUNDED AND MISSING

Another great department of the Red Cross work was the provision of supplies for the hospitals at the front. Immense stores were wanted that could not possibly be had from the Government, from X-ray outfits to tooth-brushes. The societies provided them. Garments and comforts for the wounded were sent out by the hundred thousand, not only to British armies on the Continent, but to wounded in almost every center of the war.

The British Red Cross did not stand alone. Allied organizations from the Dominions did their share splendidly. The Australasian societies liberally subscribed to the British funds, and looked well after their own men. The Australasians opened a hospital at Wimereux, staffed and maintained by Australasians, and their contingent was accompanied by an ample and adequate medical and nursing organization, which aroused great admiration.

In Canada the work of the Red Cross was taken up at the very beginning with immense enthusiasm. When the Canadian Contingent arrived in England, the ships that bore the troops carried, not merely a full medical and nursing staff, but every kind of medical comfort likely to be required.

OVERSEAS RED CROSS WORK

About the same time as the contingent reached Plymouth, Colonel Hodgetts, the Chief Commissioner of the Canadian Red Cross, arrived in London and established himself in an office in Cockspur Street. This office became a center through which a constant stream of gifts poured into the United Kingdom and into France. Large donations of money were given by the Canadians to the British Red Cross. Many motor-ambulances were purchased. Comforts of all kinds, foodstuffs and supplies, were gathered and distributed with the most lavish hand. These gifts were by no means confined to the Canadian troops. In addition to the large gifts of money, a number of motor-ambulances were presented to the British Red Cross. A coach was provided for a hospital train which Princess Christian was procuring, and a Canadian Ward was built in a hospital which the St. John Ambulance Society was constructing at the front. The Canadian Red Cross came to England to help, and it did so. It did great and much-needed work. In addition to the establishment at Le Touquet, the Canadian Red Cross made itself responsible for the construction, maintenance and administration of a great hospital at Cliveden, Mr. and Mrs. Waldorf Astor's well known Thames-side estate. Mr. Astor offered the Canadians the use of Taplow Lodge, Cliveden, and the grounds around it, and undertook sweeping structural alterations and additions to make the place suitable.

THE GREAT HOSPITAL AT CLIVEDEN

Early in 1915 the Duchess of Connaught's Canadian Red Cross Hospital, as the new establishment was
196

called, was opened with one hundred and eight beds. It was complete in every detail. The main building was a transformed tennis-court, which made as cheerful looking a hospital as could be devised. Its white walls, and its roof of green painted glass, its floors covered with green linoleum, and its abundant flowers, combined to produce a very pleasant effect. The lofty roof and the fresh country air largely robbed the place of the familiar hospital atmosphere of iodoform and antiseptics. The operating theater was one that the finest London hospitals might well have envied on account of its size, light, and perfect aseptic conditions. The accommodation was surprisingly excellent when it is remembered that it was created in a short time, out of what had been an adjunct to a big country house.

BELGIANS AT BEACHBOROUGH PARK

Beachborough Park opened in October, 1914, with close on fifty beds. Its first consignment of patients was over fifty Belgians fresh from the front, with wounds that had received little or nothing beyond first-aid. Some of the men had lain four or five days in the field before being brought in. The staff toiled over them for thirty-six hours, two nights and a day, without rest. When the Canadian troops reached the front, Beachborough Park became, as it continued from then on, a reflection of the great battles in which the Dominion troops took part. The establishment was so successful that after a few months it was determined to enlarge it, and wards were built in the grounds, enlarging the accommodation to

197

about one hundred and fifty patients. It would be impossible to detail all the places that were opened in England for the accommodation of the wounded. The Royal Army Medical Department took over numerous old buildings, schools, factories and the like, and in addition built temporary hospitals in parks and gardens on a wholesale scale. It absorbed race-tracks and transformed lunatic asylums; voluntary hospitals all over the country opened their doors to the wounded, the London Hospital alone placing three hundred beds at the disposal of the authorities. A number of private houses and nursing homes, particularly in London, were turned into special hospitals for doctors. Among the best known of these were the hospital at 27, Grosvenor Square, and Queen Alexandra's Hospital for officers at Highgate. Special sections of the community provided hospitals. The American community established and maintained a fine hospital at Paignton, Devon, in one of the most beautiful country houses of Southern England.

The claims of the Belgian people made a special appeal to the British nation, and numerous parties of surgeons and nurses went out more or less independently to help the wounded during the early fighting. The best known of these was Dr. Hector Munro, and his experiences may be taken as a notable example of others.

Dr. Munro, at the beginning of the war, abandoned for a time his practice in London and volunteered for service in Belgium. His first experiences showed him the great need of motor-ambulances for the Belgian Army, and returning to London on September 22, 1914, he issued an appeal which was to have widespread results.

He stated that he proposed to raise a small ambulance corps, with two surgeons, a staff of twenty helpers, and four cars. "I have just returned from Belgium, where I visited Ostend, Bruges, Ghent, and Antwerp, to inquire as to the need for Red Cross work there. The difficulty is to get the wounded from ten to thirty miles around Ghent into the town. There are admirable hospitals around Ghent. One large hotel has been converted by the Belgian Red Cross into *Hôpital Militaire No. 2*, and is splendidly manned with surgeons, doctors, and nurses. But it is impossible to get the wounded in there quickly enough. There are about 2,000 Uhlans wandering in the district, and there are occasional small skirmishes, ending in one or two men being killed and a dozen or so wounded. The wounded crawl away into cottages, or lie about in the open fields, where they remain unattended. Last Sunday there were 3,000 wounded to take into the town of Antwerp."

His party was quickly organized. Miss May Sinclair, the well-known novelist, acted as his secretary. Lady Dorothie Feilding, daughter of Lord Denbigh, acted as his chief of staff, and a group of men and women volunteers were enlisted. Unlike most doctors, Dr. Munro did not seek for professional nurses, but enlisted the aid of a number of eager women who had received some training in first-aid and were keen to serve.

The ambulance corps was first stationed at Ghent, and after a few days of waiting it quickly found itself in the thick of service. It soon won a high reputation for the daring of its members in penetrating into the firing-line, bringing their light cars up as near to the front as possible, and rescuing men from where danger was greatest. Their conduct during the great battle of the sea-coast in October, 1914, attracted wide notice.

The story of the work of the Munro Ambulance at Dixmude attracted widespread attention and much public support, and by December the volunteer corps had thirteen cars. It was engaged all along the line of the Belgian retreat. Eventually it settled down at Furnes, making its headquarters there, and its work extending along the line of thirty miles from Nieuport to Ypres. One of the members of the corps was wounded in the leg at Nieuport, and received the Legion of Honor. Another was poisoned from the fumes of a shell that burst near to him, and was ill for some weeks.

Soup-kitchens were established for feeding starving and exhausted men, and warm woolen underclothes and gloves were supplied for Belgian troops in the trenches. Mr. Ramsay Macdonald, M.P., worked for a time with the party.

AMERICAN HELPERS IN FRANCE

Early in the war it became evident that the French Army medical authorities would be greatly aided by some outside help. In France, where almost every able-bodied man was called to the front, it was not possible to draw to the same extent on volunteers from the country itself, as could be done in England.

RUINS OF YPRES AFTER THE BOMBARDMENT.

The old Flemish town was the center of hot fighting between the Allies and the German troops in the battles for the possession of Belgium. At the right of the picture are seen the ruins of the famous Cloth Hall, one of the most famous medieval buildings in Europe. (*Copyright by the International News Service.*)

CANADIAN TROOPS ON SALISBURY PLAIN

A portion of the Dominion contingent drilling on the plain preparatory to being reviewed by the King.

Consequently, volunteers were obtained from England and America, and a number of ambulance units got to work. One of the most notable of these was the Anglo-American Volunteer Motor-Ambulance Corps, organized by Mr. Richard Norton and placed under the command of Colonel Barry. It was formally attached to one of the northern divisions of the French Army, and it did services which, in the opinion of the French authorities themselves, it would be difficult to overestimate.

The majority of the workers in this convoy were well-to-do young Americans, who could drive, and who in some cases provided their own cars. They largely maintained themselves. This volunteer corps was representative of the great American philanthropic activity in aiding the sick, feeding the hungry, and checking disease all along the different fronts.

Nowhere was the need of Red Cross work greater than in Serbia. This country, poor and devastated by previous wars, found itself, when it had driven the Austrian armies out of its borders, in a most pitiable state. There were thousands of sick and thousands of wounded waiting attention. Great numbers of Austrian prisoners had been taken, an epidemic of typhus started among them, and among the refugees, and spread over the country with amazing virulence.

SERBIA'S PITIABLE PLIGHT

There were no Serbian trained nurses, although a certain number of Serbian ladies had begun to learn the elements of training, and there were few doctors left. Famine threatened the country. The ha'penny roll in some parts fetched a shilling. British doctors who had come to the country to help did their utmost. They were swallowed up in the magnitude of the task before them.

The sick died all over the country, in many cases with none to attend them. Wounded men, carried for days on bullock-wagons from the front—journeys every moment of which must have been exquisite agony—found no doctors to attend to them when they arrived at their stations. The country seemed to reach the very depth of possible misery.

When the cry of Serbia went out to the world, expeditions were quickly organized in Britain. The Serbian Relief Fund made renewed efforts, and was able to initiate and support many activities. Hospital parties were formed. Mrs. St. Clair Stobart, who had already done great work in Belgium and in Northern France, took a large party of doctors and trained nurses to Krajeuvitch. American doctors and philanthropists helped also.

The Red Cross parties that arrived at the front paid heavy toll among their members in deaths from typhus and typhoid as the price of their aid. But the typhus was stamped out and the worst was overcome.

CHAPTER XVII

PATRIOTIC CANADA

THE PATRIOTISM OF CANADA—A REMARKABLE
RESPONSE TO THE CALL FOR VOLUNTEERS—CAN-
ADA'S GENEROUS CONTRIBUTION — WHAT CANA-
DIANS HAVE ACCOMPLISHED.

VALCARTIER! It was significant and fitting, though
indeed it was but the accident of geographical position,
that the first great training camp of Canadian soldiers
for this war should be in Old Quebec, where France
and England settled the fate of half a continent a
hundred and fifty years ago. Men from Alaska, 4000
miles away, from British Columbia, 3000 miles away,
from the Great West and Far North—native-born
Canadians, Scots, Irish, English, naturalized Americans—gathered in French Canada to make ready for the
prodigious enterprise to which they were to consecrate
their lives and all that they were. In the province
where a conquered people secured such rights and
freedom that they never sought to free themselves from
British dominion; where twice they fought back the
American invader from British territory; there the
first contingent of eager Canadians met to complete
their equipment and make ready for an infinitely more
dramatic and crucial business than the most heated
imagination could conceive.

THE PATRIOTISM OF CANADA

It was not love of adventure which roused the Canadians. They have been first among Imperialists from the beginning of their career as a confederation, but they have never been Jingo Imperialists. A democratic people has no mind for the tinkling cymbals of aggression; but there had grown into their sensitive and alert minds the deep conviction that, as Sir Wilfrid Laurier said on an historic occasion, if we did not come closer together we must drift further apart.

The declaration of war between Britain and Germany produced a greater vibration in the Dominion than in England. The standard of education among the lowest people in Canada is higher; individual responsibility is greater. There is no dependence of class upon class, and, therefore, every man knows he must hustle for himself, so that the war became a personal thing to every Canadian from the start.

A REMARKABLE RESPONSE TO THE CALL FOR VOLUNTEERS

What happened? Just as wonderful things as the rashest, most daring minds could conceive. Young men filled the streets leading to the recruiting offices. They were not rough-riders, cow-boys and hunters alone—far from it; from college, from university, from lawyers' offices, from the merchants' and the bankers' counters, from the railway and the mine, from the schoolhouse and the farmyard, from the doctors' offices, the backwoods and the river they came offering themselves for the "Old Flag," as they called it. The Government aimed at what seemed at first a large army; that is, 30,000 men. By the time, however, that Princess Patricia's Light Infantry retired from their place of renown at Ypres with 150 men, their colors and a glory which time cannot dim, the determination came to provide an army of 150,000 men. But Canadians have always responded to their Country's call, and always will. Canadian patriotism guarantees that there will be no necessity for conscription. Canadians will come, as many as are needed, as many as can be equipped, as many in proportion as Great Britain can draw from these islands, proud to seal the bond of union in their blood.

Canada's first enthusiasm was not the mere thrill of adventure, was not a lip-service to history and the long ties of time, but the devotion of a nation, not to the people of the Mother Land, but that which the Mother Land had been, for what it had stood, and for a flag representing tradition of liberty and freedom which have been the foundation of their own health and wealth and progress.

CANADA'S GENEROUS CONTRIBUTION

From August until December of 1914 what a multitude of gifts to the Mother Land poured in from Canada! There were bags of flour by the million, thousands of tons of cheese, hundreds of thousands of bushels of potatoes, horses, all kinds of grain, fruit and vegetables, and gifts of money. Political differences were composed. Sir Wilfrid Laurier, the French-Canadian ex-Prime Minister, took to the platform to encourage recruiting, to explain the causes of the war, to guide his fellow-countrymen into the paths of duty, while his political foe, Prime Minister Borden, was in England in conference with its Government. A burning faith and enthusiasm inspired the Canadian people.

So wonderful was the outburst it might have seemed that the glow, the determination, could not last. It not only lasted, it grew greater as the months went by. In the dark days of August, 1914, when Great Britain suddenly found herself confronted with her armed and well-prepared antagonist, the silver lining to the black clouds that hung over the Dominion was the splendid consistency of the people. Everyone in Great Britain who knew anything of Greater Britain knew that the Dominions would be loyal and true. But even the seers who had visions, and the dreamers of dreams, had failed to imagine anything so great as what actually took place. From August 4th it was no longer a case of the people of Greater Britain helping Great Britain in her war. It was the people of Greater Britain taking their share in their own war, making common purpose and finding common strength in their unity.

Valcartier was a marvel of its kind, a camp built up from nothing in a very few weeks, with permanent shower baths, electric light, a good water supply throughout the lines, and conveniences lacking in many camps that have been established for years. The Dominion Government resolved that the Canadian troops were to be completely equipped in a way surpassed by no other army in the world. No money was to be spared. Accordingly, the personal equip-

206

ment of the men was brought to a point of excellence that excited general admiration on their arrival in Europe.

WHAT CANADIANS HAVE ACCOMPLISHED

From Valcartier the Canadian troops were transferred to Salisbury Plains, in England, for an exceedingly thorough course of training. Then came inspection by the King and Lord Kitchener; then suddenly they were marched away, not knowing where they were going, and then almost as suddenly—Ypres, Neuve Chapelle, the second battle of Ypres, Festubert, Givenchy, Langemark, and the military capacity of the Canadians was established at once and for evermore!

The world came to know that a Canadian division had saved the situation at Ypres; had heard of an initiative, a resolution and an almost fanatical courage which was as great as any veteran troops the oldest military nation had ever shown. The world heard with what splendid fury lost guns were recovered in the face of terrific fire; how points were held under punishment of German artillery such as no troops had ever been obliged to face before; what the Princess Patricia's Light Infantry did at St. Eloi. All this was done by other Canadian troops as a matter of course, but as a matter of honor also. When Lieutenant Campbell and Private Vincent, with a little company, fought in a German trench until only the two were left, and Campbell fought his machine-gun resting on Vincent's back until he could fight no longer, and crawled away in a dying condition, while Vincent dragged the gun to safety, no surprise was felt, because the quality of

207

the Canadian had become an asset of the whole Empire. The quality of the Australian and the New Zealander is no less—not by the tiniest fraction; but the Canadians were the first to get their chance to receive the baptism of fire; were the first to prove that the men of the oversea Dominions have the root of the matter in them, and are good enough to fight with the best men that are fighting anywhere. Said one of the Second Contingent in London to one of the first who had come back from the field of battle: "We've had a hell of a time living down your reputation in England!" The reply was: "You'll have a hell of a time living up to it in France!"

That sense of humor is part of the Canadian equipment; it belongs to his elemental shrewdness, comradeship and common sense, and that is why he gets along with the British soldier so well. They respect each other; they swear at each other now and then, but they swear *by* each other all the time. They recognize that they have drawn life and character from the same spring. The Canadians are a hardy race—sober, industrious, tenacious. They have gripped this problem with both hands; they will stay.

The admiration of the British Army for the Canadian troops has frequently been remarked during the war. It is no surface thing—it is deep and sincere, and no words can give adequate expression to the splendid, magnificent work they have been doing.

PREMIER BORDEN'S PATRIOTIC SPEECH

Premier Borden of Canada well expressed the spirit of the Dominion in a notable speech delivered at the

THREE THOUSAND BRITISH INFANTRY WITHSTAND NINE THOUSAND PRUSSIAN CAVALRY.

At Le Cateau, the men of the 12th Infantry Brigade performed a noteworthy piece of work, standing against the German Cavalry Division of the guards—the crack mounted division of the German army. There were some 9,000 superb Prussian horsemen against, perhaps, 3,000 British foot-soldiers. It was a terrible charge, but the pride of the German cavalry was thrown b... ..ish ...d ... of th.... ... ...t th.y turned and fled.

RELIEF MAP OF EUROPE, SHOWING THE TREMENDOUS FORCE

LAND AND SEA OPERATIONS AT THE BEGINNING OF THE WAR

THE GLORIOUS CHARGE OF THE NINTH LANCERS.

An incident of the retreat from Mons to Cambrai. A German battery of eleven guns posted in a wood and disguised with quantities of forage, had caused havoc in the British ranks. All attempts at silencing the guns having proved ineffectual, the Ninth Lancers rode straight at them, across the open, through a hail of shell from the other German batteries, and cut down all the gunners and put every gun out of action. The whole of the Allied forces rang with praise of the charge.

Canada Club of London in August, 1915. There was a large and distinguished gathering, including the High Commissioners of sister Dominions. The toast to the Premier was received with great enthusiasm, and cheers were given for Sir Robert and also Lady Borden.

Replying, the Premier said he was grateful for the reception and for the way they received the name of Lady Borden. She would have crossed the Atlantic and been present if she had not been occupied in duties at home which she thought more useful to the work of the Red Cross and other associations.

CANADA'S HIGH AIM

The work done by the Canada Club, as well as that of other Canadians not members of the club, throughout the British Isles in providing comforts for the men in the field, and in other ways, was one for which the Premier said he was profoundly grateful, and was intensely appreciated by the people themselves in Canada, who in that regard had done not a little since the outbreak of the war. The constant aim and purpose of the Canadian Government had been to co-operate with the Government of the United Kingdom and overseas Dominions in an endeavor to bring the war to an honorable and triumphant conclusion.

In that purpose the work of Sir George Perley in London had been of the highest possible advantage to the Dominion. The object of Canada at the commencement of the war, said the Premier, was, of course, to throw as great a force as possible into the field at the earliest possible moment, and there they were unprepared for war even to a greater degree than the British Isles themselves.

A CAUSE FOR PRIDE

He confessed some pride in the fact that within six weeks after the commencement of hostilities they were able to place at Valcartier 33,000 of the best that Canada could produce, fully armed and equipped. Many of these had since gone to the front, and he believed had done their duty to the fullest possible extent. There were present in the Premier's audience distintinguished representatives from Australia, South Africa and New Zealand, and he asked that he might be permitted to extend, as had already been extended, this Government's congratulations and the congratulations of Canada on what their soldiers, in all their triumphs, had accomplished. Later in the war, he said, troops from those Dominions would fight side by side on the continent of Europe with British troops and troops from Canada. He knew the men from Canada welcomed the comradeship of the men from those three Dominions.

THE EAGER CANADIANS

The Premier proceeded to allude to the numbers despatched from Canada. Dwelling on the eagerness of the men to go to the front, he said that when he was in Boulogne, after a certain number of reinforcements had been sent from Shorncliffe, there were found dozens of men who had not been included, but who had stolen away to get to Boulogne. He might also allude to an incident which occurred in western Canada, when some men, not included in a detachment for Valcartier, forcibly took possession of a railway car and were not discovered until well on the journey.

The Premier dwelt on his trip to the front, also the hospitals, remarking that it was satisfactory to find in those institutions that the arrangements were all that could be desired. He had met a man who threw aside all business activities, leaving his affairs to take care of themselves, and enlisted at the opening of the war. He passed through the second battle of Ypres untouched, but was severely wounded at Festubert, where he received four bullets in his right arm, from which he had not yet recovered, four in his left shoulder and three in his left leg. The Premier was astonished to see he had recovered to the degree he had.

"When I met him I asked him," continued Premier Borden, "whether the surgeon had succeeded in extracting all the bullets at one operation? He replied: 'Well, he missed a few the first time.' Then he went on to tell me how the second operation became necessary. The spirit of the wounded was splendid."

PROOF OF IMPERIAL UNITY

Continuing, the Premier remarked he was persuaded of the unity of the Empire by what he had seen during the past twelve months and in what he thought the should see in the future it would be more strikingly manifest than ever before. He did not think anyone could gainsay that, and, considering the lack of organization in the ties which bound the Empire together, and the remarkable powers of self-government with which all the overseas nations of the Empire had been entrusted, and which they held as a right and not as grace, he did feel that, in the co-operation between the overseas Dominions and the Government, these Islands had been successful beyond what they could have anticipated, and he was sure that condition would continue to the end.

A CLOSER ORGANIZATION

There might come a time in the future, he predicted, when they would have to consider matters of better organization between these Islands and the Dominions. To those who thought such a task was impossible he would commend the example of the men who founded the Dominion of Canada, because if ever a task seemed impossible that which they undertook must have so seemed, yet it has been a remarkable success.

His hearers would agree with him, he was confident, that the Canadian national spirit was asserted, and in the past had asserted itself in a manner which would satisfy all. Those difficulties were overcome at the inception of the Dominion, and surely difficulties which seemed to stand in the way of better organization of the affairs of the British Empire can be overcome by the wise counsel and co-operation of the statesmen of these Islands and Dominions.

The Premier said he held the profound conviction, that regiment for regiment and man for man the allied forces could more than hold their own with the most efficient troops of the enemy. In this war, in which all the uses of applied science were being turned to destruction, the first duty of this Empire was to place themselves on an equal footing.

A COURAGEOUS COUNTRY

In this most important regard, Premier Borden asserted, Britons were taking the necessary steps. If they were inclined to be discouraged by the fall of some fortress, he hoped they would remember the great work accomplished for them by the navy in securing the pathways of the seas. "If I should bring today a message from the people of Canada it would be that not for one single moment will they be discouraged by any reverse; not for one single moment will they relax their determination or efforts to bring this war to a triumphant and honorable conclusion, which is our due."

After that he believed the Empire would march forward to a nobler and greater future. He ventured to believe the work of the Empire was not yet done, but that the future opened up an opportunity for usefulness and influence which perhaps none now could see.

CHAPTER XVIII

A CRIME AGAINST CIVILIZATION: THE TRAGIC DESTRUCTION OF THE LUSITANIA

AN UNPRECEDENTED CRIME AGAINST HUMANITY—
THE LUSITANIA: BUILT FOR SAFETY—GERMANY'S
ANNOUNCED INTENTION TO SINK THE VESSEL—
LINER'S SPEED INCREASED AS DANGER NEARED—
SUBMARINE'S PERISCOPE DIPS UNDER SURFACE—
PASSENGERS OVERCOME BY POISONOUS FUMES—
BOAT CAPSIZES WITH WOMEN AND CHILDREN—
HUNDREDS JUMP INTO THE SEA—THE LUSITANIA
GOES TO HER DOOM—INTERVIEW WITH CAPTAIN
TURNER.

NO THINKING man—whether he believes or disbelieves in war—expects to have war without the horrors and atrocities which accompany it. That "war is hell" is as true now as when General Sherman so pronounced it. It seems, indeed, to be truer today. And yet we have always thought—perhaps because we hoped—that there was a limit at which even war, with all its lust of blood, with all its passion of hatred, with all its devilish zest for efficiency in the destruction of human life, would stop.

Now we know that there is no limit at which the makers of war, in their frenzy to pile horror on horror, and atrocity on atrocity, will stop. We have seen a nation despoiled and raped because it resisted an

214

invader, and we said that was war. But now out of the sun-lit waves has come a venomous instrument of destruction, and without warning, without respite for escape, has sent headlong to the bottom of the everlasting sea more than a thousand unarmed, unresisting, peace-bent men, women and children—even babes in arms. So the Lusitania was sunk. It may be war, but it is something incalculably more sobering than merely that. It is the difference between assassination and massacre. It is war's supreme crime against civilization.

AN UNPRECEDENTED CRIME AGAINST HUMANITY

The horror of the deadly assault on the Lusitania does not lessen as the first shock of the disaster recedes into the past. The world is aghast. It had not taken the German threat at full value; it did not believe that any civilized nation would be so wanton in its lust and passion of war as to count a thousand non-combatant lives a mere unfortunate incidental of the carnage.

Nothing that can be said in mitigation of the destruction of the Lusitania can alter the fact that an outrage unknown heretofore in the warfare of civilized nations has been committed. Regardless of the technicalities which may be offered as a defense in international law, there are rights which must be asserted, must be defended and maintained. If international law can be torn to shreds and converted into scrap paper to serve the necessities of war, its obstructive letter can be disregarded when it is necessary to serve the rights of humanity.

215

The irony of the situation lies in the fact that from the ghastly experience of great marine disasters the Lusitania was evolved as a vessel that was "safe." No such calamity as the attack of a torpedo was foreseen by the builders of the giant ship, and yet, even after the outbreak of the European war, and when upon the eve of her last voyage the warning came that an attempt would be made to torpedo the Lusitania, her owners confidently assured the world that the ship was safe because her great speed would enable her to outstrip any submarine ever built.

Limitation of language makes adequate word description of this mammoth Cunarder impossible. The following figures show its immense dimensions: Length, 790 feet; breadth, 88 feet; depth, to boat deck, 80 feet; draught, fully loaded, 37 feet, 6 inches; displacement on load line, 45,000 tons; height to top of funnels, 155 feet; height to mastheads, 216 feet. The hull below draught line was divided into 175 water-tight compartments, which made it—so the owners claimed—"unsinkable." With complete safety device equipment, including wireless telegraph, Mundy-Gray improved method of submarine signaling, and with officers and crew all trained and reliable men, the Lusitania was acclaimed as being unexcelled from a standpoint of safety, as in all other respects.

Size, however, was its least remarkable feature. The ship was propelled by four screws rotated by turbine engines of 68,000 horse-power, capable of developing a sea speed of more than twenty-five knots per hour regardless of weather conditions, and of

THREE BRITISH CRUISERS SUNK BY SUBMARINES.

The "Aboukir," "Hogue" and "Cressy" sunk by torpedoes on September 22. The horrors of modern warfare are illustrated by the notice issued after this disaster by the British Admiralty, which reads in part, "No act of humanity, whether to friend or foe, should lead to neglect of the proper precautions and dispositions of war, and no measure can be taken to save life which prejudice the military situation." (*Copyright by the Sun News Service.*)

SINKING OF A TORPEDOED BATTLESHIP.

As the British vessel "Aboukir" was sinking after being torpedoed by a German submarine, one of the sailors described the last moment as follows: "The captain sings out an order just like on any ordinary occasion, 'If any man wishes to leave the side of the ship he can do so, every man for himself,' then we gave a cheer and in we went."

maintaining without driving a schedule with the regularity of a railroad train, and thus establishing its right to the title of "the fastest ocean greyhound."

On Saturday May 1, 1915, the day on which the Cunard liner Lusitania, carrying 2,000 passengers and crew, sailed from New York for Liverpool, the following advertisement, over the name of the Imperial German Embassy, was published in the leading newspapers of the United States:

NOTICE!

TRAVELERS intending to embark on the Atlantic voyage are reminded that a state of war exists between Germany and her allies and Great Britain and her allies; that the zone of war includes the waters adjacent to the British Isles; that, in accordance with formal notice given by the Imperial German Government, vessels flying the flag of Great Britain, or of any of her allies, are liable to destruction in those waters and that travelers sailing in the war zone on ships of Great Britain or her allies do so at their own risk.

IMPERIAL GERMAN EMBASSY.
WASHINGTON, D. C., April 22, 1915.

The advertisement was commented upon by the passengers of the Lusitania, but it did not cause any of them to cancel their bookings. No one took the matter seriously. It was not conceivable that even the German military lords could seriously plot so dastardly an attack on non-combatants.

When the attention of Captain W. T. Turner, commander of the Lusitania, was called to the warning, he laughed and said: "It doesn't seem as if they had scared many people from going on the ship by the looks of the passenger list."

Agents of the Cunard Line said there was no truth in reports that several prominent passengers had received anonymous telegrams warning them not to sail on the Lusitania. Charles T. Bowring, president of the St. George's Society, who was a passenger, said that it was a silly performance for the German Embassy to do.

Charles Klein, the American playwright, said he was going to devote his time on the voyage to thinking of his new play, "Potash and Perlmutter in Society," and would not have time to worry about trifles.

Alfred G. Vanderbilt was one of the last to go on board.

Elbert Hubbard, publisher of the Philistine, who sailed with his wife, said he believed the German Emperor had ordered the advertisement to be placed in the newspapers, and added jokingly that if he was on board the liner when she was torpedoed, he would be able to do the Kaiser justice in the Philistine.

The early days of the voyage were unmarked by incidents other than those which have interested ocean passengers on countless previous trips, and little apprehension was felt by those on the Lusitania of the fate which lay ahead of the vessel.

218

The ship was proceeding at a moderate speed, on Friday, May 7, when she passed Fastnet Light, off Cape Clear, the extreme southwesterly point of Ireland that is first sighted by east-bound liners. Captain Turner was on the bridge, with his staff captain and other officers, maintaining a close lookout. Fastnet left behind, the Lusitania's course was brought closer to shore, probably within twelve miles of the rock-bound coast.

LINER'S SPEED INCREASED AS DANGER NEARED

Her speed was also increased to twenty knots or more, according to the more observant passengers, and some declare that she worked a sort of zigzag course, plainly ready to shift her helm whenever danger should appear. Captain Turner, it is known, was watching closely for any evidence of submarines.

One of the passengers, Dr. Daniel Moore, of Yankton, S. D., declared that before he went downstairs to luncheon shortly after one o'clock he and others with him noticed, through a pair of marine glasses, a curious object in the sea, possibly two miles or more away. What it was he could not determine, but he jokingly referred to it later at luncheon as a submarine.

While the first cabin passengers were chatting over their coffee cups they felt the ship give a great leap forward. Full speed ahead had suddenly been signaled from the bridge. This was a few minutes after two o'clock, and just about the time that Ellison Myers, of Stratford, Ontario, a boy on his way to join the British Navy, noticed the periscope of a submarine about a mile away to starboard. Myers and his companions saw Captain Turner hurriedly give orders to the helmsman and ring for full speed to the engine room.

The Lusitania began to swerve to starboard, heading for the submarine, but before she could really answer her helm a torpedo was flashing through the water toward her at express speed. Myers and his companions, like many others of the passengers, saw the white wake of the torpedo and its metal casing gleaming in the bright sunlight. The weather was ideal, light winds and a clear sky making the surface of the ocean as calm and smooth as could be wished by any traveler.

SUBMARINE'S PERISCOPE DIPS UNDER SURFACE

The torpedo came on, aimed apparently at the bow of the ship, but nicely calculated to hit her amidships. Before its wake was seen the periscope of the submarine had vanished beneath the surface.

In far less time than it takes to tell, the torpedo had crashed into the Lusitania's starboard side, just abaft the first funnel, and exploded with a dull boom in the forward stoke-hole.

Captain Turner at once ordered the helm put over and the prow of the ship headed for land, in the hope that she might strike shallow water while still under way. The boats were ordered out, and the signals calling the boat crews to their stations were flashed everywhere through the vessel.

Several of the life-boats were already swung out, according to some survivors, there having been a life-saving drill earlier in the day before the ship spoke Fastnet Light.

Down in the dining saloon the passengers felt the ship reel from the shock of the explosion and many were hurled from their chairs. Before they could recover themselves, another explosion occurred. There is a difference of opinion as to the number of torpedoes fired. Some say there were two; others say only one torpedo struck the vessel, and that the second explosion was internal.

PASSENGERS OVERCOME BY POISONOUS FUMES

In any event, the passengers now realized their danger. The ship, torn almost apart, was filled with fumes and smoke, the decks were covered with débris that fell from the sky, and the great Lusitania began to list quickly to starboard. Before the passengers below decks could make their way above, the decks were beginning to slant ominously, and the air was filled with the cries of terrified men and women, some of them already injured by being hurled against the sides of the saloons. Many passengers were stricken unconscious by the smoke and fumes from the exploding torpedoes.

The stewards and stewardesses, recognizing the too evident signs of a sinking ship, rushed about urging and helping the passengers to put on life-belts, of which more than 3,000 were aboard.

On the boat deck attempts were being made to lower the life-boats, but several causes combined to impede the efforts of the crew in this direction. The port side of the vessel was already so far up that the boats on that side were quite useless, and as the starboard boats were lowered the plunging vessel—she was still under headway, for all efforts to reverse the engines proved useless—swung back and forth, and when they struck the water were dragged along through the sea, making it almost impossible to get them away.

BOAT CAPSIZES WITH WOMEN AND CHILDREN

The first life-boat that struck the water capsized with some sixty women and children aboard her, and all of these must have been drowned almost instantly. Ten more boats were lowered, the desperate expedient of cutting away the ropes being resorted to to prevent them from being dragged along by the now halting steamer.

The great ship was sinking by the bow, foot by foot, and in ten minutes after the first explosion she was already preparing to founder. Her stern rose high in the air, so that those in the boats that got away could see the whirring propellers, and even the boat deck was awash.

Captain Turner urged the men to be calm, to take care of the women and children, and megaphoned the passengers to seize life-belts, chairs—anything they could lay hands on to save themselves from drowning. There was never any question in the captain's mind that the ship was about to sink, and if, as reported, some of the stewards ran about advising the passengers not to take to the boats, that there was no danger of the vessel going down till she reached shore, it was done without his orders. But many of the survivors have denied this, and declared that all the crew, officers, stewards and sailors, even the stokers, who dashed up from their flaming quarters below, showed the utmost bravery and calmness in the face of the disaster, and sought in every way to aid the panic-stricken passengers to get off the ship.

HUNDREDS JUMP INTO THE SEA

When it was seen that most of the boats would be useless, hundreds of passengers donned life-belts and jumped into the sea. Others seized deck chairs, tubs, kegs, anything available, and hurled themselves into the water, clinging to these articles.

The first-cabin passengers fared worst, for the second and third-cabin travelers had long before finished their midday meal and were on deck when the torpedo struck. But the first-cabin people on the D deck and in the balcony, at luncheon, were at a terrible disadvantage, and those who had already finished were in their staterooms resting or cleaning up preparatory to the after luncheon day.

The confusion on the stairways became terrible, and the great number of little children, more than 150 of them under two years, a great many of them infants in arms, made the plight of the women still more desperate.

LUSITANIA GOES TO HER DOOM

After the life-boats had cut adrift it was plain that a few seconds would see the end of the great ship. With a great shiver she bent her bow down below the surface, and then her stern uprose, and with a horrible sough the liner that had been the pride of the Cunard Line, plunged down in sixty fathoms of water. In the last few seconds the hundreds of women and men, a great many of them carrying children in their arms, leaped overboard, but hundreds of others, delaying the jump too long, were carried down in the suction that left a huge whirlpool swirling about the spot where the last of the vessel was seen.

Among these were Elbert Hubbard and his wife, Charles Frohman, who was crippled with rheumatism and unable to move quickly; Justus Miles Forman, Charles Klein, Alfred G. Vanderbilt and many others of the best-known Americans and Englishmen aboard.

Captain Turner stayed on the bridge as the ship went down, but before the last plunge he bade his staff officer and the helmsman, who were still with him, to save themselves. The helmsman leaped into the sea and was saved, but the staff officer would not desert his superior, and went down with the ship. He did not come to the surface again.

Captain Turner, however, a strong swimmer, rose after the eddying whirlpool had calmed down, and, seizing a couple of deck chairs, kept himself afloat for three hours. The master-at-arms of the Lusitania, named Williams, who was looking for survivors in a boat after he had been picked up, saw the flash of the captain's gold-braided uniform, and rescued him, more dead than alive.

INTERVIEW WITH CAPTAIN TURNER

Despite the doubt as to whether two torpedoes exploded, or whether the first detonation caused the big liner's boilers to let go, Captain Turner stated that there was no doubt that at least two torpedoes reached the ship.

"I am not certain whether the two explosions—and there were two—resulted from torpedoes, or whether one was a boiler explosion. I am sure, however, that I saw the first torpedo strike the vessel on her starboard side. I also saw a second torpedo apparently headed straight for the steamship's hull, directly below the suite occupied by Alfred G. Vanderbilt."

When asked if the second explosion had been caused by the blowing up of ammunition stored in the liner's hull, Captain Turner said:

"No; if ammunition had exploded that would probably have torn the ship apart and the loss of life would have been much heavier than it was."

Captain Turner declared that, from the bridge, he saw the torpedo streaking toward the Lusitania and tried to change the ship's course to avoid the missile, but was unable to do so in time. The only thing left for him to do was to rush the liner ashore and beach her, and she was headed for the Irish coast when she foundered.

According to Captain Turner, the German submarine did not flee at once after torpedoing the liner.

"While I was swimming about after the ship had disappeared I saw the periscope of the submarine rise amidst the débris," said he. "Instead of offering any help the submarine immediately submerged herself and I saw nothing more of her. I did everything possible for my passengers. That was all I could do."

CHAPTER XIX

AMERICA IN THE GREAT WAR

DECLARATION OF WAR AGAINST THE IMPERIAL
GERMAN GOVERNMENT—A MASTER STATE OF THE
WORLD—WHAT WE FIGHT FOR—WHAT WE FIGHT
AGAINST—ALLIES IN A COMMON CAUSE—OUR
ALLIES WELCOME US—THE HOUR OF DOOM TO
TYRANNY—AMERICA TRUE TO HER TRADITIONS.

WITH DUE solemnity and a full appreciation of the
momentous nature of its decision, Congress, backed
by the stand the President had taken when diplomatic
relations with Germany were severed, and by the
sentiments of the people and the press, declared war
on the Empire of Germany April 6, 1917.

The President's message to Congress assembled in
extra session April 2d, was a masterpiece in its force-
ful and convincing appeal to all classes, races, and
interests. Few more felicitous State documents can
be recalled in our history.

A MASTER STATE OF THE WORLD

With one brave and sagacious utterance, President
Wilson led the American people to the high and sure
ground of a lasting and beneficent influence as a
Master State of the world.

It was but a new and resplendent chapter in the
epic story of America. Colonial America became
independent under Washington, continental under
Jefferson, united under Lincoln, and now cosmo-

politan, to a degree never hitherto attained, under Woodrow Wilson.

After a dispassionate restatement of our case against the German Government, the President in his address to Congress said:

"There is one choice we can not make, we are incapable of making: We will not choose the path of submission and suffer the most sacred rights of our Nation and our people to be ignored or violated. The wrongs against which we now array ourselves are not common wrongs; they cut to the very roots of human life."

"With a profound sense of the solemn and even tragical character of the step I am taking, and of the grave responsibilities which it involves, but in unhesitating obedience to what I deem my constitutional duty, I advise that the Congress declare the recent course of the Imperial German Government to be in fact nothing less than war against the Government and people of the United States; that it formally accept the status of belligerent which has thus been thrust upon it, and that it take immediate steps not only to put the country in a more thorough state of defense, but also to exert all its power and employ all its resources to bring the Government of the German Empire to terms and end the war."

WHAT WE FIGHT FOR

After two years and a half of patience and concession, the United States was compelled to take up arms in defense of its sovereignty and in behalf of an imperiled civilization.

The issues of this conflict are not the creation of a few months. They did not arise wholly from a recent series of injuries and aggressions. They are fundamental. They concern the security of this republic and the preservation of the principles upon which it is founded.

In his address to Congress President Wilson voiced the sentiments of the Nation in the following words: "We shall fight for the things which we have always carried nearest our hearts—for democracy, for the right of those who submit to authority to have a voice in their own government, for the rights and liberties of small nations, for a universal dominion of right, by such a concert of free peoples as shall bring peace and safety to all nations."

This was America's answer to the world's cry for freedom and security—an answer that is a blessing to all now living and will be a benediction to future generations.

WHAT WE FIGHT AGAINST

Since that memorable day when the Stars and Stripes were first unfurled to proclaim that a people had been born to be the torch bearers of liberty, Old Glory has never lacked for brave defenders, and has never been unfurled in an unrighteous or unsuccessful war. This fact is our grandest national heritage, and we, today, are under a solemn obligation to maintain this tradition. America's entrance into the Great War was a beacon light of hope to the men defending human rights on the far-flung battlefields of the world, a definite promise of the future to little nations sturdily fighting against German militarism for their liberty. It is against this German militarism which threatens human liberty everywhere, and makes world-peace impossible, that we also fight with the Allied Nations of Europe.

Our aims and purposes when we entered the conflict are clearly set forth in these ringing words of the President:

"We have no selfish ends to serve. We desire no conquest, no dominion. We seek no indemnities for ourselves, no material compensation for the sacrifices we shall truly make. We are but one of the champions of the rights of mankind. We shall be satisfied when those rights have been as secure as the faith and the freedom of the nations can make them."

ALLIES IN A COMMON CAUSE

History must henceforth identify the American Nation with the brave peoples overseas who are defending themselves against the most terrible foe that ever menaced civilization. Their victory is our victory. The glory of their achievements adds lustre to our own.

The great feats of the British navy now have a keen inspiration for us; the awful siege of Verdun now has a deep meaning for us; the valorous defense of Ypres by Canadian troops, and the terrible drive along the Somme are glorious events which will make future generations of America thrill with boundless pride. Because by our entry into the conflict and our participation in it, we become united to our Allies by the strongest tie that can bind nations together—the tie of a common cause. That cause is human liberty and the defense of those principles and ideals which ennoble individuals and nations.

OUR ALLIES WELCOME US

Long ago there sailed from Halifax a unit recruited from the Americans living in Canada. The unit was called the American Legion. While they did not bear the Stars and Stripes to the front, they bore in their hearts that deathless spirit of freedom which makes free men brothers wherever they meet. Tommy Atkins and Jean Baptiste, Guiseppi and Ivan as well as Fritz and Hans have long since learned from the Americans serving in the various military units now afield just how Yankee Doodle acts in the fight to the finish.

They remember how Corp. Victor Chapman, airman, killed over the battlefields of Verdun while defending two other aviators, smilingly died. They have not forgotten the words of Lieut. Kiffin Rockwell, mortally wounded in combat in the air, "I pay my debt for LaFayette and Rochambeau." These and other members of the American Escadrille, the birdmen, flying for France, and hundreds of other Americans have long since immortalized the courage of Yankee Doodle on the battlefields of Europe.

THE HOUR OF DOOM TO TYRANNY

The news of America's declaration of war on the Imperial German Government was followed by great rejoicing among our Allies. It was as if the sad world smiled again. Old Glory waved along the Paris Boulevards; American patriotic songs were sung in the cafés; men of the immortal American Flying Corps were embraced by French soldiers on the battlefield; and cheered by the people wherever they appeared; the king and queen of England joined in singing "The Star Spangled Banner" in St. Paul's Cathedral, London, where thousands had gathered to commemorate America's entry into the war. Italy, through her great D'Annunzio, felicitated us; Russia, lately free from Romanoff bondage, assured·us of her loyalty and friendship. Every nation engaged in battle against the most ruthless and terrible foe that ever ravaged the world welcomed us as an ally. And in that hour when all the great free peoples of the earth drew close together and America, the youngest and richest, unsheathed her keen, true sword in the cause of right and took her stand, back to back with her Allies, it was the hour of doom for oppression and tyranny.

AMERICA TRUE TO HER TRADITIONS

As might be expected, the newspapers of the entire country vigorously supported the President. The New York "Tribune" pointed out that it has not been our habit to yield to intimidation:

"We fought the Beys and Pashas and the Barbary States when they tried to make us pay tribute for the privilege of navigating the waters of the western Mediterranean. When we were a weak, impoverished Nation, . . . we declared war on Great Britain because Great Britain abridged and abolished our rights. We are a rich and powerful Nation now, though still woefully unprepared for either offense or defense. But our

lamentable condition of unpreparedness . . . could
not excuse us from facing Germany's challenge as
firmly and courageously as the feeble, unorganized
United States of Madison's time faced the challenge of
Great Britain."

"President Wilson has done the thing which Washington would have done, which Lincoln would have done,
and what any other American President would have
done." Thus spoke the New York "Herald" (Ind.).
The New York "Sun" (Ind.) said the Nation had made
no attempt to blind itself to the possibilities of the
future, nor had it ignored the hard measures which
maintenance of its position may entail. "Its patriotic
purpose is expressed with sobriety and from the out-
givings of its spokesman the blatant note of demagogy
is happily absent." And the response to the President's
address, as the "Times" asserted, "has been made
with one voice. He has the support of a united
people."

In times of stress and danger the American people
require from their Chief Magistrate neither incon-
clusive interpretation nor indeterminate consultation.
All they ask is masterful leadership based upon mutual
faith of the President in his country and of the country
in its President. Thomas Jefferson's famous declaration was re-echoed in the hearts of united Americans
when war against Germany was declared. It is as
follows:

"As an American, faithful to American ideals of
justice, liberty and humanity, and confident that the
Government has exerted its most earnest efforts to
keep us at peace with the world, I hereby declare my

absolute and unconditional loyalty to the Government of the United States, and pledge my support to you in protecting American rights against unlawful violence upon land and sea, in guarding the nation against hostile attacks, and in upholding international right.

"And for the support of this Declaration, with a firm reliance on the protection of Divine Providence, We mutually pledge to each other [and to you our President] our Lives, our Fortunes, and our sacred Honor."

CHAPTER XX

AMERICA'S FIRST ACHIEVEMENT IN THE GREAT WAR

THE SEA FIGHT—SECRETARY OF THE NAVY DANIELS
ISSUES STATEMENT—CONVOYS ANSWER WITH HEAVY
GUNFIRE—HOPED TO SLAUGHTER LARGE NUMBERS
—CONCERN FELT OVER LEAK TO GERMANY.

ON THE Fourth of July, 1917, there was announced to the world America's first notable victory in the World War. The news was both timely and appropriate. For several days the country had felt that troop movements toward France must be under way though the newspapers, with one exception, had patriotically refrained from printing details of the sailing of the transports. Nevertheless there was keen anxiety throughout the land both among government officials and private citizens who knew that our overseas expedition must pass through the submarine danger zone.

THE SEA FIGHT

It was a source of the greatest satisfaction and pride to all the country to learn that American warships had beaten off two attacks by fleets of German submarines directed at our troop transports bearing

234

the last of the Pershing expedition to France. The fire of the American ships not only drove off the attacking submarines but is known to have sunk at least one and probably more of the German "sea snakes."

Both of the attacks were made in force, showing that the Germans had information of the coming of the transports and had planned to get them.

The Germans made their first attack in force the night of June 22d, at 10.30 o'clock, at a point far out in the Atlantic Ocean, which was presumably free from submarines. The convoy protected the transports by using their guns so effectively that the torpedo fire of the U-boats was scattered and ineffective. The second attack was made by German submarines beyond the rendezvous, where the transports and their convoy were to be picked up by United States destroyers sent out by Vice-Admiral Sims to furnish additional protection for them through the submarine war zone.

The first news of the battle was given out by the committee on public information.

This announcement was issued:

The Navy Department at 5 o'clock this afternoon received word of the safe arrival at a French port of the last contingent of General Pershing's expeditionary force. At the time the information was released announcement also was made that the transports were twice attacked by submarines on the way across.

No ship was hit, not an American life was lost, and while the navy gunners report the sinking of one submarine only, there is reason to believe that others were destroyed in the first night attack.

AMERICA'S FIRST ACHIEVEMENT

Secretary Daniels made this statement:

It is with the joy of a great relief that I announce to the people of the United States the safe arrival in France of every fighting man and every fighting ship.

Now that the last vessel has reached port, it is safe to disclose the dangers that were encountered and to tell the complete story of peril and courage.

The transports bearing our troops were twice attacked by German submarines on the way across. On both occasions the U-boats were beaten off with every appearance of loss. One was certainly sunk, and there is reason to believe that the accurate fire of our gunners sent others to the bottom.

For purposes of convenience the expedition was divided into contingents, each contingent including troopships and a naval escort designed to keep off such German raiders as might be met.

An ocean rendezvous had also been arranged with the American destroyers now operating in European waters in order that the passage of the danger zone might be attended by every possible protection.

The first attack took place at 10.30 on the night of June 22d.

What gives it peculiar and disturbing significance is that our ships were set upon at a point well this side of the rendezvous and in that part of the Atlantic presumably free from submarines.

The attack was made in force, although the night made impossible any exact count of the U-boats gathered for what they deemed slaughter.

CONVOYS ANSWER WITH HEAVY GUNFIRE

The high-seas convoy, circling with their searchlights, answered with heavy gunfire, and its accuracy stands proved by the fact that the torpedo discharge became increasingly scattered and inaccurate. It is not known how many torpedoes were launched, but five were counted as they sped by bow and stern.

A second attack was launched a few days later against another

Copyright by Harris & Ewing.

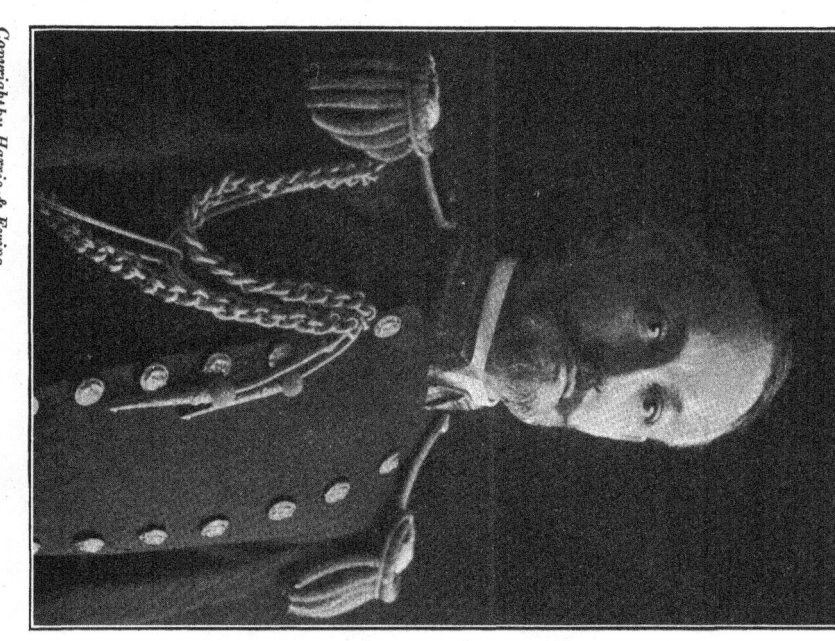

VICE-ADMIRAL WILLIAM S. SIMS, U. S. N.

Who was sent in command of the first fleet of destroyers which the United States contributed to help rid the seas of German submarines.

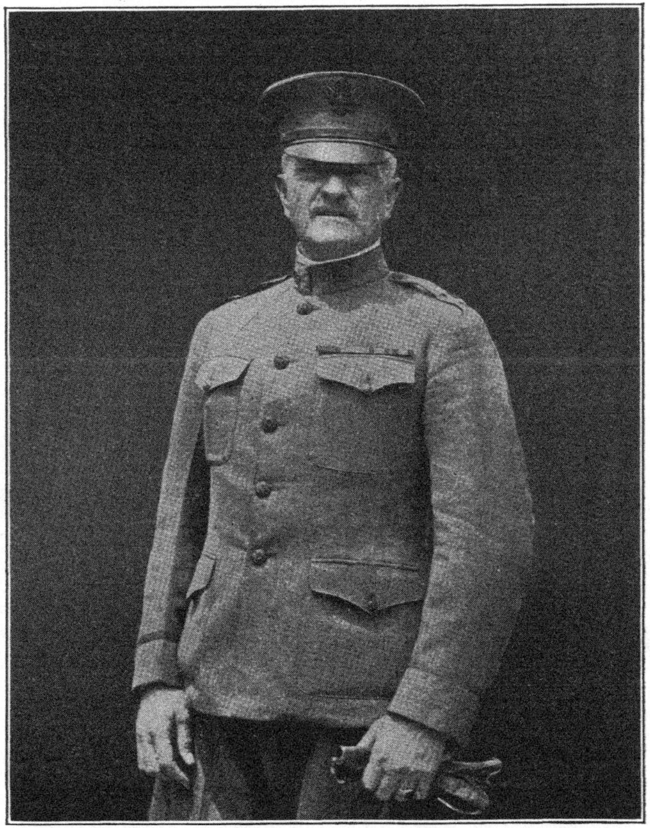

Copyright by Harris & Ewing.

MAJOR-GENERAL JOHN J. PERSHING.

Who was selected to lead the first American expeditionary force to France.

THE UNITED STATES NAVY IN ACTION.

U. S. Destroyers beating off German submarines while escorting the Adriatic to Queenstown.

contingent. The point of assault was beyond the rendezvous, and our destroyers were sailing as a screen between the transports and all harm. The results of the battle were in favor of American gunnery.

Not alone did the destroyers hold the U-boats at a safe distance, but their speed also resulted in the sinking of one submarine at least. Grenades were used in firing, a depth-charge explosive timed to go off at a certain distance under water. In one instance, oil and wreckage covered the surface of the sea after a shot from a destroyer at a periscope, and the reports make claim of sinking.

Protected by our high-seas convoy, by our destroyers and by French war vessels, the contingent proceeded and joined the others in a French port.

The whole nation will rejoice that so great a peril is passed for the vanguard of the men who will fight our battles in France. No more thrilling Fourth of July celebration could have been arranged than this glad news that lifts the shadow of dread from the heart of America.

Secretary of War Baker gave out the following letter to Secretary Daniels covering the army's thanks to the navy:

Word has just come to the War Department that the last ships convoying General Pershing's expeditionary force to France arrived safe today. As you know, the navy assumed the responsibility for the safety of these ships on the sea and through the danger zone. The ships themselves and their convoys were in the hands of the navy, and now that they have arrived and carried, without the loss of a man, our soldiers who are the first to represent America in the battle of democracy, I beg leave to tender to you, to the Admiral and to the navy the hearty thanks of the War Department and of the army. This splendid achievement is an auspicious beginning, and it has been characterized throughout by the most cordial and effective co-operation between the two military services.

HOPED TO SLAUGHTER LARGE NUMBERS

The German Admiralty is believed to have taken extraordinary precautions to play havoc with the American transports. It is the belief of naval officers that the lull in the German submarine warfare that immediately preceded the sailing of the expedition was caused by the calling in of German submarines for refilling with torpedoes and supplies as part of a campaign in which they hoped to slaughter a large number of the American troops in the first large contingent sent to France, for the moral effect of such a victory. Vice-Admiral Sims was in charge of the arrangements for the protection of the expedition. He was placed in command of all the war vessels in Irish waters and given full responsibility for the protection of the expedition.

The various contingents of the expedition were convoyed from the United States by warships of various types. At secret points of rendezvous they were met by destroyers sent out by Vice-Admiral Sims to give them strong protection through the submarine war zone, and later they were met by French warships. The plans worked out under the direction of Vice-Admiral Sims proved completely successful.

CONCERN FELT OVER LEAK TO GERMANY

The satisfaction of officials over the safe arrival in France of all the transports that composed the first American expeditionary force was tempered by concern over the apparent fact that the German Government had advance information of the probable locations of the transport fleet on the days that it was attacked by the German U-boats. How the German Government got this information was not known, but there was a suspicion that it went out of New York about the time that the transport fleet sailed.

When United States troops were arriving at American ports preparatory to sailing to France as part of the expedition under General Siebert a New York newspaper printed a story that was plain notice that the troops were about to sail. On the following day the same newspaper printed an interview with a Red Cross official in New York, in which he complained of the poor accommodations on the trains that had brought the troops to the seaboard. This interview indicated that the transports carrying the troops had just put to sea. Much indignation was expressed over the publications, but the government made no statement to indicate that it deprecated them.

It was believed that as a result of these publications the government had the transports remain in the vicinity of the home coast for several days after they had cleared from the ports of departure in order, if possible, to throw German submarines off the track. That this ruse was not successful was shown by the attacks made by the flotillas of U-boats.

CHAPTER XXI

THE DOWNFALL OF CZARISM

CAUSES OF THE REVOLUTION—THE POPULAR UP-
RISING — THE NEW GOVERNMENT — THE NEW
GOVERNMENT'S POLICY—ABDICATION OF THE CZAR
—RUSSIA OF THE FUTURE.

ON FRIDAY, March 16, 1917, the world was
electrified by the sudden announcement of the successful Russian Revolution.   Two days earlier there
were intimations of serious unrest and of an impending
political crisis, but that the most absolute autocracy
in the world could crumble and be entirely shorn of
power in one short week practically without a struggle
and be replaced by a modern democratic government,
without serious loss of life or damage to property
seemed incredible.

CAUSES OF THE REVOLUTION

Back of the unrest among the Russian people
was the feeling, which gained strength with every
day, that there was a vicious circle at court among
the higher nobility that was strongly pro-German
and that treachery was rampant even in the higher
offices of the military establishment.   Information
had been furnished the enemy, army supplies had
been stolen and sold, munitions were faulty and the

240

supply irregular, the hospital service subject to constant criticism.

There was a sinister force back of the conspiracy against Russia's best interests in the person of the monk Gregory Rasputin, who, starting as Siberian peasant, had aquired a gradually widening influence through his so-called cures effected by hypnotic sug-

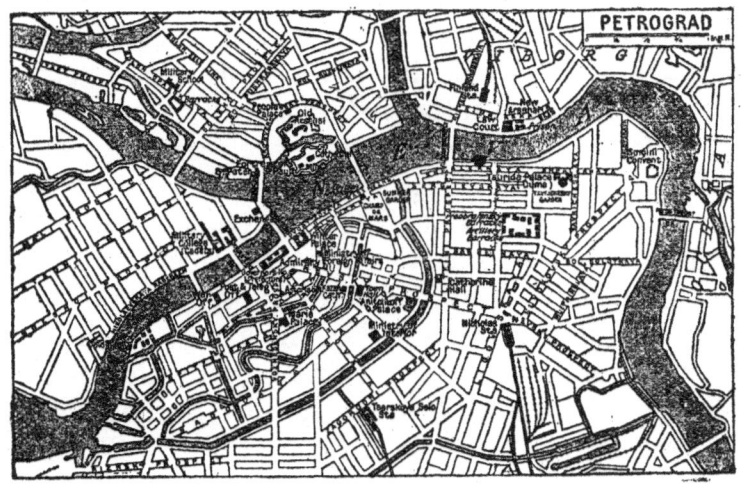

THE CAPITAL OF THE NEW DEMOCRACY.

Plan of Petrograd showing streets and buildings which were the scenes of notable events during the Revolution of March, 1917. The Taurida Palace, home of the Duma, where the Provisional Government was set up; the Fortress of St. Peter and St. Paul; the British Embassy; the Winter Palace, afterwards appropriated for National uses; the Arsenal, Barracks, and thoroughfares at the corners of which barricades were built during the street fighting.

gestion, which finally took him to Petrograd and into the high favor of the Czarina and to a large extent of the Czar. To Rasputin's influence was due the dismissal of Grand Duke Nicholas from the post of Commander-in-Chief and the appointment of Boris Sturmer to the position of Prime Minister, and of

Protopopoff to that of Minister of the Interior. It was strongly suspected that Rasputin was in the pay of Germany or at least of the pro-German and reactionary elements in the government.

Protopopoff's rule became increasingly distasteful to patriotic Russians whose sole aim was the winning of the war. In company with certain bureaucrats who were strongly suspected of pro-German tendencies, he gradually forced the empire toward a Revolution born of hunger which would leave Germany and Austria-Hungary victorious in the eastern theatre of war.

In a determined effort to save their country, some leading members of the Royal House decided to dispose of the most sinister and notorious figure in Russian history. Driving up to Rasputin's house in Petrograd, they carried him off and ordered him to shoot himself as a penalty for his crimes. In the affray which took place the monk was killed. But the evil which he had done was too great to be dissipated by his death.

In November, 1916, the Prime Minister, Stürmer, was denounced as a traitor who had sold himself to Germany. The succeeding ministry proved as bad or worse and the impression gained ground that influential persons in the government were intriguing to have Russia desert the Allies and conclude a separate peace. On March 8, 1917, a group of workingmen in Petrograd decided on a general strike as a protest against the serious food shortage. For some time past there had been threats of such a strike but the leaders did not expect it since the people at large well knew that any such interruption of the making of munitions would be of great benefit to the enemy.

THE POPULAR UPRISING

The food situation had been growing steadily worse for months in spite of the well-known fact that huge quantities of grain and other provisions were stored in the interior. When the government announced that it would be necessary to go without bread altogether for several days the temper of the crowd, already overstrained, broke. At first the unrest was expressed in an unusually quiet way, the crowds parading the streets in a demonstration to demand bread. The Duma was actively debating the food question and demanding satisfaction from the Minister of Agriculture with growing impatience. On November 10th the military commander of the Petrograd district issued a proclamation warning all citizens not to assemble in the streets or create disorder under threat of being shot down by the troops. This added flame to the fire, but the grand explosion came when the Czar, who was absent from the capital, issued two ukases suspending the sittings of the Duma and the Council of the Empire. Immediately the revolution became a fact. The Duma refused to dissolve and its president, Michael V. Rodzianko, telegraphed to the Czar requesting a withdrawal of the order and warning him that the consequences of a refusal would be serious. The Czar started immediately for Petrograd but it was too late—the revolution was full grown. Troops ordered to break up parades of the people did their duty in a half-hearted way. When ordered to fire on the crowd they revolted, shot their officers and joined the revolution. Regiment after regiment went over and like wildfire the revolt spread to other large cities of Russia. In Petrograd the police remained loyal to the Imperial Government and there was some fighting between the police and soldiers which soon resulted in the rout and disappearance of the police. Revolting troops captured the Fortress of St. Peter and St. Paul and the various government buildings with little or no resistance until they came to the small district containing the Admiralty Office, the War Office, St. Isaac's Cathedral and the Military Hotel. The Council of Ministers had gathered for a last conference in the Admiralty Building guarded by the last regiments still loyal to the old regime. The revolutionary troops made a fierce attack upon the defenders, pouring rifle and machine gun fire upon them and for several hours the fiercest battle of the day raged. The people in the streets fled to the nearest shelter as the streets all about the Admiralty Building were swept with a hail of bullets. Suddenly there came a lull in the battle and then victorious shouts from the revolutionary troops announcing the surrender of the defending forces. The ministers were then arrested and thrown into jail.

THE NEW GOVERNMENT

A new government was immediately formed by the Duma. The Premier chosen was Prince Georges E. Lvoff, one of the most popular men in Russia, head of the Army Commissary and of the Zemstvo Committees. The Foreign Minister was M. Paul N. Milukoff, for many years leader of the Russian Liberals and familiar to Americans through his professorship

244

STREET FIGHTING IN PETROGRAD.
Students and soldiers firing at police across the Moika Canal during the Revolution of March, 1917.

A RUSSIAN COSSACK CHARGE IN THE CARPATHIANS.

Some of the stubbornest and most eagerly contested engagements of the great war took place on the snow covered heights of the Carpathians. This illustration shows a charge of a famous Cossack regiment upon an Austrian battery. The Cossacks are numbered among the finest cavalry organizations in the world and are fearless and relentless fighters. Their horses are

at the University of Chicago. Another powerful member of the new ministry was Alexander F. Kerensky, deputy from Saratoff to the Duma, who was appointed Minister of Justice. The young lawyer had always been a friend and leader of the working-men and his appointment did much to bring together the labor party and the Moderate Democratic Party and prevent a split in the ranks of the Revolutionary Party.

THE NEW GOVERNMENT'S POLICY

The new government immediately issued an appeal to the people stating its policy, which included a general amnesty for political and religious offenses, liberty of speech and of the press, abolition of all social, religious and national restrictions, the establishment of a constitutional assembly based on universal suffrage, and various army reforms.

ABDICATION OF THE CZAR

The next step of the new government was to force the abdication of the Czar. His Majesty's train on which he was returning to Petrograd was stopped at Pskoff station to receive the envoys of the people, M. Gutchkoff and M. Choulgine. Entering the royal train they found waiting the Count Chamberlain, Baron Fredericks, Count Narishkia, and General Nicholas V. Russky, a member of the Council of the Empire: Soon the Emperor entered, wearing the uniform of one of the Caucasian Regiments, and shook hands quite calmly with the Duma committee. M. Gutchkoff then related to the Emperor the events of the previous days and ended by saying that it would be useless to send troops from the front to Petrograd as they would immediately go over to the revolutionists, and that the only thing for him to do was to abdicate the throne in favor of his young son, the Grand Duke Alexis, with his brother, the Grand Duke Michail as Regent. After thinking the matter over for some time, the Czar said that he could not bear to be separated from his son and would therefore abdicate in favor of his brother Grand Duke Michail. This was satisfactory to the committee and the Emperor retired to another car and wrote his act of abdication. This was on March 15, 1917 at 11.48 in the evening.

RUSSIA OF THE FUTURE

Thus passed the heavy pall of Czarism from the fair land of Russia. One more government of the people, for the people and by the people had triumphed over autocracy and Russia awoke in a dawn of new opportunity, aglow with ambition and dedicated to the high resolve that Russian freedom should never perish.

CHAPTER XXII

THE CANADIANS' GLORIOUS FEAT AT LANGEMARCK

THE CRUCIAL TEST OF CANADA'S MEN—WONDERFUL
STORY OF HEROISM AS TOLD BY SIR MAX AITKEN—
A REMARKABLE PERFORMANCE—QUIET PRECEDING
STORM—SECOND BATTLE OF YPRES—LINE NEVER
WAVERED—OFFICER FELL AT HEAD OF TROOPS—
FORTUNES OF THIRD BRIGADE—IN DIRE PERIL—
OVERWHELMING NUMBERS—PUT TO TEST—CAPTURE
OF ST. JULIEN—A HERO LEADING HEROES.

THE FIGHT of the Canadians at Langemarck and
St. Julien in April, 1915, makes such a battle story as
has sufficed, in other nations, to inspire song and
tradition for centuries. In the words of Sir John
French, the Canadians, by holding their ground when
it did not seem humanly possible to hold it, "saved the
situation," kept the enemy out of Ypres, kept closed
the road to Calais, and made a failure of German
plans that otherwise were about to be successful.

The Canadian soldiers have indeed shown that they
are second to none. They were put to as supreme a
test as it would be possible for any army to meet with,
for they fought overwhelming numbers under conditions that seemed to ensure annihilation. They fought
on, and failed neither in courage, discipline, nor
tenacity, although thousands of them fell.

247

The story of their unflinching heroism was told by Sir Max Aitken, the record officer serving with the Canadian division in France:

"The recent fighting in Flanders, in which the Canadians played so glorious a part, cannot of course be described with precision of military detail until time has made possible the co-ordination of relevant facts, and the piecing together in a narrative both lucid and exact of much which, so near the event, is confused and blurred. But it is considered right that the mourning in Canada for husbands, sons or brothers who have given their lives for the Empire should have with as little reserve as military considerations allow the rare and precious consolation which, in the agony of bereavement, the record of the valor of their dead must bring, and indeed the mourning in Canada will be very widely spread, for the battle which raged for so many days in the neighborhood of Ypres was bloody, even as men appraise battles in this callous and life-engulfing war. But as long as brave deeds retain the power to fire the blood of Anglo-Saxons, the stand made by the Canadians in those desperate days will be told by fathers to their sons.

A REMARKABLE PERFORMANCE

"The Canadians have wrested the trenches over the bodies of the dead and earned the right to stand side by side with the superb troops who, in the first battle of Ypres, broke and drove before them the flower of the Prussian Guards. Looked at from any point the performance would be remarkable. It is amazing to soldiers when the genesis and composition of the

Canadian division are considered. It contained no doubt a sprinkling of South African veterans, but it consisted in the main of men who were admirable raw material, but who, at the outbreak of war, were neither disciplined nor trained as men count discipline and training in these days of scientific warfare. It was, it is true, commanded by a distinguished English general. Its staff was supplemented, without being replaced, by some brilliant British staff officers. But in its higher and regimental commands were to be found lawyers, college professors, business men and real estate agents, ready with cool self-confidence to do battle against an organization in which the study of military science is the exclusive pursuit of laborious lives.

"With what devotion, with a valor how desperate, with resourcefulness how cool and how frightful, the amateur soldier of Canada confronted overwhelming odds, may perhaps be made clear, even by a narrative so incomplete as the present.

"The salient of Ypres has become familiar to all students of the campaign in Flanders. Like all salients it was, and was known to be, a source of weakness to the forces holding it, but the reasons which have led to its retention are apparent, and need not be explained.

"On Thursday, April 22, 1915, the Canadian division held a line of roughly five thousand yards, extending in a northwesterly direction from the Ypres-Roulers railway, to the Ypres-Poekappelle road, and connecting at its terminus with the French troops. The division consisted of three infantry brigades in addition to the artillery brigades. Of the infantry brigades the first was in reserve, the second was on the right, and the third established contact with the allies at the point indicated above.

"The day was a peaceful one, warm and sunny, and except that the previous day had witnessed a further bombardment of the stricken town of Ypres, everything seemed quiet in front of the Canadian line. At five o'clock in the afternoon a plan carefully prepared was put into execution against our French allies on the left. Asphyxiating gas of great intensity was projected into their trenches, probably by means of force pumps and pipes laid out under the parapets. The fumes, aided by a favorable wind, floated backwards, poisoning and disabling over an extended area those who fell under their effect. The result was that the French were compelled to give ground for a considerable distance. The glory which the French army has won in this war would make it impertinent to labor on the compelling nature of the poisonous discharges under which the trenches were lost. The French did, as everyone knew they would do, all that stout soldiers could do, and the Canadian division, officers and men, look forward to many occasions in the future in which they will stand side by side with the brave armies of France.

"The immediate consequence of this enforced withdrawal was, of course, extremely grave. The third brigade of the Canadian division was without any left, or, in other words, its left was in the air. It became imperatively necessary greatly to extend the Canadian lines to the left rear. It was not, of course, practicable to move the first brigade from reserve at a moment's

MAP ILLUSTRATING THE BATTLE OF LANGEMARCK.
Shaded Portion Indicates German Gain.

notice, and the line, extended from five to nine thousand
yards, was not naturally the line that had been held by
the allies at five o'clock, and a gap still existed on its left.

251

"The new line, of which our recent point of contact with the French formed the apex, ran quite roughly to the south and west. As shown above, it became necessary for Brigadier-General Turner, commanding the third brigade, to throw back his left flank southward to protect his rear. In the course of the confusion which followed upon the readjustment of position, the enemy, who had advanced rapidly after his initial successes, took four British 4.7 guns in a small wood to the west of the village of St. Julien, two miles in the rear of the original French trenches.

SECOND BATTLE OF YPRES

"The story of the second battle of Ypres is the story of how the Canadian division, enormously outnumbered, for they had in front of them at least four divisions, supported by immensely heavy artillery, with a gap still existing, though reduced, in their lines, and with dispositions made hurriedly under the stimulus of critical danger, fought through the day and through the night, and then through another day and night; fought under their officers until, as happened to so many, these perished gloriously, and then fought from the impulsion of sheer valor because they came from fighting stock.

"The enemy, of course, was aware, whether fully or not may perhaps be doubted, of the advantage his breach in the line had given him, and immediately began to push a formidable series of attacks upon the whole of the newly-formed Canadian salient.

"If it is possible to distinguish when the attack was everywhere so fierce, it developed with particular intensity at this moment upon the apex of the newly-formed line running in the direction of St. Julien. It has already been stated that four British guns were taken in a wood comparatively early in the evening of the 22d. In the course of that night, and under the heaviest machine-gun fire, this wood was assaulted by the Canadian Scottish, sixteenth battalion, of the third brigade, and the tenth battalion of the second brigade, which was intercepted for this purpose on its way to a reserve trench. The battalions were respectively commanded by Lieutenant-Colonel Leckie, and Lieutenant-Colonel Boyle, and after a most fierce struggle in the light of a misty moon they took the position at the point of the bayonet. At midnight the second battalion, under Lieutenant-Colonel Watson and the Toronto regiment, Queen's Own (third battalion), under Lieutenant-Colonel Rennie, both of the first brigade, brought up much-needed reinforcements, and though not actually engaged in the assault, were in reserve.

LINE NEVER WAVERED

"All through the following days and nights these battalions shared the fortunes and misfortunes of the third brigade. An officer, who took part in the attack, describes how the men about him fell under the fire of the machine guns, which, in his phrase, played upon them 'like a watering pot.' He added quite simply, 'I wrote my own life off,' but the line never wavered. When one man fell another took his place, and with a final shout the survivors of the two battalions flung themselves into the wood.

"The German garrison was completely demoralized, and the impetuous advance of the Canadians did not cease until they reached the far side of the wood and entrenched themselves there in the position so dearly gained. They had, however, the disappointment of finding that the guns had been blown up by the enemy, and later on the same night, a most formidable concentration of artillery fire, sweeping the wood as a tropical storm sweeps the leaves from a forest, made it impossible for them to hold the position for which they had sacrified so much.

"The fighting continued without intermission all through the night and to those who observed the indications that the attack was being pushed with ever-growing strength, it hardly seemed possible that the Canadians, fighting in positions so difficult to defend, and so little the subject of deliberate choice, could maintain their resistance for any long period. At 6 A. M. on Friday it became apparent that the left was becoming more and more involved and a powerful German attempt to outflank it developed rapidly. The consequences if it had been broken or outflanked need not be insisted upon. They were not merely local.

"It was therefore decided, formidable as the attempt undoubtedly was, to try and give relief by a counter-attack upon the first line of German trenches, now far, far advanced from those originally occupied by the French. This was carried out by the Ontario first and fourth battalions of the first brigade, under Brigadier-General Mercer, acting in combination with a British brigade. It is safe to say that the youngest private in the rank, as he set his teeth for the advance, knew the task in front of him, and the youngest subaltern knew all that rested upon its success.

OFFICER FELL AT HEAD OF TROOPS

"It did not seem that any human being could live in the shower of shot and shell which began to play upon the advancing troops. They suffered terrible casualties. For a short time every man seemed to fall, but the attack was pressed even closer and closer. The fourth Canadian battalion at one moment came under a particularly withering fire. For a moment, not more, it wavered. Its most gallant commanding officer, Lieutenant-Colonel Birchall, carrying, after an old fashion, a light cane, coolly and cheerfully rallied his men, and at the very moment when his example had infected them fell dead at the head of his battalion.

"With a hoarse cry of anger they sprang forward (for, indeed, they loved him) as if to avenge his death. The astonishing attack which followed, pushed home in the face of direct frontal fire, made in broad daylight by battalions whose names should live forever in the memories of soldiers, was carried to the first line of German trenches. After a hand-to-hand struggle the last German who resisted was bayoneted, and the trench was won.

"The measure of this success may be taken when it is pointed out that this trench represented in the German advance the apex in the breach which the enemy had made in the original line of the allies, and that it was two and a half miles south of that line.

255

This charge, made by men who looked death indifferently in the face, for no man who took part in it could think that he was likely to live, saved the Canadian left. But it did more; up to the point where the assailants conquered or died, it secured and maintained during the most critical moment of all the integrity of the allied line. For the trench was not only taken, it was thereafter held against all comers, and in the teeth of every conceivable projectile, until the night of Sunday, the 25th, when all that remained of the war-broken but victorious battalions was relieved by fresh troops.

FORTUNES OF THIRD BRIGADE

"It is necessary now to return to the fortunes of the third brigade, commanded by Brigadier-General Turner, which, as we have seen, at five o'clock on Thursday was holding the Canadian left and after the first attack assumed the defense of the new Canadian salient. at the same time sparing all the men it could to form an extemporized line between the wood and St. Julien. This brigade also was, at the first moment of the German offensive, made the object of an attack by the discharge of poisonous gas. The discharge was followed by two enemy assaults. Although the fumes were extremely poisonous, they were not, perhaps, having regard to the wind, so disabling as on the French lines (which ran almost east to west), and the brigade, though affected by the fumes, stoutly beat back the two German assaults.

"Encouraged by this success, it rose to the supreme effort required by the assault of the wood, which has already been described. At 4 A. M. on the morning of Friday, the 23d, a fresh emission of gas was made both upon the second brigade, which held the line running northeast, and upon the third brigade, which, as has been fully explained, had continued the line up to the pivotal point, as defined above, and had then spread down in a southeasterly direction. It is perhaps worth mentioning, that two privates of the forty-eighth Highlanders, who found their way into the trenches commanded by Colonel Lipsett, ninetieth Winnipeg Rifles, eighth battalion, perished of the fumes, and it was noticed that their faces became blue immediately after dissolution.

"The Royal Highlanders of Montreal, thirteenth battalion, and the forty-eighth Highlanders, fifteenth battalion, were more especially affected by the discharge. The Royal Highlanders, though considerably shaken, remained immovable upon their ground. The forty-eighth Highlanders, who no doubt received a more poisonous discharge, were for the moment dismayed and indeed their trench, according to the testimony of very hardened soldiers, became intolerable. The battalion retired from the trench, but for a very short distance, and for an equally short time. In a few moments they were again their own. They advanced upon and occupied the trenches which they had momentarily abandoned.

IN DIRE PERIL

"In the course of the same night the third brigade, which had already displayed a resource, a gallantry, and a tenacity, for which no eulogy could be excessive, was exposed (and with it the whole allied cause) to a peril still more formidable.

"It has been explained, and indeed the fundamental situation made the peril clear, that several German divisions were attempting to crush, or drive back this devoted brigade, and in any event to use their enormous numerical superiority to sweep around and overwhelm our left wing at a point in the line which cannot be precisely determined. The last attempt partially succeeded, and in the course of this critical struggle, German troops in considerable, though not in overwhelming, numbers swung past the unsupported left to the brigade and, slipping in between the wood and St. Julien, added to the torturing anxieties of the long-drawn-out struggle by the appearance, and indeed for the moment the reality, of isolation from the brigade base.

"In the exertions made by the third brigade during this supreme crisis, it is almost impossible to single out one battalion without injustice to others, but though the efforts of the Royal Highlanders of Montreal, thirteenth battalion, were only equal to those of the other battalions who did such heroic service, it so happened by chance that the fate of some of its officers attracted special attention.

"Major Norsworthy, already almost disabled by a bullet wound, was bayoneted and killed while he was rallying his men with easy cheerfulness. The case of Captain McCuaig, of the same battalion, was not less glorious, although his death can claim no witness. This most gallant officer was seriously wounded in a hurriedly constructed trench. At a moment when it

258

would have been possible to remove him to safety, he absolutely refused to move, and continued in the discharge of his duty. But the situation grew instantly worse, and peremptory orders were received for an immediate withdrawal. Those who were compelled to obey them were most insistent to carry with them, at whatever risk to their own mobility and safety, an officer to whom they were devotedly attached. But he, knowing, it may be, better than they, the exertions which still lay in front of them, and unwilling to inflict upon them the disabilities of a maimed man, very resolutely refused, and asked of them one thing only, that there should be given to him as he lay alone in the trench, two loaded Colt revolvers to add to his own, which lay in his right hand as he made his last request. And so, with three revolvers ready to his hand for use, a very brave officer waited to sell his life, wounded and racked with pain, in an abandoned trench.

"On Friday afternoon the left of the Canadian line was strengthened by important reinforcements of British troops, amounting to seven battalions. From this time forward the Canadians also continued to receive further assistance on the left from a series of French counter-attacks pushed in a northeasterly direction from the canal bank.

OVERWHELMING NUMBERS

"But the artillery fire of the enemy continually grew in intensity, and it became more and more evident that the Canadian salient could no longer be maintained against the overwhelming superiority of

259

numbers by which it was assailed. Slowly, stub-bornly, and contesting every yard, the defenders gave ground until the salient gradually receded from the apex near the point where it had originally aligned with the French, and fell back upon St. John.

"Soon it became evident that even St. Julien, exposed from right and left, was no longer tenable in the face of overwhelming numerical superiority. The third brigade was therefore ordered to retreat further south, selling every yard of ground as dearly as it had done since five o'clock on Thursday. But it was found impossible, without hazarding far larger forces, to disentangle the detachment of the Royal High-landers of Montreal, thirteenth battalion, and of the Royal Montreal Regiment, fourteenth battalion. The brigade was ordered, and not a moment too soon, to move back. It left these units with hearts as heavy as those of his comrades who had said farewell to Captain McCuaig.

"The German line rolled, indeed, over the deserted village, but for several hours after the enemy had become master of the village the sullen and persistent rifle fire which survived showed that they were not yet master of the Canadian rear guard. If they died, they died worthy of Canada. The enforced retirement of the third brigade (and to have stayed longer would have been madness) reproduced for the second brigade, commanded by Brigadier-General Curry, in a singu-larly exact fashion the position of the third brigade itself at the moment of the withdrawal of the French.

SECOND BRIGADE PUT TO TEST

"The second brigade, it must be remembered, had retained the whole line of trenches, roughly five hundred yards, which it was holding at five o'clock on Thursday afternoon, supported by the incomparable exertions of the third brigade, and by the highly hazardous deployment in which necessity had involved that brigade. The second brigade had maintained its lines. It now devolved upon General Curry, commanding this brigade, to reproduce the tactical maneuvers by which earlier in the fight the third brigade had adapted itself to the flank movement of overwhelming numerical superiority. He flung his left flank round and his record is that in the very crisis of this immense struggle he held his line of trenches from Thursday at five o'clock until Sunday afternoon, and on Sunday afternoon he had not abandoned his trenches. There were none left. They had been obliterated by artillery. He withdrew his undefeated troops from the fragments of his field fortifications, and the hearts of his men were as completely unbroken as the parapets of his trenches were completely broken. Such a brigade!

"It is invidious to single out any battalion for special praise, but it is perhaps necessary to the story to point out that Lieutenant-Colonel Lipsett, commanding the ninetieth Winnipeg Rifles, eighth battalion, of the second brigade, held the extreme left of the brigade position at the most critical moment.

"The battalion was expelled from the trenches early on Friday morning by an emission of poisonous gas, but recovering in three-quarters of an hour, it counter-attacked, retook the trenches it had abandoned

and bayoneted the enemy, and after the third brigade
had been forced to retire, Lieutenant-Colonel Lipsett
held his position, though his left was in the air, until
two British regiments filled up the gap on Saturday
night.

CAPTURE OF ST. JULIEN

"The individual fortunes of those two brigades
have brought us to the events of Sunday afternoon,
but it is necessary, to make the story complete,
to recur for a moment to the events of the
morning.

"After a very formidable attack the enemy succeeded in capturing the village of St. Julien, which has
so often been referred to in describing the fortunes of
the Canadian left. This success opened up a new and
formidable line of advance, but by this time further
reinforcements had arrived. Here again it became
evident that the tactical necessities of the situation
dictated an offensive movement, as the surest method
of arresting further progress.

"General Alderson, who was in command of the
reinforcements, accordingly directed that an advance
should be made by a British brigade which had been
brought up in support. The attack was thrust through
the Canadian left and center, and as the troops making
it swept on, many of them going to certain death, they
paused an instant, and with deep-throated cheers for
Canada gave the first indication to the division of the
warm admiration which their exertions had excited in
the British army.

"The advance was indeed costly, but it could not

be gainsaid. The story is one of which the brigade may be proud, but it does not belong to the special account of the fortunes of the Canadian contingent. It is sufficient for our purpose to notice that the attack succeeded in its object, and the German advance along the line, which was momentarily threatened, was arrested.

"We had reached, in describing the events of the afternoon, the points at which the trenches of the second brigade had been completely destroyed. This brigade and the third brigade, and the considerable reinforcements which by this time filled the gap between the two brigades, were gradually driven, fighting every yard, upon a line running, roughly, from Fortuin, south of St. Julien, in a northeasterly direction towards Passchendale. . Here the two brigades were relieved by two British brigades, after exertions as glorious, as fruitful, and, alas! as costly, as soldiers have ever been called upon to make.

"Monday morning broke bright and clear, and found the Canadians behind the firing line. This day, too, was to bring its anxieties. The attack was still pressed, and it became necessary to ask Brigadier-General Curry whether he could once more call upon his shrunken brigade.

A HERO LEADING HEROES

"'The men are tired,' this indomitable soldier replied, 'but they are ready and glad to go again to the trenches.' And so once more, a hero leading heroes, the general marched back the men of the second brigade, reduced to a quarter of its original strength, to the apex of the line as it existed at that moment.

"This position he held all day Monday. On Tuesday he was still occupying reserve trenches, and on Wednesday was relieved and retired to billets in the rear.

"Such, in the most general outline, is the story of a great and glorious feat of arms. A story told so soon after the event, while tendering bare justice to units whose doings fell under the eyes of particular observers, must do less than justice to others who played their part—and all did—as gloriously as those whose special activities it is possible, even at this stage, to describe. But the friends of men who fought in other battalions may be content in the knowledge that they, too, shall learn, when time allows, the exact part which each unit played in these unforgettable days."

CHAPTER XXIII

VIVID EXPERIENCES OF T. F. TRUSLER AT YPRES

LOST HIS MEMORY — REPORTED MISSING — ASPHYX-
IATING GAS CLOUD—FIGHTING TEN TO ONE—INTO
BATTLE WITH A SONG—CROSSING A CANAL UNDER
FIRE—INTO HURRICANE OF FIRE—HOW WAR MAKES
HEROES—A PERILOUS ESCAPE—SAVING THE DAY AT
YPRES—STORIES ABOUT SPIES.

OF ALL the strange personal experiences encountered in the war, perhaps none surpass those of Gunner Thomas F. Trusler in their peculiar combination of mystery, adventure and courage. To have lost all recollection of his earlier life, to have passed unscathed through the thickest of the three days' terrific fighting at the battle of Ypres, in which he and his comrades won the commendation of General French that they had accomplished the impossible, and finally to have had his leg shattered by a bursting shell from the enemy, incapacitating him for further service—this, in brief reflects only the main high-lights in Trusler's career as a gun-layer in the Third Battery of the Third Brigade of the Canadian Field Artillery.

LOST HIS MEMORY

Young Trusler went as a gun-layer with the first Canadian contingent which reached France late in 1914. At that time the German General Staff was

265

perfecting its scheme to break through to Calais by way of Ypres. Trusler first came under fire near Vlamartinghe, just west of Ypres. His division was acting as a reserve force. What befell him there is related in his own words:

I have been told by men who served with me on my gun that we all saw a huge German aeroplane fly over us. Soon thereafter there came a rain of high explosive shells from a big German gun. Several of our boys were killed, and the fact that I was not was a miracle. One of the shells fell within ten or twenty feet of me, I was told, but did not explode. The concussion, however, was terrific, and it dazed and stupefied me.

I remember awakening in a base hospital with the wounded all about me. I felt myself all over and could find nothing smashed, so I sat up in my cot. Then I got out of it and stood up and asked why I was there. A physician told me what had happened to me and sent me back to my brigade, which he located by the insignia on my uniform. When I got back I didn't seem to recollect anything or anybody.

Some of the men of my gun company saw me and took me back to my quarters. It was necessary for me to make friends with my companions again. They called me "Howie"—a nickname—and soon I became known as "Howie Trusler." That fact made it difficult for my parents to locate me, because when I was asked my name I spelled it "Tressler."

REPORTED MISSING

Consequently "T. F. Trusler" went on the rolls of the missing. Consequently also, I failed to get mail from my fiancée and my parents. It was not until last summer, when I was wounded in the leg so badly that I was sent to England, that I made any attempt to find out who I was. I confided my story to an English woman of high rank who was interested in the hospital. She made inquiries among the officers of my brigade, and they remembered "Trusler" who came out with the contingent.

My parents were communicated with and my mother remembered an old scar on my foot. Sure enough the scar was there. Even when I returned to Montreal I didn't recognize my mother and don't yet. My people had a great deal of trouble getting me back. I had been signing myself Tressler, instead of Thomas Frederick Trusler, and when my uncle came up to fetch me, the military authorities were not going to let him have me. At last they decided to send a man down to Montreal with us. When I saw my father and mother they were perfect strangers to me. I just shook hands with them and said, "I'm pleased to meet you." I learned I was engaged to be married before I left for the front and on my return home my fiancée was at the station with my mother and father. I didn't recognize any of them, but they took me home.

Although I cannot remember what happened before January, 1915, I have a vivid recollection of what has happened since.

After I returned to my gun company from the field hospital I resumed active duty, and passed through the battle of Ypres. My recollection of that terrific three-day fighting will never leave me.

The idea of the Germans was to break through the Allies' lines around Ypres and get to Calais, from which point they could have struck directly at England. Like all general attacks, the German advance was preceded by a heavy artillery bombardment. The purpose of the bombardment is to tear up the wire entanglements, break up the enemies' trenches, and demoralize the men. Then the infantry get out and make their attack. Many attacks have failed because the wire entanglements have not been broken up.

We expected an attack from the direction of Boesinghe, because we had gotten news from our aeroplanes, that the Germans were massing troops in Belgium and that they were coming towards Ypres.

About five o'clock of the evening of April 23, we were getting quite bored, for we were in the reserve force along the Poperinghe road, three miles west of Ypres. The dull monotony was rudely broken by the sudden appearance of swarms of French colonial troops, Singalese and Zouaves, rushing in from the front trenches, clutching at their throats, holding their sides, rolling on the ground, gasping for breath, eyes bloodshot and staring, many of them bleeding at the mouth, but most of them unable to explain the cause of their peculiar actions. Along with them came scores of refugees, men, women and children, bearing with them all they could take from their burning and wrecked homes.

ASPHYXIATING GAS CLOUD

They told us that they noticed three balls of white smoke go up from the German lines, and immediately

CONQUERING THE ALPS.

Immense labor and great ingenuity were required to haul the monster Italian guns up the steep mountain sides to their positions. Once in place, however, they justified the effort required by raining down huge shells on the Austrian positions

WOMEN AT WORK THAT MEN MIGHT FIGHT

A busy scene in one of the munition workshops. The women in the foreground are testing shells for accuracy of size and those in the background are turning the shells on engine lathes.

afterwards a big heavy cloud of smoke started to roll over and over—something like a storm in China; that is the nearest you can come to it—and those clouds just rolled straight over until they got near the French lines, and then the soldiers began to get the smell of some kind of gas in their nostrils.

You know chloride of lime—if you just get a sharp smell of it. This gas had a faint smell of that. And then again the effect is something as though you put your hands over your mouth and your nose until you can't get any breath. It's an awful feeling. You want to get a breath. That is how this thing is. Just the same as a man being hung about seven hours a day.

This compelled the French first line to retire, causing them to form a fresh line running from Steenstraate to Langemarck, north of Pilkem. They fell back gradually to this new line owing to the gas fumes, their reserves being taken back with them. The wind was blowing in a southeasterly direction at that time and the Germans could only gas part of the French line then. Gradually as the strange gas affected the French they begin to fall back more and more.

The Germans could not gas the Canadians to any great extent because of the wind; but they had succeeded in smashing the French line very seriously into open country, and what few villages were there had been blown to pieces by high explosive shells. Their idea was to get that line beaten back, so they could send in their troops and cut off the Canadian line.

FIGHTING TEN TO ONE

The Germans were in overwhelming numbers. There were fifteen to twenty thousand Canadians, and I know from an official source that the Germans had from four to five divisions in action. Each division consists of forty thousand men, so that they had somewhere around 150,000 to 200,000.

The Canadians did not see the joke of being cut off and wiped out. Their original line was five thousand yards in length. Therefore they extended their line in due course to nine thousand yards, passing their men up this line and extending them parallel with St. Julien.

Until that time we had never heard of asphyxiating gas and were at a loss to make out what it all meant. The order "stand to your arms" was quickly passed along to the reserves. The Montreal Highlanders were the first to get on the move. It takes longer to get artillery wagons on the move, and while we were working at feverish haste the Highlanders went by, each man singing and smiling, although they must have known that many of them would never return.

At seven o'clock the artillery forces were all ready and waiting for the order to move forward. I shall never forget the scene at the moment. From the city of Ypres there arose high in the heavens huge jets of flame, while overhead shells burst by the hundreds, and in our ears were the din of falling walls and all sorts of indescribable noises.

INTO BATTLE WITH A SONG

It was a wonderful sight. Coming down this road were men and women, with children hanging to their arms. There were the French Colonial troops holding their throats. Then you would see the Forty-eighth Highlanders with their kilts swinging, waving their bayonets. They knew they were going forward to what these other people were running away from. We just dropped our lines and stood by and gave them a good cheer. It was a terrible sight, but it was beautiful. Some of them were singing. They were singing "When the Boys Come Home." It's a mighty catchy song, especially at a time like that:

> *Keep the home fires burning*
> *While your hearts are yearning;*
> *Though the boys are far from home*
> *They dream of you.*
> *There's a silver lining*
> *Through the dark clouds shining;*
> *Turn the dark cloud inside out*
> *Till the boys come home.*

These fellows were singing this song with a zest— no fear, no trembling knees, nor any sign of cowardice. We were watching them keenly, and in our absorption we let some of our horses get away; the sergeant-major turned and said, "Where the devil are those horses going?" Of course, everybody jumped, and we tied up the lines and put them on the wagons. Then orders came, "Prepare for action!"

We removed the breech and muzzle covers, uncapped the shells, and got the fuses all set. We knew something was going to happen, because we were getting shells all ready to go into action, which is only done when action is right at hand.

When the order came to move forward we urged our horses with a cheer and a song, our batteries tearing along the road with the speed and noise of fire-engines.

As we neared Ypres we overtook the infantry, which made way for the guns, lining up on either side of the road, the men with their caps on, their bayonets swinging high in the air, shrieking and singing wildly as we tore along.

CROSSING A CANAL UNDER FIRE

It was necessary for us to make a detour south and east of Ypres in order to get to the main road leading to our damaged front. It also was necessary to cross the Yser Canal, about half a mile south of the town, on a pontoon bridge. The first gun got over safely, when along came a German shell and destroyed it.

Under a deadly fire, for the Germans had the range, we waited while the engineers worked to construct another bridge. Two long thick poles were placed across the narrow canal and cross-ways on them timbers and logs were piled. The second gun went across precariously, but the third was upset by a rolling log, the cannon carriage falling on one side of the narrow bridge and the six horses on the other. While the cannon and horses seemed to be see-sawing this way and that across the bridge, a shell put an end to all the trouble.

There was a terrific roar, a terrific splash, and then the men were seen and heard struggling and shrieking in the muddy water of the canal, with the horses, wagons and guns. There was no attempt at rescue. The Engineer Corps went calmly about its work of stringing in new pontoons while the stream of traffic was temporarliy diverted to the other bridge, and so alternately one or the other of these bridges was being blown up. When we finally got across the bridge and started on the gallop for the front, a new menace awaited us. Aeroplanes buzzing over our heads were dropping star shells, lighting up the wooded roads with a weird blue light; they were also dropping high-explosive bombs on the road to cut us off in our work of rescue.

INTO HURRICANE OF FIRE

This was followed by a perfect hurricane of shells, and the last gun to attempt the crossing went into the water. Emerging from a wood, we ran into a murderous gun-fire from German infantry and machine guns. My gun and others of our battery were hurled into this open fire-swept field, swung around and in less than two minutes opened fire on the Germans.

A field gun is equipped with a metal shield fastened to the hub of the gun carriage for the protection of the gunners. The gun protrudes through the shield, and there are also openings in it for the use of the gun-layer in sighting and firing the gun. The gun-layer, a kind of chief gunner, operates the gun while the other gunners pass along the shells and load them into the breech. The guns are lined up six inches apart because of the wheel hubs, so there is an open space between the shields. Sometimes as a fellow was passing a shell a bullet would hit it, and up would go the shell and kill all the gun crew around. We had twelve men and before we had been in action thirty-five minutes we had five completely blown to pieces.

Each of our shells contained three hundred bullets, and at a range of two hundred and fifty yards one can readily imagine how the Germans fell. Yet under this torrent of steel they came on and on with fixed bayonets, only to be beaten down, torn to pieces and piled in heaps. Advancing over their own dead, regiment after regiment was hurled against us. They got so near us on several occasions that the infantry were ordered up to repel them.

That was the first hand-to-hand fighting that I saw. It was awful to see men with the blood lust on them killing and not caring. Finally we halted them, but the German infantry remained hidden behind a deep fringe of trees with their own dead piled up against them. Our guns could not do effective work because of the trees. Therefore we were ordered to use high-explosive shells.

HOW WAR MAKES HEROES

I shall never forget how these shells were brought to us. The ammunition wagon containing them came galloping across the open field under a heavy fire, the men lashing their horses and yelling like mad. They took a hedge there something like three feet high, jumping clean over it, wagon and all. The horses were simply crazed. Some of them had been hit with bullets, and when they neared our guns the men could not stop them. It looked as though they would go right on to the German lines. There was only one thing to do: the rider of the leading horses drew his revolver and shot them dead. They went down, with the other horses and men and the wagon rolling over and over them. One poor fellow was found with the hoof of a horse driven through his face. With the high-explosive shells we tore the trees to bits and left the whole place open; then our infantry, quickly following up the advantage, drove the Teutons back.

Our boys were yelling like a lot of wild Indians, waving their hats, until they got right up to the German trenches, and they went at them with bayonets. Some of the Germans threw up their arms and would not fight at all. At last I saw one of our fellows catch hold of a German, and you could see he was saying something like "For God's sake, why don't you fight?" and threw him down and kicked him out of the way. And that is what was going on right along the line. Their nerves had gone altogether. But you can't blame those men. They were doing their piece for their country. Under the circumstances a man will lose his head very easily.

A PERILOUS ESCAPE

Meantime our line was badly pressed near St. Julien, and after the arrival of fresh British and Canadians our battery was ordered there. We went right through the town. Then we began to straighten out the line, but again the Germans renewed their terrific attacks, and they drove our troops right back onto St. Julien. We had to retire with our guns, fighting desperately

275

all the way. On and on came the German infantry, and the retreat was sounded, but not for me. My gun and two others, and seven hundred men of the Montreal Highlanders, were ordered to remain in the town to cover the retreat.

Our first feelings upon being left alone were, "Well it looks as though we're finished." Just as we were thinking that, an officer came up and said, "What the devil are you men standing there for?" Bang! Off would go another shell. We were thoroughly played out, but we kept fighting. Sometimes one of the men sitting at a gun would almost drop over with exhaustion, and then an officer would say, "What are you doing? Going to sleep? Why don't you go to sleep at the right time?" And the fellow would turn around, smile, and pull the lever again.

I lost seven men during the night. One fellow got out of action about the easiest I ever saw. He was sitting on the gun and just put his hand on top of the shield, when a rain of bullets took off all his fingers. He just turned round, smiled, and said, "I'm hit." He got up out of the seat, walked a few spaces, and dropped.

The Germans saw that the town was being evacuated and at daylight advanced in tremendous numbers. The Germans didn't expect to meet with any resistance in the town at all, so they marched in singing. We wiped out with our three guns the first two regiments. Then we were ordered to retreat while the Highlanders went forward. The Highlanders were almost annihilated and we stopped and gave them assistance.

Never did I see such a hail of bullets. The Germans

276

Infan ry of the first Canadian Contingent passing Stonehenge on their way from Salisbury Plain to London.

Canadian transport and field artillery embarking at Quebec for England.

Parade of Canadian Highlanders on Salisbury Plain.

KING GEORGE AT THE FRONT

The King is here seen greeting Canadian general officers on a visit to the scene of action.

came on in thousands. The spokes in the wheels of the gun carriages were nearly all broken and one brave company of Germans got right up to our gun. It was saved by a French-Canadian whose name, strange to say, was McConnell. With the butt of a short rifle he killed three Germans who attempted to get behind the bullet shield of the gun. At last the Germans were checked and we saved our three guns.

SAVING THE DAY AT YPRES

Gradually we got back under cover, and so fell back into the original line again, and we fought in the general action that went on until close to seven o'clock on Sunday. When we went back some of our fellows had their clothes almost completely torn off; there was hardly a man that was not wounded; they were covered with blood, and they looked a perfect wreck. They had had nothing to eat for three days, and when they passed through the British troops, the British soldiers all turned around and gave three cheers for the Canadians. We did not realize until then what we had actually done: we saved the whole situation, fighting against overwhelming odds for three days and nights. Out of our battery of 313 men, with their reserves, we had fifty-two left at the finish of that action.

I saw a very amusing incident at Ypres. In one of the trenches, they had sandbags placed all over the ground and in the sandbags is a small opening at which a man stands with his rifle resting on a pivot so that he can train it along the enemy's trench by moving it back and forth. Just back of him there was a rod standing up with a bell on it—an ordinary door bell. Well, occasionally they would ring the bell, and almost always some German in the opposite trench would stick up his head out of curiosity to see what the ringing was—thinking perhaps it was a stray cow, or something like that. Instantly the man with the rifle would spot him—and then there was one more dead German.

STORIES ABOUT SPIES

Spying at the front is the most dangerous of all occupations. The Germans are very clever at it, and one method of sending news between the lines is by trained dogs. One night one of our sentries saw a dog dart past him. He called to the animal, thinking the dog would make an excellent mascot for the battery. The dog came back, wagging his tail, and the sentry took him to his quarters.

The following morning one of the men remarked on the thickness of the plain leather collar worn by the dog. An examination revealed that the collar was hollow, and in it we found a message in cipher. Instantly an officer was summoned, the dog was put on a long wire leash and driven out of camp. He went direct to a barber shop, where the men were in the habit of lounging and talking when off duty. The barber, whom we thought to be a Belgian, was a German spy and afterward was put to death.

I was quartered soon after that on an outpost guarding general headquarters. Not even the King of England could have passed the road we guarded unless he had a passport. Toward evening a handsome

278

automobile of English make containing two staff officers approached. The sentry on duty saluted with fixed bayonet and asked for passports. One of the officers got out of the machine and reached his hand into a leather case. Instead of drawing out a passport, he drew out a revolver and shot at the sentry. He missed and the sentry shot him dead. Meantime another sentry killed the other supposed officer. Both men were Germans. In their automobile was a quantity of high explosives.

Another case was that of a dispatch rider from another division. "You know," he said one day, "we had one of our sights blown up last week, one just like that," and he picked up a gun-sight and turned it around to look at it. Then he said, "I'll bet you a dollar the Germans haven't any sights like that." The section officer was standing right near and he said, "What do you know about sights? You're a dispatch rider. You stop there!" pulling out his revolver, "you shouldn't know anything about sights at all." Although he spoke with a Canadian accent, the dispatch rider turned out to be a German.

I was responsible for catching one spy. I happened to go to a little place at the back of the line, and asked for a drink of water. A Frenchman came to the door. I said, "Will you give me some water?" He motioned as though he did not understand me, but I saw that he did not want to give me a drink. After many efforts I simply could not make him appear to know what I wanted. I went back later with some others from our division, and just for fun we drew our revolvers and stuck them in the doorway. Then we all walked inside the house, and started to look around. We happened to look down on the floor and saw a wire running along the base of the wall; we traced it up the wall, through the ceiling, right over the top of the roof and down the other side of the house into the ground. On further investigation we found it ran back into the German lines. It was afterwards found that though the man spoke French fluently, he was from Alsace and was a spy. If he had given me a drink he would probably not have been found out.

CHAPTER XXIV

CANADIAN HEROISM IN THE WAR

MANY INSTANCES OF CANADIAN VALOR—CORPORAL
HARMON'S STORY—GLORY OF THE BLACK WATCH
— CANADIANS FIGHT IN FIERCEST SECTIONS —
CANADIAN SOLDIERS POPULAR EVERYWHERE—WIN
MANY MEDALS BY HEROIC DEEDS.

THE MOST impartial observers on the battlefields
of Europe are as one in their praises of the courage
and efficiency of a Canadian soldier. The course of
the war furnishes many instances of marked heroism
on the part of Canadian troops. Langemarck is a
glorious page in Canadian history; but Langemarck
is only one. True, the feat of the Canadian battalion
in that engagement was of such tremendous importance in holding back the enemy against seemingly
impossible odds that it may well be reserved for
special treatment later in this narrative; but many
other notable examples of the bravery, discipline, and
determination of Canadian soldiers are at hand to
quote.

CORPORAL HARMON'S STORY

Corporal Burdette W. Harmon, of Woodstock,
N. B., who was in the Marine and Fisheries Depart-
ment at Ottawa, when he enlisted with the Royal
Canadian Engineers of the First Canadian Contingent,

gives one of the most remarkable and complete descriptions of the fighting that has yet been penned.

It was in the engagement in which Corporal Burdette was wounded that the First Canadian Battalion lost six hundred of their seven hundred and fifty men. Corporal Harmon was wounded eight times by a German bomb when he was caught alone by the Germans away down their trenches after a portion of the Huns' line had been blown up by a Canadian mine.

"We knew for several days before June 15," said Corporal Harmon, "that an attack was imminent. The bombardments, while largely sporadic, had been very destructive, because we had some very heavy howitzers hammering away at the enemy's trenches. The night before the attack, part of our company placed two eighteen-pounders within one hundred and fifty feet of the German trenches. This was a very clever trick, and the boys who took part in it deserve credit.

"Seven of us were told off to report to Col. Hill of the First Battalion. He talked to us for over an hour, and explained by maps the plan of attack. There were to be five bombing parties, one sapper to be attached to each party. The two remaining were to look for leads and cut them. At two o'clock in the afternoon we fell in with our respective platoons, and marched towards the 'Duke's Hill.'

LIKE A SEWER DITCH

"We had to round in and out for a mile and a half, in what was exactly like a deep sewer ditch. At 4.30 p. m., we were in the front trench, and prepared to rest until six—the mine was to go up at six. At 5.30 the artillery lieutenant in charge of the field gun told us to pull away the sand bag barrier that hid his gun from the Germans. We expected a fusilade of shot as we exposed ourselves in the gradually increased opening. We were agreeably surprised. The move drew a very slight addition of rifle fire. That gun began to speak. We were right under the muzzle— what a noise! It was sure ear-splitting. I stood and watched the gunner. Without hat, shirt only, and sleeves rolled up, he flung those shells into the breach with marvelous skill. Crouched on bended knees, with sweat rolling down his face, he looked to me like a warrior king of old. He truly was a hero. He fired twenty shots, and was then blown to pieces by a shell that exploded backwards when he opened the breech. Our grim giant, of which we were proud, was stark and cold. It was depressing to be deprived of such an encouragement at such a time. Some score of German crack shots with machine guns were hidden within one hundred and fifty feet.

"Lieutenant James spoke calmly. 'Boys, in a minute the mine goes up.' I climbed on the firing platform to be ready for a quick spring up the three-step ladder. I called Corporal Talbot in charge of the bombing infantry, to come up near me, in order that the men might better follow, having his familiar figure as a guide.

A FIERCE EXPLOSION

"And now the explosion! Can you imagine it? Three thousand pounds of an explosive, as powerful as nitro-glycerine. Lumps of earth as big as barrels went hundreds of feet in the air. I watched it with childish curiosity. The sun, a crimson red, was setting. The rays glistened in the falling curtain, and lit it up so that it looked like many rainbows. Now the Angel of Death began to reap. A large lump beat the man behind me to his knees. Lieutenant James falls, killed.

"Our trench is rocked and buried and some scores of our own men are killed and wounded. The rainbow has no interest. I bend my head and each moment expect to have my brains knocked out. At last the sky ceased to rain lumps of earth. We leap for the parapet. I notice that Talbot is beside me and we rush forward. As quick as we were, others were much quicker. The short space between the trenches is already filled with charging Canadians. A few fall as we rush forward. I stop for a second beside the yawning crater and try to estimate its extent. I conjectured it was sixty feet deep, and two hundred feet across. I ran on and the first German I ran across was a little fellow, about twenty, with his leg shattered. He was in the edge of the crater, high up on the mound. Horror and fear were painted on his face. With a broken leg he could not move, and he piteously moved his hand to surrender. I thought of all the vows I had sworn, and I knelt to shoot him. Thank God, I did not do it, but ran on.

"The next sight almost made me laugh. About twenty hands seemed to move from the earth. They did not have time to run down their trench and they waited for our rush with hands up. We stopped to shoot a few who were running through the grass towards their second line. Talbot and I did not bother with the prisoners. Our job was to bomb down the front line trench as far as possible.

RAN DOWN THE TRENCH

"We ran down the trench for about fifty yards and came across a group of about six infantry with another engineer named Boyle. Boyle was boss and he told us that the lieutenant had told them to stay there. Some of us were chagrined. Our orders were to go down the trench to 'hell.' Colonel Hill's orders surely were more reliable than the commands of a lieutenant. A big splendid looking sergeant says, 'Come on, who will follow me.' I ran after him followed by the bunch, Boyle included—he didn't lack spunk. He thought the word of a lieutenant was a command from God. We ran down the trench for about one hundred yards.

"We came across two huge cables about one inch in diameter, made of many small wires and the whole insulated. Boyle asks how we are to cut these; mine clippers were no good. I told him to get a shovel and put it under the cable. We hammered with another shovel until the cable was almost cut. He goes ahead with that job, and the sergeant, aided by myself, and others, builds a barricade. Boyle had the cables almost cut by this time and I asked him to go back for reinforcements. He started back, and in a few minutes, about ten men came along. We climbed over our barricade and advanced. We must have gone over one hundred yards when I noticed that the sergeant

285

and myself were alone. He was ahead and one would think he was hunting deer.

"We passed dead and dying Germans, but did not stop to look in dugouts. It is risky to pass such places, but we thought them empty and chanced it. The sergeant stopped and seized me by the shoulder, 'Do you see them opposite?' he said. The trench was built like a snake fence, and they were in the opposite angle.

"I saw several heads and one fellow' out of the trench. The sergeant and I started to shoot, shoulder to shoulder. He fired about four rounds when I felt a pull and heard a thud. I turned my eyes and saw the sergeant bent forward on his rifle, with his head blown off just above the eyes. Blood and brains rolled down his face, and his rifle was stained a bright scarlet from the stock to the muzzle. In a glance I had seen that he was dead.

"I was alone, and down the German trench. It did not take me long to decide what to do. I 'beat' it back over dead Germans and around corners further than any Germans would dare come, until I met three or four of our fellows behind our barricade. We wanted to see what would happen. In a few minutes about ten men came along. They said, 'Come on, boys, we have orders to advance.' I started ahead with the leader. By the time we reached the dead body of the sergeant, German shrapnel and snipers had thinned the bunch to four.

TO BUILD BARRICADE

"I told the fellow with me how the sergeant died. He lifted his face from the butt of his rifle, and laid him tenderly in the bottom of the trench. He cut his wire clippers from his neck and handed them to me. The three of us then started to build a barricade. As we worked two awful explosions seemed to lift us off our feet. I mentally figured that shrapnel could not forever continue to fall at that particular spot. A second report, almost split my ear drums. My rifle is torn from my hand, and I feel a sharp pain in my right hand and side. Someone shouts, 'They are bombing us.' That is warning enough.

"We have no bombs and are as helpless as children. We run back along the trench, and at last come to where our infantry form a continuous line. What an encouragement. I stop to rest, nearly reeling with exhaustion. The strain had been great and that bomb had hit me in eight places—many merely scratches though. I felt that I had a right to have a rest. I asked the fellows if it would discourage them if I retired. I said I was wounded and exhausted. They said for me to go back, so I retired a few yards down the trench and crawled into a dug-out.

"I dwell on this point because my conscience troubles me. I should not have left those fellows—as a matter of life or death I could have used my rifle with a measure—though small I admit—of efficiency. I am minutely truthful in this letter, and I wish to point out to anyone who finds anything praiseworthy in my conduct, that when I retired to that dug-out, while yet able to hold a rifle, I nullified any credit due to me. In that were two wounded—I must be honest with all— not any worse off than I was.

"The order now came to retire. How hard it was to

leave our wounded Canadians in the trench. Most probably the Germans bayoneted them as their bombing party made headway. Our bombs were exhausted. The seventh division had not gained ground on the left and we were being caught on three sides. Hence the order to retire.

"Now I am at the Duchess of Connaught hospital. I am fully recovered, and mean to get back to France, though it may be eight weeks yet.

"You might give this letter the publicity which in your judgment is proper. It is written from an altruistic motive, and not one of egotism. I want no cheap notoriety, and I regret the way the Ottawa correspond-'ents dressed up Allen's letter.

"In the attack the First Battalion lost 600 men out of 750. Those figures are but ciphers to you, but they seem to me to personify scores of battle-torn Canadians. On land and sea fate never offers to the lips of men a more bitter chalice than that offered to the lips of a helpless comrade as he sees his friends pass him and hears the steady advance of the cracking bombs, and already in anticipation feels the saw-toothed bayonet plunged between his ribs.

"The sun was red and just sinking to the west. Who in Canada does not hear them calling, yes calling, calling and moaning for help—ENLIST."

GLORY OF THE BLACK WATCH

When this war is over the history of the famous Black Watch will have to be rewritten. The glorious past will in no way have faded, but the more recent achievements of the historic regiment, with its many battalions, will shed additional lustre on the name.

In that new history no story will be more renowned than the stand of the Thirteenth Battalion of the Canadian division at Ypres.

There are some incidents in the story of the Black Watch that are well worth re-telling. No man who intends to join the Seventy-third could hear without a thrill of pride the story of the assault on Ticonderoga in 1758.

ABERCROMBIE'S FORCE

The Black Watch was one of the regiments which formed a part of the force commanded by General Abercrombie in the war against the French. They advanced on Ticonderoga, in June, through the forest. The scouts had reported the place indifferently fortified, and held by some 5,000 French with 3,000 more coming up. Abercrombie's force consisted of 6,337 regulars and 9,000 provincials. But the scouts were wrong. Ticonderoga was practically impregnable. The British, however, attacked with great vigor, notwithstanding the fact that they were under a terrible disadvantage. They had no artillery and the fort was protected by an abattis composed of large trees.

The Forty-second had been detailed as part of the reserve. They were held back and compelled to stand aside and see the attacking force rush up time after time, only to be driven back by the withering fire that came from behind the abattis. The dead were strewn about the ground and the cries and groans of the wounded were horrible there in the bright sunlight of the clearing. At last they could stand the inaction no longer. Disregarding commands they started forward.

Broadswords in hand they crossed the open space. They reached the abattis. With their swords they hacked and hewed at the trees. In frenzied rage they forced a way. A few actually got beyond the barricade. All were instantly killed, however.

FIVE HOURS' FIGHT

A writer who was present afterwards told the story: "The Highlanders, screaming with rage, rushed time after time on us, and it was not till their general sounded the retreat three times that they were prevailed on to abandon the attack."

The fight lasted five hours and the regiment lost 647 killed and wounded out of a total of 1,100. An officer who witnessed the struggle wrote:

"I am penetrated with the great loss and immortal glory acquired by the Highlanders engaged in this affair. Impatient for the fray, they rushed forward to the entrenchments into which many of them actually mounted. Their intrepidity was rather animated than damped by witnessing their comrades fall on every side. They seemed more anxious to avenge the fate of their deceased friends than careful to avoid a like death."

The following year the Black Watch again advanced against this stronghold and this time, after a fight of but half an hour, added to their glories by capturing it.

CHAPTER XXV

WOMAN'S PART IN THE GREAT WAR

COURAGE OF THE WOMEN—EQUIPPING A MILITARY
HOSPITAL — THE FIRST PATIENT — WOUNDED SOL-
DIERS BY THE HUNDREDS—HOW FAST A NURSE
SOMETIMES MUST WORK—CHEERFULNESS OF THE
WOUNDED—DIFFICULTIES OF THE WORK—"WHERE
IS THE THERMOMETER?"—FEW DEATHS IN THE
HOSPITAL — THE HARDEST TRIAL — FAITH IN
HUMANKIND.

SOME OF the most vivid experiences of the war
occur in the hospitals where the wounded are cared
for. The following account of a war nurse's experiences
is typical of thousands of other brave women who helped
to ease pain and suffering among the men who have
fallen in the name of liberty:

"Don't worry about me or about the children!" I
heard the voice near me in the crowd, and turned to
where a woman was bidding her soldier-husband
good-by. Around them stood three children—boys
aged, I should say, about five, seven and twelve years.
A mist covered my eyes. It was almost more than I
could endure, the farewell of these soldiers to their
families. But there was no mist in the eyes of the
woman. Rather a light!

"Don't worry about the children," she repeated.
"I'll bring them up, and bring them up to fight for

their country, too. You—you think of 1870! Remember father in 1870! I'll remember the children!"

COURAGE OF THE WOMEN

Here was a woman's courage unsurpassed. She was doing her part, and with what a spirit! I determined to do mine. I would not return to America, as I had planned. For three years I had lived in France. For three years this country had been my friend. And now I would be its friend. I would offer my services as a nurse.

When I spoke to the head surgeon of the American Ambulance Hospital in Neuilly, whom I knew, he said that they were going to take a certain number of "auxiliaries," as he called them—women untrained, who were to work under the direction of the trained nurses.

"You are sure you want to come?" he questioned me.

"Yes—sure."

"But you know, as yet, we have no extra beds for the nurses."

"But I have one in my apartment," I said.

He gave me another searching look, then replied: "Well, I advise you to get that this afternoon. Listen!" I did. Far in the distance we could hear, faint but unmistakable, the booming of the guns of battle. "The Germans are within fifteen miles of Paris. Tonight, I think, the gates of Paris will be closed. It is well—if you wish to come—to come immediately."

I waited for no more. I hastened to my apartment, miles away in another quarter. I packed my suitcase.

292

I called a fiacre. We strapped my cot on the side, together with my few things. We rode through the gates of Paris—the gates that were closed that night!

EQUIPPING A MILITARY HOSPITAL

I saw my bed carried up into a medium-sized room in which there were eight other cots, and that was the only furniture. No chairs, no tables, no bureaus, and certainly no mirrors. For weeks I slept in this room with the other eight nurses, using our suitcases as chairs and tables and chests of drawers. Since that time there has been a place fixed in the other part of the building for nurses' quarters. We even have a bathtub, which was a personal gift from a good friend of the hospital. The nurses who come now do not appreciate it. But those who are left of the sixty who had five tin basins to wash in—to bathe in—we appreciate it!

"In a little over a week we must be ready for wounded." The order came from the head nurse standing almost ankle-deep in the débris that covered the floors, for the building had never been used, and shavings and plaster and mortar had to be swept out and mopped up—and I had to help do it, on my knees. Beds were moved in for the wounded, but no bedding. We had ordered dozens of blankets. But we couldn't get them. We expected twenty-five dozen chairs. We got four dozen. We were short of money; we were short of help; but we were long on hope. The hospital grew almost in a night to meet the needs of the Great War, but its growing pains were great and many. Still, it proved the stuff of which we were

293

made. In the personnel of the hospital was an American woman whose name is socially prominent in many countries. Associated with her were friends. To many of them, I imagine, this was the first essay out of a drawing-room atmosphere. And they made good —most of them. I take off my hat to the American woman whose sense of organization, of bringing order out of chaos, is born in her, or is absorbed from her organizing husband.

THE FIRST PATIENT

Finally, in some way or other, we did get ready, and the word went around that we might expect the wounded that night.

The moments were tense. They were so tense we were fairly hysterical. Hour passed hour. Finally we heard the sound of the ambulance coming into the grounds. We rushed—one over the other—down the stairs to the receiving room. We met the stretcher as it was being brought in. I say *the* stretcher, for there was only one. Our first patient! His wound? There was not any. Only an attack of heart trouble, due to fear.

Now I can laugh about it. But *then* I cannot tell you the pain of that disappointment. I suppose it was due to the last glimmer of that romantic tradition which made me look forward with beating heart to that first moment.

WOUNDED SOLDIERS BY THE HUNDREDS

But the wounded began to come in hundreds. Many from the Battle of the Marne that had decided the fate of Paris—from the Field of the Five Thousand Dead. They came with shattered faces—some with half faces; with frozen feet dropping off them; with fractured legs and arms and brains. Oh! such sights— such sights! And not only did I have to look at them; I had to care for them. Heaped into days I got years of training. Carefully directed by the trained nurse over me, and by the surgeons, I looked after some of these men.

I remember especially one afternoon, two weeks after the hospital opened. The head nurse was in the operating room. I was alone in the ward with ten wounded men—I with my two weeks' experience.

One was an Irishman, with the humor and grit of the Celt. He had just come in from an operation for a fractured arm. And he wouldn't keep covered.

"Sister," he said in his semi-consciousness, "Sister, where be I?"

"In the hospital," I answered.

"Sister—sure, an' if I had a wife, what would she say if she could see me now?"

HOW FAST A NURSE SOMETIMES MUST WORK

As I looked up to answer, I caught sight of Pierre in the far corner. He was trying to get up. I dropped the blankets of the Irishman and rushed to him. I knew he was in a critical condition, and delirious. In his skull was a hole as big as a dollar from which his brain protruded. He thought he was again on the battle-line, and was arising to meet his enemy.

As I persuaded him to return to his bed, the door opened. The orderlies brought in an operation case—

295

a Frenchman, whose jugular vein, lacerated by a bullet, had been sewed. Was I ready for him? they asked. I had to be, regardless of Pierre and my joking Irishman. But as I laid his head on the pillow I saw on the pillow of Pierré a red spot—a bright, spreading spot. The cerebral hemorrhage that we had feared had come.

I opened the door—called, signaled for a doctor, bade one of the convalescents whose arm was in a sling care for the Irishman, while I rushed to Pierre. The door opened again. The nurse came in with a patient whose leg had just been amputated.

This was what war nursing meant, and I had been a nurse two weeks!

CHEERFULNESS OF THE WOUNDED

Yet, curiously enough, we had lots of gaiety, due to the wounded. They are seldom depressed. And they cannot understand the surprise of the visitors to find them gay. Too, they are eternally bored by the usual question: "Do you want to go back to the trenches?" Most of them do.

It was during the first days that I made the acquaintance of the English "Tommy"—that unquenchable spirit of bravery and bravado. No one can be sad with Tommy in the ward. The first one I had was Sergeant Walker. He came in with his leg off.

"Where was it amputated?" I asked.

"Sure—and in the field, Miss," he answered.

"In the field?" I exclaimed, astonished. "Who did it?"

"I did."

"You? What do you mean? Tell me about it?"

"Well, you see, Miss, I was ordered to 'old a position with me men. And, sure, while we was a 'olding of it, waitin' for reinforcements—for some of us had to be sacrificed if the retreat 'ad to come, and it 'ad to, Miss—along came one of those whizzin' shells and 'it me in the leg. But I 'ad orders to stick to me post, me and me men, an' we stuck, until there was only three of us left. Then we started to retreat. And, sure, Miss, as I started, I felt 'ampered in me goin'. I looked down and there was me leg a hangin' by a piece of flesh. Well, now, Miss, I was never one to be 'ampered. So I outs with me jackknife, and I cuts the piece of flesh and dropped me leg. Then I hobbled along as far as I could, in a dash for safety—a dash, Miss," he laughed.

He had not bled to death for the simple reason that the stump of his leg had been seared by the heat of the obus. He was awarded the Victoria Cross—and he could not understand why!

DIFFICULTIES OF THE WORK

Few of us got any sleep during the first weeks. I can still see the face of the surgical nurse as she rushed from the operating room on the first floor, which came to be known as the "clean" operating room, to that on the third floor, known as the "dirty" operating room. Which merely meant that some of the men were so dirty when they arrived—so covered with gangrene and filth—that it was not safe to take them to the operating room for fear of infection. So another room without any appliances had to be opened in another part of the building. This building, which is

297

a block long and half a block deep, has no elevator, so the nurse had to carry her bandages and instruments up and down stairs from one room to the other. She deserves a medal. I wonder how many lives she saved.

"WHERE IS THE THERMOMETER?"

"Where is the thermometer?" was a frequent cry, for there was only one then.

"Why, ward 232 had it last, I think."

I went to 232. "Thermometer," I cried.

"Just gave it to nurse in 370."

I rushed up another flight of stairs,

"Give me the thermometer quick," I demanded.

"Can't—using it now," came back the reply.

"You'll give me that if it's at the point of the bayonet," I insisted, and I meant it, too. "I've got a boy down there with hemorrhage temperature, I think." I took the thermometer and rushed back to Antoine. He had developed high temperature, as I found by the thermometer. Before I could tell the doctor, the hemorrhage came. There was no way that I knew to stop the blood, for one could not put a turn-gat on his back where they had taken a bullet from his spine. I had to think fast, I knew. I sat down by him and thrust my hand into that wound—it was that large— at the same time sending one of the convalescents for the doctor. I was covered with blood to my elbow— but we saved Antoine's life.

FEW DEATHS IN THE HOSPITAL

Not many died in our hospital because of our superior surgical staff, although, for the same reason, we got the most severe cases. However, that is a curious thing—when a man dies in the ward it affects the other men in the ward; it affects the whole hospital for days. They don't get over it. They don't forget it.

"But you've seen soldiers die and soldiers killed by the hundreds," I said to one of them who was brooding over the death of the man in the cot next to his.

"Yes, I know," he answered; "but this is different." They seem to feel that when they are in action they are not so impotent against death.

I could understand when I saw my first "death." Always I had been spared that. I was afraid of death.

"You are to go to the room on the fourth floor— the isolation room—there is a man dying with gaseous gangrene." They were my orders. I said nothing, but as I closed the door of the ward, I had only one impulse. It was to run. Then I thought of the man there alone—and went to him.

THE HARDEST TRIAL

He was lying on a bed near a window. He opened his eyes as I came in. They were wonderful eyes, brown and soft and questioning—haunting eyes. But he said no words. For three hours I sat by his side and watched death creep up. They were the longest hours I have ever spent. He opened his eyes again. "Wife," he murmured, then "Children." I understood. "Yes," I answered. "I will write to them."

The door opened. The rector came in. In his hand was the English prayer-book. I stood up. Again the soldier opened his eyes and listened to the beautiful words of the prayer. And as he listened he held out his hand toward mine, reaching out at the end for some touch. It almost overpowered me, that groping at the last for a human touch. I had never seen him before. He had never seen me. But we drew together in that hour, and so we stayed until his hand relaxed.

As I closed the door and staggered to my room I thought ludicrously enough of a conversation I had heard of two young girls who had come to France to nurse. They had made a great fête of it. Before they left America they gave "tea" to their society friends and sold their party dresses for the benefit of the soldiers. They were coming to be nurses! To hold officers' hands and comfort them! Did they know that this was what it meant?

FAITH IN HUMANKIND

But I am afraid I'm giving a wrong impression. For it is not all sad, as I have said. There were always the soldiers to cheer one. Most of our patients were French—not such French as you know or as I knew. There is a new spirit. The traditional mask of their frivolity has been discarded—the fiber of their spirits has been uncovered. Mingling with them are Senegalese and Arabs, many of whom can speak little French.

One Arab I remember particularly well. He had been wounded in the head and for weeks he scarcely spoke a word. But gradually he gained confidence in me, and began to talk with the few French words he knew. One day when we were alone he said:

"What's the war all about, nurse? Is it about a king? And is the king in Germany or in France?"

300

He had been a shepherd of the hills and knew nothing of worldly things. As simply as I could I tried to tell him, and he seemed satisfied.

When I see the fineness and the courage of "my" soldiers I wonder how I could ever have lacked faith in humankind—in the godliness of the most simple, yes, even sometimes the most evil—of men who are purifying themselves in this war.

"Greater love hath no man than this" kept ringing ever in my ears as they told me that Jean could not live throughout the night. We knew he had to die, but we could not speak of it. He had been brought to us three days before—a hero. Jean was a gunner. In one of the attacks of the enemy his comrades had been forced slowly to retreat because of their inferior numbers. But Jean stood by his gun. Regularly, unflinchingly, he kept his gun shooting. He was hit in one leg—but his hands were all right and the gun went on. He was hit in the other leg. Still his hands were all right, and the gun went on. The enemy, hearing, meeting that incessant, regular fire, thought that reinforcements had come, and withdrew. Alone and unaided Jean won that engagement.

Jean had been sent to us. All we could do was to make his last hours as comfortable as we could. His wife was sent for. She came and sat by his bedside. The next day the colonel came to pin on his breast the *medaille militaire*, the highest honor that can be given to a soldier of France.

"I want to kiss it first," whispered Jean. He took it in his hands and reverently touched his lips to it. And then the colonel pinned it on his breast.

And now they told me Jean was dying. I took some roses which were on my table and went to him. His wife was weeping by his side.

"I've brought a brave man some roses," I said.

"Oh, nurse, I'm afraid he's past knowing or caring now," she answered, sobbing.

"Then I give them to you—the wife of a brave man."

"Yes—I know. But at what a price! What a price I have had to pay for it!" But even as she spoke—and again when I caught the gleam of the *medaille* pinned alone on the black curtains of the carriage that bore Jean to his last resting place—I thought what it would mean to her; of what it would mean to her children; of what it would mean to the small village where he lived—to the children who would gather around it—this emblem of great love.

Did I ever regret that I—an American girl—came to the French wounded? No, never. For it is by such bravery—such spirit—that we catch enough light to rise.

CHAPTER XXVI

A BATTLE IN THE AIR

HOW ZEPPELIN AND AEROPLANE FIGHT FOR SUPREM-
ACY—HUNTING THEIR PREY—HOW THEY AVOID
THE ZEPPELIN'S FIRE—READY FOR THE FINAL
BLOW.

OUT OF the gray dawn mist the huge pencilled
Zeppelin emerges, her engines thrashing fiercely. She
is late in getting back from her night raid, and the
captain has seen two ominous black spots in the sky to
the rearward.

Aeroplanes! Since the news of the night raid was
flashed to the Allies aerial stations men and machines
have been preparing for the grim task of intercepting
the Zeppelin on the return journey, when daylight
would give aeroplanes their full power of attack. While
it is yet dark two of the most daring pilots start, and
by clever airmanship they make a course which should
give them a strategic position when the Zeppelin
appears.

But the crafty enemy has taken another course, and
when dawn breaks he is not to be seen by the aerial
watchers. Masses of fleecy clouds render observation
difficult, and hope has almost disappeared when suddenly
one of the pilots sees the Zeppelin loom through a cloud
bank several miles ahead. Heeling over at a terrific
angle, the little craft swing round in pursuit, climbing

303

as they go so as to get the "hawk position" over the enemy ship.

HUNTING THEIR PREY

The Zeppelin has disappeared! Somewhere in that upper world of coldness and rudely-disturbed silence the ship is traveling through billowy clouds, now touched by the glorious lights of the new day. A reek of burned oil fouls the pure air, and the roar of engines in full throttle pulsates into space.

Like swallows in pursuit of flies the aeroplanes hunt high and low for the enemy, and not until after one long despairing dive to earth is the vessel sighted. It has cleverly been using the clouds for cover, and by the liberal sacrifice of gas and ballast it has danced up and down in the air to elude the hunters. In these tactics the Zeppelin has the advantage of quick movements. A brilliant burst of sunlight suddenly reveals the ship to the aviators, and the Zeppelin captain also discovers the enemy as they wheel round to pursue. The aeroplanes are at a lower level, and they promptly start climbing. The Zeppelin leaps upwards, and setting her elevation planes seeks to gain a still greater advantage in height.

HOW THEY AVOID THE ZEPPELIN'S FIRE

It looks as if pursuit were hopeless, but the aeroplanes hold on grimly. Steadily they gain in forward speed. Their engines are fresh, whilst the Zeppelin motors are feeling the long strain of high-speed running. When the affair settles into a stern chase the Zeppelin guns open fire. The airmen are prepared for this and keep as close as possible in the wake of the German ship, thus masking the guns in the forward cabin. But the Zeppelin, learning a lesson from previous encounters, has guns in the rear cabin, and despite the disadvantage of shooting in a line parallel with the keel they make rapid practice on the aeroplanes. Now the situation is growing desperate for the Zeppelin. All the ballast has been thrown out, petrol is running short, and the engines are showing signs of increasing weakness and irregular running. The engineers mutter and make signs to each other.

Undeterred by the guns, one aeroplane has already climbed to the same level as the airship and is steadily rising to a height where it will be concealed from the Zeppelin guns by the body of the ship itself. This Zeppelin has tried and discarded the gun-mounting on the top of the ship, and the captain can only storm with impotent rage as the aeroplane climbs to a higher level. A great burst of forward speed can alone save him from being overtaken by the enemy.

Now the second aeroplane has risen also above the fire zone, though one ragged wing shows a wound. As a balloon the Zeppelin can rise no higher, for all her ballast has been sacrificed, and the captain decides to bring his elevating planes back to the normal and stake all on a high-speed flight in a horizontal course. He is encouraged in this by the sight of the German lines below him with the landmarks which he knows so well. Puffs of smoke tell him that the aeroplanes are being shelled by German gunners, who very quickly have guessed what the situation is. Some of the shells burst so close to him that his opinion of the gunners is not flattering, and yet he knows that if something is not done to the airmen he is doomed.

READY FOR THE FINAL BLOW

The firing soon ceases. A few moments of intense agony follow as the crew look at each other with horror-stricken eyes. What is happening above them?

From their little cabins there is no possibility of an upward survey, for the great body of the ship looms above them, shutting out the overhead view. But they can picture those two gaunt birds flying after them remorselessly as Fate, and inch by inch gaining upon them. When the Zeppelin lies beneath the aeroplanes a bomb will drop on the ship's back, and then——

In a frenzy the captain plunges the ship downward and swings her to the right with a swerve which threatens to break her spine. But the elephantine manœuvre avails little. The birds above him can dive and swerve with the grace of swallows whilst his giant ship lumbers like a derelict balloon.

"Harbor!" shouts one of the crew, pointing to the familiar long building far below. In the coolness of despair the man levels his glasses. and he discerns men running and signaling.

A wireless message is picked up by the Zeppelin operator—"Two aeroplanes above you."

The captain suddenly falls into a seat, burying his face in his hands and sobbing hysterically. His nerve has broken.

"How long they are!" yells a stolid fellow looking upward.

But as he speaks there is a dull thud, and then a sheet of flame, spreading with lightning speed, envelops them. The burning hydrogen consumes them with appalling fury, and in a few instants the great ship, crumbling and melting, hurtles to earth like a blazing meteor.

From the earth many guns speak. They but serve for the firing salute over the graves of the fallen.

Two black specks in the sky rock under the concussions of the bursting shells, but keep on their way.

A few instants later the sickening crash of the Zeppelin carcase paralyzes the gunners with horror. Only a German knows what it is to see a Zeppelin fall. It is an omen of doom.

CHAPTER XXVII

A MARCH THROUGH THE NIGHT

WHAT IT MEANS TO THE MEN THEMSELVES —
DAWN AT LAST—GUARDING PRECIOUS WATER —
BACK FROM THE FIRING LINE—STORIES BY THE
WAYSIDE.

THIS DESCRIPTION of a movement of a large body of troops at night, written by a Canadian officer at the front, gives a good word picture of what the movement of a division from one position to another means to the men themselves:

For the last few days we have been moving day and night from one place to another in an atmosphere of slaughter. Great aggressive attacks against the enemy have been hourly launched. Here and there success; here and there disaster; everywhere terrible bloodshed and sacrifice of human life. We, as yet, being reserve, have not been engaged, but are close to the scene of the fray. Almost every minute of the day we meet men who have been in the fighting, and are eloquent with tales of the battle. To give you an idea of what a big movement means I will briefly sketch our activities during the last few days. As you know, we retired from the fighting line to a charming town some seven or eight miles to the rear. We were taken there to rest for eight days, but forty-eight hours had not gone by before there sprang up in all directions signs of military activity of an unusual nature. All officers were assembled, and particulars and explanations given secretly of a long-contemplated move. Of course, all instructions were given in the strictest confidence, so that this aspect of our movements and knowledge of our military intentions I cannot divulge. I can only say that the information was of a dramatic nature, thrilling all of us with excitement. The result of the conference was that on the same night everyone "stood to" in a constant state of readiness. By midnight we were supposed to move off for the front, but the order was cancelled and we "stood easy." However, on the following night we did move, and soon after starting we learned that the whole division was on the march.

Of course it is quite a complicated business to move a division to a certain point. Each unit, from a regiment upwards, has its allotted time to pass a point. For instance, each of the battalions of our brigade had to pass the brigade headquarters at a certain time. We had to pass at 12.14 a. m., another regiment at 12.7 a. m., and so on. Then the brigades in their turn have to pass a certain point at set time.

Thus each unit falls in behind the other at scheduled time. The following fact shows how slowly large bodies of troops move, especially in the night time. It took us from twelve o'clock noon until four a. m. to travel six miles to the place where we were to billet.

The march was exhausting. Men were allowed to smoke, but not to talk. The effect is very weird and impressive—one interminable length of men tramping slowly and stolidly along—whither? To what? They

309

knew not. This ignorance of what may be forth-coming and the influence of the night combine to keep the men silent.

DAWN AT LAST

Every now and then motor-cycles and machines would tear by, momentarily illuminating the lines and showing them as gaping and irregular. Every hundred yards or so there would be a check, and almost imme-diately afterwards the line would continue to move. One moment one is moving quickly; another, haltingly and slow. Here and there you would hear the grouser spitting out curses in a loud whisper. Up and down the lines go the officers, encouraging the men to keep up. In spite of our utmost energy the men straggle and gradually get further and further apart, for it is very, very difficult to keep close together in the dark when marching. Suddenly comes a halt. Down the lines dash the officers, closing up the men and forming their fours. At last dawn begins to break, and soon a gay daylight spreads, bringing relief to all. Weary we arrive at our destination. Men are hurried into the buildings, and ground allotted to them. They are immediately placed under cover, so that no enemy aeroplanes may learn that we are moving troops. By five o'clock thousands of troops were concealed in all directions.

GUARDING PRECIOUS WATER

The first thing we did on arrival was to place sen-tries on all the water supplies, for water was scarce. Nobody was allowed to wash, and for the most part

310

everybody had to exist for the day on the water they had in their bottles.

Save for the sentries, everybody, in a very short time, was sleeping. At 5 a. m. the stillness was suddenly broken by terrific firing in the distance. This got louder and louder, and lasted for nearly two hours. We surmised, of course, that a big attack was on. This was confirmed later in the day—in the afternoon—when little batches of wounded men began to pass.

BACK FROM THE FIRING LINE

Just as night was falling we got the order to "Stand to," and within a quarter of an hour were marching towards the firing line. We did not go far but in the short distance we did travel we were passed by hundreds of men, singly and in groups, straggling back from the battle line. Here was a group whose regiment had been almost annihilated; there was another dazed and scared. They had seen terrible, terrible sights, and had fearful tales to mutter. They and their comrades had been sent to capture a trench. It was thought that the Germans at that point had been completely wiped out by our artillery fire. They rushed forward—it was but eighty yards to the trench —only to find the trench crowded with Germans, who allowed them to get close up to the wire entanglements and then withered them with rifle and machine-gun fire. In five minutes 250 were mowed down. The remainder lay down and tried to conceal themselves. Of those who lay down this group alone lived to tell the tale, and they were nearly crazy with the strain of lying there twelve hours, expecting death every moment. When night came they managed to crawl back to safety.

STORIES BY THE WAYSIDE

In addition there were terrible and dreadful tales of wounded lying helpless and parched with thirst and delirious with pain, waiting through the long night till aid could be given them. Then here and there was the grand story of the heroic man: one going from safety to almost certain death to fetch in a wounded comrade. Another giving up his water bottle in the early morning to the wounded comrade by his side. All night long we heard stories of the ebb and flow of bloody encounters. Here a division had routed the enemy and advanced; there a division had been practically wiped out. The grand outstanding feature of the whole thing was that, whatever they had gone through, all were ready to return to the hell for the sake of their country. Yes, indeed, the spirit is fine.

Since that stirring night we have been shifted three times, and any moment expect to do our share. Everybody is cheery and determined to do his bit to his utmost.

CHAPTER XXVIII

JAMES BRYCE'S REPORT ON SYSTEMATIC MASSACRE IN BELGIUM

REPORT OF COMMISSION TO INVESTIGATE GERMAN OUTRAGES — A HARROWING RECITAL — TELLS OF MASSACRES—"KILLED IN MASSES"—THE TALE OF LOUVAIN—TREATMENT OF WOMEN AND CHILDREN— CALLS KILLING DELIBERATE—"SPIRIT OF WAR DEIFIED"—THE COMMISSION'S CONCLUSIONS.

VISCOUNT BRYCE, former British Ambassador at Washington, was appointed chairman of a special government commission to investigate and report on "outrages alleged to have been committed by German troops." Associated with Lord Bryce on the commission were Sir Frederick Pollock, Sir Edward Clarke, Sir Alfred Hopkinson, H. A. L. Fisher, Vice-Chancellor of the University of Sheffield; Harold Cox, and Kenelm E. Digby. The commission was appointed by Premier Asquith on January 22, 1915. The document is considered as probably the most severe arraignment made of the German military sweep across Belgium, mainly because of the position of Viscount Bryce as a historian, and also because of the care with which the investigation was made, the great number of witnesses whose testimony was examined, and the mass of evidence submitted with the report of the commission.

313

The report makes an official document of sixty-one printed pages, or upward of 30,000 words, accompanied by maps showing the various routes of the army and the chief scenes of desolation. It states at the outset that 1,200 witnesses have been examined, the depositions being taken by examiners of legal knowledge and experience, though without authority to administer an oath. The examiners were instructed not to "lead" the witnesses, and to seek to bring out the truth by cross-examination and otherwise. The commission also submitted extracts from a number of diaries taken from the German dead, chiefly German soldiers and in some cases officers.

A HARROWING RECITAL

Taking up conditions at Liège at the outset of the war, the report gives a harrowing recital of occurrences at various points in the devastated territory. At Herve on August 4, 1914, the report says, "the murder of an innocent fugitive civilian was a prelude to the burning and pillage of the town and of other villages in the neighborhood; to the indiscriminate shooting of civilians of both sexes and to the organized military execution of batches of selected males. Thus some fifty men escaping from burning houses were seized, taken outside the town and shot. At Melen, in one household alone the father and mother (names given) were shot, the daughter died after being repeatedly attacked and the son was wounded.

"In Soumagne and Micheroux very many civilians were summarily shot. In a field belonging to a man named E——, fifty-six or fifty-seven were put to death.

A German officer said, 'You have shot at us.' One of the villagers asked to be allowed to speak, and said, 'If you think these people fired, kill me, but let them go.' The answer was three volleys. The survivors were bayoneted. Their corpses were seen in the field that night by another witness. One at least had been mutilated. These were not the only victims in Soumagne. The eye-witness of the massacre saw, on his way home, twenty bodies, one that of a girl thirteen. Another witness saw nineteen corpses in a meadow.

"At Heure le Romain all the male inhabitants, including some bed-ridden old men, were imprisoned in the church. The burgomaster's brother and the priest were bayoneted. The village of Vise was completely destroyed. Officers directed the incendiaries. Antiques and china were removed from the houses before their destruction, by officers, who guarded the plunder, revolver in hand.

TELLS OF MASSACRES

"Entries in a German diary show that on August 10 the German soldiers gave themselves up to debauchery in the streets of Liège, and on the night of the 20th a massacre took place in the streets. . . . Though the cause of the massacre is in dispute, the results are known with certainty. The Rue des Pitteurs and houses in the Place de l'Université and the Quai des Pecheurs were systematically fired with benzine; and many inhabitants were burned alive in their houses, their efforts to escape being prevented by rifle fire. Twenty people were shot while trying to escape, before the eyes of one of the witnesses. The Liège

Fire Brigade turned out, but was not allowed to extinguish the fire. Its carts, however, were usefully employed in removing heaps of civilian corpses to the Town Hall."

Taking up the Valleys of the Meuse and Sambre, the report gives lengthy details of terrible conditions described by witnesses at Andenne, and says:

"About four hundred people lost their lives in this massacre, some on the banks of the Meuse, where they were shot according to orders given, and some in the cellars of the houses where they had taken refuge. Eight men belonging to one family were murdered. Another man was placed close to a machine gun which was fired through him. His wife brought his body home on a wheelbarrow. The Germans broke into her house and ransacked it.

"A hair-dresser was murdered in his kitchen where he was sitting with a child on each knee. A paralytic was murdered in his garden. After this came the general sack of the town. Many of the inhabitants who escaped the massacre were kept as prisoners and compelled to clear the houses of corpses and bury them in trenches. These prisoners were subsequently used as a shelter and protection for a pontoon bridge which the Germans had built across the river and were so used to prevent the Belgian forts from firing upon it.

"A few days later the Germans celebrated a 'fête nocturne' in the square. Hot wine, located in the town, was drunk, and the women were compelled to give three cheers for the Kaiser and to sing 'Deutschland über Alles.'"

"KILLED IN MASSES"

Similar details are recited at much length in reference to the districts of Namur, Charleroi and the town of Dinant. At the latter point, the report says, "Unarmed civilians were killed in masses. We have no reason to believe that the civilian population of Dinant gave any provocation or that any other defense can be put forward to justify the treatment inflicted upon its citizens."

The commission stated that it had received a great mass of evidence on "scenes of chronic outrage" in the territory bounded by the towns Aerschot, Malines, Vilvorde and Louvain. It stated that the total number of outrages was so great that the commission could not refer to them all.

"The commission is specially impressed by the character of the outrages committed in the smaller villages. Many of these are exceptionally shocking and cannot be regarded as contemplated or prescribed by responsible commanders of the troops by whom they were commanded. Evidence goes to show that deaths in these villages were due not to accident but to deliberate purpose. The wounds were generally stabs or cuts, and for the most part appear to have been inflicted with a bayonet.

"In Sempst the corpse of a man with his legs cut off, who was partly bound, was seen by a witness, who also saw a girl of seventeen in great distress dressed only in a chemise. She alleged that she herself and other girls had been dragged into a field, stripped naked and attacked, and that some of them had been killed with a bayonet."

317

Taking up conditions at Aerschot and the surrounding district during September, the report says:

"At Haecht several children had been murdered; one of two or three years old was found nailed to the door of a farmhouse by its hands and feet, a crime which seems almost incredible, but the evidence for which we feel bound to accept. At Eppeghem the body of a child of two was seen pinned to the ground with a German lance. The same witness saw a mutilated woman alive near Weerde on the same day."

A chapter is given to the terrible conditions at Louvain, where the report states, "massacre, fire and destruction went on. . . . Citizens were shot and others taken prisoners and compelled to go with the troops. Soldiers went through the streets saying, 'Man hat geschossen' (some one has fired on us).

THE TALE OF LOUVAIN

"The massacre of civilians at Louvain was not confined to its citizens. Large crowds of people were brought into Louvain from the surrounding districts, not only from Aerschot and Gelrod, but also from other places. For example, a witness describes how many women and children were taken in carts to Louvain, and there placed in a stable. Of the hundreds of people thus taken from the various villages and brought to Louvain as prisoners, some were massacred there, others were forced to march along with citizens of Louvain through various places, some being ultimately sent to the Belgian lines at Malines, others were taken in trucks to Cologne, others were released.

"Ropes were put around the necks of some and they

were told they would be hanged. An order then came that they were to be shot instead of hanged. A firing squad was prepared, and five or six prisoners were put up, but were not shot. . . . This taking of the inhabitants in groups and marching them to various places must evidently have been done under the direction of a higher military authority. The ill-treatment of the prisoners was under the eyes and often under the direction or sanction of officers, and officers themselves took part in it. . . . .

"It is to be noticed that cases occur in the depositions in which humane acts by individual officers and soldiers are mentioned, or in which officers are said to have expressed regret at being obliged to carry out orders for cruel action against the civilians. Similarly, we find entries in diaries which reveal a genuine pity for the population and disgust at the conduct of the enemy. It appears that a German non-commissioned officer stated definitely that he 'was acting under orders and executing them with great unwillingness.' A commissioned officer on being asked at Louvain by a witness, a highly educated man, about the horrible acts committed by the soldiers, said he 'was merely executing orders,' and that he himself would be shot if he did not execute them."

Another division of the report is on the "killing of non-combatants in France." This is not as detailed as the case of Belgium, as the commission states that the French official report gives the most complete account as to the invaded districts in France. It adds:

"The evidence before us proves that, in the parts

of France referred to, murder of unoffending civilians and other acts of cruelty, including aggravated cases of felonious attack, carried out under threat of death, and sometimes actually followed by murder of the victim, were committed by some of the German troops."

TREATMENT OF WOMEN AND CHILDREN

A special chapter is given to the treatment of women and children. The latter, it is said, frequently received milder treatment than the men. But many instances are given of "calculated cruelty, often going the length of murder, towards the women and children." A witness gives a story, very circumstantial in its details, of how women were publicly attacked in the market place of the city, five young German officers assisting. The report goes on: "In the evidence before us there are cases tending to show that aggravated crimes against women were sometimes severely punished. These instances are sufficient to show that the maltreatment of women was not part of the military scheme of the invaders, however much it may appear to have been the inevitable result of the system of terror deliberately adopted in certain regions.

"It is clearly shown that many offences were committed against infants and quite young children. On one occasion children were even roped together and used as a military screen against the enemy, on another three soldiers went into action carrying small children to protect themselves from flank fire. It is difficult to imagine the motives which may have prompted such acts. Whether or not Belgian civilians fired on German soldiers, young children at any rate did not fire."

320

Many instances are given of the use of civilians as screens during the military operation. Cases of the Red Cross being misused for offensive military purposes, and of abuse of the white flag are also given. As to the latter the report says: "There is in our opinion sufficient evidence that these offences have been frequent, deliberate and in many cases committed by whole units under orders. All the facts mentioned are in contravention of The Hague Convention, signed by the Great Powers, including France, Germany, Great Britain and the United States, in 1907."

A division of the report is given to diaries of German soldiers. The entry of a sergeant of the First Guards Regiment, who received the Iron Cross, says, under date of August 10: "A transport of 300 Belgians came through Duisburg in the morning. Of these, eighty, including the Oberburgomaster, were shot according to martial law." The diary of a member of the Fourth Company of Jagers says, under date of August 23: "About 220 inhabitants and the village were burned." Another diary, by a member of the Second Mounted Battery, First Kurhessian Field Artillery Regiment, No. 11, records an incident which happened in French territory near Lille on October 11: "We had no fight, but we caught about twenty men and shot them." The commission says of this last diary: "By this time killing not in a fight would seem to have passed into a habit."

The report adds that the most important entry was contained in diary No. 19. This contained no name and address, but names referred to in the diary indicate that the entries were made by an officer of the First

Regiment of Foot Guards. The entry made at Bermeton on August 24 says: "We took about 1,000 prisoners; at least 500 were shot. The village was burned because inhabitants had also shot. Two civilians were shot at once."

"If a line is drawn on ᴗ map from the Belgian frontier to Liège and continued to Charleroi, and a second line drawn from Liège to Malines, a sort of figure resembling an irregular Y will be formed. It is along this 'Y' that most of the systematic (as opposed to isolated) outrages were committed. If the period from August 4 to August 30 is taken it will be found to cover most of these organized outrages. Termonde and Alost extend, it is true, beyond the 'Y' lines, and they belong to the month of September. Murder, assault, arson and pillage began from the moment when the German army crossed the frontier. For the first fortnight of the war the towns and villages near Liège were the chief sufferers. From August 19 to the end of the month outrages spread in the direction of Charleroi and Malines and reached their period of greatest intensity.

"There is a certain significance in the fact that the outrages around Liège coincide with the unexpected resistance of the Belgian army in that district, and that the slaughter which reigned from August 19 to the end of the month is contemporaneous with the period when the German army's need for a quick passage through Belgium at all costs was deemed imperative.

"In all wars occur many shocking and outrageous acts of men of criminal instincts whose worst passions are unloosed by the immunity which the conditions of warfare afford. Drunkenness, moreover, may turn even a soldier who has no criminal habits into a brute, and there is evidence that intoxication was extremely prevalent among the German army, both in Belgium and in France. Unfortunately little seems to have been done to repress this source of danger.

CALLS KILLING DELIBERATE

"In the present war, however—and this is the gravest charge against the German army—the evidence shows that the killing of non-combatants was carried out to an extent for which no previous war between nations claiming to be civilized (for such cases as the atrocities perpetrated by the Turks on the Bulgarian Christians in 1876, and on the Armenian Christians in 1895 and 1896, do not belong to that category) furnishes any precedent. That this killing was done as part of a deliberate plan is clear from the facts hereinbefore set forth regarding Louvain, Aerschot, Dinant and other towns. The killing was done under orders in each place. It began at a certain fixed date. Some of the officers who carried out the work did it reluctantly, and said they were obeying directions from their chiefs. The same remarks apply to the destruction of property. House burning was part of the program; and villages, even large parts of a city, were given to the flames as part of the terrorizing policy.

"Citizens of neutral states who visited Belgium in December and January report that the German authorities do not deny that non-combatants were systematically killed in large numbers during the first weeks of the invasion, and this, so far as we know, has never been officially denied.

"The German government has, however, sought to justify these severities on the grounds of military necessity and has excused them as retaliation for cases in which civilians fired on German troops. There may have been cases in which such firing occurred, but no proof has ever been given, or, to our knowledge, attempted to be given, of such cases, nor of the stories of shocking outrages perpetrated by Belgian men and women on German soldiers. . . .

"We gladly record the instances where the evidence shows that humanity has not wholly disappeared from some members of the German army and that they realized that the responsible heads of that organization were employing them not in war but in butchery: 'I am merely executing orders, and I should be shot if I did not execute them,' said an officer to a witness at Louvain. At Brussels another officer said, 'I have not done one hundredth part of what we have been ordered to do by the high German military authorities.'

"That these acts should have been perpetrated on the peaceful population of an unoffending country which was not at war with its invaders, but merely defending its own neutrality, guaranteed by the invading power, may excite amazement and even incredulity. It was with amazement and almost with incredulity that the commission first read the depositions relating to such acts. But when the evidence regarding Liège was followed by that regarding Aerschot, Louvain, Andenne, Dinant, and the other towns and villages, the cumulative effect of such a mass

324

of concurrent testimony became irresistible, and we were driven to the conclusion that the things described had really happened. The question then arose how they could have happened.

"The explanation seems to be that these excesses were committed—in some cases ordered, in others allowed—on a system and in pursuance of a set purpose. That purpose was to strike terror into the civil population and dishearten the Belgian troops, so as to crush down resistance and extinguish the very spirit of self-defense. The pretext that civilians had fired upon the invading troops was used to justify not merely the shooting of individual franc-tireurs, but the murder of large numbers of innocent civilians, an act absolutely forbidden by the rules of civilized warfare.

"SPIRIT OF WAR DEIFIED"

"In the minds of Prussian officers war seems to have become a sort of sacred mission, one of the highest functions of the omnipotent state, which is itself as much an army as a state. Ordinary morality and the ordinary sentiment of pity vanish in its presence, superseded by a new standard which justifies to the soldier every means that can conduce to success, however shocking to a natural sense of justice and humanity, however revolting to his own feelings. The spirit of war is deified. Obedience to the state and its war lord leaves no room for any other duty or feeling. Cruelty becomes legitimate when it promises victory. Proclaimed by the heads of the army, this doctrine would seem to have permeated the officers and affected even the private soldiers, leading them to justify the killing of non-combatants as an act of war, and so accustoming them to slaughter that even women and children become at last the victims.

"It cannot be supposed to be a national doctrine, for it neither springs from nor reflects the mind and feelings of the German people as they have heretofore been known to other nations. It is specifically military doctrine, the outcome of a theory held by a ruling caste who have brooded and thought, written and talked and dreamed about war until they have fallen under its obsession and been hypnotized by its spirit.

"The doctrine is plainly set forth in the German official monograph on the usages of war on land, issued under the direction of the German staff. This book is pervaded throughout by the view that whatever military needs suggest becomes thereby lawful, and upon this principle, as the diaries show, the German officers acted.

"If this explanation be the true one, the mystery is solved, and that which seemed scarcely credible becomes more intelligible though not less pernicious. This is not the only case that history records in which a false theory, disguising itself as loyalty to a state or to a church, has perverted the conception of duty and become a source of danger to the world."

THE COMMISSION'S CONCLUSIONS

The conclusions of the commission, as to the various detailed recitals, are as follows:

"We may now sum up and endeavor to explain the character and significance of the wrongful acts done by the German army in Belgium.

"It is proved, first, that there were in many parts of Belgium deliberate and systematically organized massacres of the civil population accompanied by many isolated murders and other outrages.

"Second—That in the conduct of the war generally innocent civilians, both men and women, were murdered in large numbers, women attacked and children murdered.

"Third—That looting, house burning and the wanton destruction of property were ordered and countenanced by the officers of the German army, that elaborate provision had been made for systematic incendiarism at the very outbreak of the war, and that the burning and

"THEIR FIRST SUCCESS."

"At Morfontaine, near Longwy, the Germans shot two fifteen-year-old children who had warned the French gendarmes of the enemy's arrival."—The Newspapers.

destruction were frequently where no military necessity could be alleged, being, indeed, part of a system of general terrorization.

"Fourth—That the rules and usages of war were frequently broken, particularly by the using of civilians, including women and children, as a shield for advancing forces exposed to fire, to a less degree by killing the wounded and prisoners, and in the frequent abuse of the Red Cross and the white flag.

"Sensible as they are of the gravity of these conclusions, the commission conceive that they would be
doing less than their duty if they failed to record them
as fully established by the evidence. Murder, lust and
pillage prevailed over many parts of Belgium on a
scale unparalleled in any war between civilized nations
during the last three centuries.

"Our function is ended when we have stated what
the evidence establishes, but we may be permitted to
express our belief that these disclosures will not have
been made in vain if they touch and rouse the conscience
of mankind, and we venture to hope that as soon as the
present war is over, the nations of the world in council
will consider what means can be provided and sanctions
devised to prevent the recurrence of such horrors as
our generation is now witnessing."

CHAPTER XXIX

PITIFUL FLIGHT OF A MILLION WOMEN

By Philip Gibbs
Of the London Daily Chronicle

THE GERMAN ADVANCE UPON PARIS—THE PRIZE
OF PARIS—HEROIC EFFORTS OF FRENCH SOLDIERS
—GERMANS BALKED OF THEIR PRIZE—SIXTY MILES
OF FUGITIVES — TERROR IN EYES — PARIS THE
BEAUTIFUL.

[The following article is reproduced by the courtesy of the
New York Times.]

AT LEAST a million German soldiers—that is no
exaggeration of a light pen, but the sober and actual
truth—were advancing steadily upon the capital of
France. They were close to Beauvais when I escaped
from what was then a death-trap. They were fighting
our British troops at Creil when I came to that town.
Upon the following days they were holding our men in
the Forest of Compiègne. They had been as near to
Paris as Senlis, almost within gunshot of the outer forts.

"Nothing seems to stop them," said many soldiers
with whom I spoke. "We kill them and kill them, but
they come on."

The situation seemed to me almost ready for the
supreme tragedy—the capture or destruction of Paris.
The northwest of France lay very open to the enemy,

abandoned as far south as Abbéville and Amiens, too lightly held by a mixed army corps of French and Algerian troops with their headquarters at Aumale.

Here was an easy way to Paris.

Always obsessed with the idea that the Germans must come from the east, the almost fatal error of this war, the French had girdled Paris with almost impenetrable forts on the east side, from those of Ecouen and Montmorency, by the far-flung forts of Chelles and Champigny, to those of Susy and Villeneuve, on the outer lines of the triple cordon; but on the west side, between Pontoise and Versailles, the defenses of Paris were weak. I say, "were," because during the last days thousands of men were digging trenches and throwing up ramparts. Only the snakelike Seine, twining into a Pegoud loop, forms a natural defense to the western approach to the city, none too secure against men who have crossed many rivers in their desperate assaults.

THE PRIZE OF PARIS

This, then, was the Germans' chance; it was for this that they had fought their way westward and southward through incessant battlefields from Mons and Charleroi to St. Quentin and Amiens and down to Creil and Compiègne, flinging away human life as though it were but rubbish for death-pits. The prize of Paris, Paris the great and beautiful, seemed to be within their grasp.

It was their intention to smash their way into it by this western entry and then to skin it alive. Holding this city at ransom, it was their idea to force France to her knees under threat of making a vast and desolate ruin of all those palaces and churches and noble buildings in which the soul of French history is enshrined.

I am not saying these things from rumor and hearsay, I am writing from the evidence of my own eyes after traveling several hundreds of miles in France along the main strategical lines, grim sentinels guarding the last barriers to that approaching death which was sweeping on its way through France to the rich harvest of Paris.

THE ANXIOUS HOUR.

There was only one thing to do to escape from the menace of this death. By all the ways open, by any way, the population of Paris emptied itself like rushing rivers of humanity along all the lines which promised anything like safety.

Only those stayed behind to whom life means very little away from Paris and who if death came desired to die in the city of their life.

Again I write from what I saw and to tell the honest truth from what I suffered, for the fatigue of this hunting for facts behind the screen of war is exhausting to all but one's moral strength, and even to that.

I found myself in the midst of a new and extraordinary activity of the French and English armies. Regiments were being rushed up to the center of the allied forces toward Creil, Montdidier, and Noyon.

This great movement continued for several days, putting to a severe test the French railway system, which is so wonderfully organized that it achieved this mighty transportation of troops with clockwork regularity. Working to a time-table dictated by some great brain in the headquarters of the French army, there were calculated with perfect precision the conditions of a network of lines on which troop trains might be run to a given point. It was an immense victory of organization, and a movement which heartened one observer at least to believe that the German death-blow would again be averted.

HEROIC EFFORTS OF FRENCH SOLDIERS

I saw regiment after regiment entraining. Men from the Southern Provinces, speaking the patois of the South; men from the Eastern Departments whom I had seen a month before, at the beginning of the war, at Chalons and Epernay and Nancy, and men from the southwest and center of France, in garrisons along the Loire. They were all in splendid spirits and utterly undaunted by the rapidity of the German advance.

"It is nothing, my little one," said a dirty, unshaved gentleman with the laughing eyes of a D'Artagnan; "we shall bite their heads off. These brutal 'bosches' are going to put themselves in a 'guet-apens,' a veritable death-trap. We shall have them at last."

Many of them had fought at Longwy and along the heights of the Vosges. The youngest of them had bristling beards, their blue coats with turned-back flaps were war-worn and flanked with the dust of long marches; their red trousers were sloppy and stained, but they had not forgotten how to laugh, and the gallantry of their spirits was a joy to see.

They are very proud, these French soldiers, of fighting side by side with their old foes. The English now, after long centuries of strife, from Edward, the Black Prince, to Wellington, are their brothers-in-arms upon the battle-fields, and because I am English they offered me their cigarettes and made me one of them. But I realized even then that the individual is of no account in this inhuman business of war.

It is only masses of men that matter, moved by common obedience at the dictation of mysterious far-off powers, and I thanked Heaven that masses of men were on the move rapidly in vast numbers and in the right direction to support the French lines which had fallen back from Amiens a few hours before I left that town, and whom I had followed in their retirement, back and back, with the English always strengthening their left, but retiring with them almost to the outskirts of Paris itself.

Only this could save Paris—the rapid strengthening of the allied front by enormous reserves strong enough to hold back the arrow-shaped battering ram of the enemy's main army.

Undoubtedly the French headquarters staff was

working heroically and with fine intelligence to save the situation at the very gates of Paris. The country was being swept absolutely clean of troops in all parts of France, where they had been waiting as reserves.

It was astounding to me to see, after those three days of rushing troop trains and of crowded stations not large enough to contain the regiments, how an air of profound solitude and peace had taken possession of all these routes.

In my long journey through and about France and circling round Paris I found myself wondering sometimes whether all this war had not been a dreadful illusion without reality, and a transformation had taken place, startling in its change, from military turmoil to rural peace.

Dijon was emptied of its troops. The road to Châlons was deserted by all but fugitives. The great armed camp at Châlons itself had been cleared out except for a small garrison. The troops at Tours had gone northward to the French center. All our English reserves had been rushed up to the front from Havre and Rouen.

There was only one deduction to be drawn from this great, swift movement—the French and English lines had been supported by every available battalion to save Paris from its menace of destruction, to meet the weight of the enemy's metal by a force strong enough to resist its mighty mass.

GERMANS BALKED OF THEIR PRIZE

It was still possible that the Germans might be smashed on their left wing, hurled back to the west between Paris and the sea, and cut off from their line of communications. It was undoubtedly this impending peril which scared the enemy's headquarters staff and upset all its calculations. They had not anticipated the rapidity of the supporting movement of the allied armies, and at the very gates of Paris they saw themselves balked of their prize, the greatest prize of the war, by the necessity of changing front.

To do them justice, they realized instantly the new order of things, and with quick and marvelous decision did not hesitate to alter the direction of their main force. Instead of proceeding to the west of Paris they swung round steadily to the southeast in order to keep their armies away from the enveloping movement of the French and English and drive their famous wedge-like formation southward for the purpose of dividing the allied forces of the west from the French army of the east. The miraculous had happened, and Paris, for a little time at least, was unmolested.

After wandering along the westerly and southerly roads I started for Paris when thousands and scores of thousands were flying from it. At that time I believed, as all France believed, that in a few hours German shells would be crashing across the fortifications of the city and that Paris the beautiful would be Paris the infernal. It needed a good deal of resolution on my part to go deliberately to a city from which the population was fleeing, and I confess quite honestly that I had a nasty sensation in the neighborhood of my waistcoat buttons at the thought.

SIXTY MILES OF FUGITIVES

Along the road from Tours to Paris there were sixty unbroken miles of people—on my honor, I do not exaggerate, but write the absolute truth. They were all people who had despaired of breaking through the dense masses of their fellow-citizens camped around the railway stations, and had decided to take the roads as the only way of escape.

The vehicles were taxicabs, for which the rich paid fabulous prices; motor cars which had escaped military requisition, farmers' carts laden with several families and piles of household goods, shop carts drawn by horses already tired to the point of death because of the weight of the people who crowded behind, pony traps and governess carts.

Many persons, well dressed and belonging obviously to well-to-do bourgeoisie, were wheeling barrows like costers, but instead of trundling cabbages were pushing forward sleeping babies and little children, who seemed on the first stage to find new amusement and excitement in the journey from home; but for the most part they trudged along bravely, carrying their babies and holding the hands of their little ones.

They were of all classes, rank and fortune being annihilated by the common tragedy. Elegant women whose beauty is known in Paris salons, whose frivolity, perhaps, in the past was the main purpose of their life, were now on a level with the peasant mothers of the French suburbs and with the "midinettes" of Montmartre, and their courage did not fail them so quickly.

I looked into many proud, brave faces of these delicate women, walking in high-heeled shoes, all too frail for the hard, dusty roadways. They belonged to the same race and breed as those ladies who defied death with fine disdain upon the scaffold of the guillotine in the great Revolution.

They were leaving Paris now, not because of any fears for themselves—I believe they were fearless—but because they had decided to save the little sons and daughters of soldier fathers.

This great army in retreat was made up of every type familiar in Paris.

Here were women of the gay world, poor creatures whose painted faces had been washed with tears, and whose tight skirts and white stockings were never made for a long march down the highways of France.

Here also were thousands of those poor old ladies who live on a few francs a week in the top attics of the Paris streets which Balzac knew; they had fled from their poor sanctuaries and some of them were still carrying cats and canaries, as dear to them as their own lives.

There was one young woman who walked with a pet monkey on her shoulder while she carried a bird in a golden cage. Old men, who remembered 1870, gave their arms to old ladies to whom they had made love when the Prussians were at the gates of Paris then.

It was pitiful to see these old people now hobbling along together—pitiful, but beautiful also, because of their lasting love.

Young boy students, with ties as black as their hats and rat-tail hair, marched in small companies of comrades, singing brave songs, as though they had no fear in their hearts, and very little food, I think, in their stomachs.

Shopgirls and concierges, city clerks, old aristocrats, young boys and girls, who supported grandfathers and grandmothers and carried new-born babies and gave pick-a-back rides to little brothers and sisters, came along the way of retreat.

TERROR IN EYES

Each human being in the vast torrent of life will have an unforgettable story of adventure to tell if life remains. As a novelist I should have been glad to get their narratives along this road for a great story of suffering and strange adventure, but there was no time for that and no excuse.

When I met many of them they were almost beyond the power of words. The hot sun of this September had beaten down upon them—scorching them as in the glow of molten metal. Their tongues clave to their mouths with thirst.

Some of them had that wild look in their eyes which is the first sign of the delirium of thirst and fatigue.

Nothing to eat or drink could be found on the way from Paris. The little roadside cafés had been cleared out by the preceding hordes.

Unless these people carried their own food and drink they could have none except of the charity of their comrades in misfortune, and that charity has exceeded all other acts of heroism in this war. Women gave their last biscuit, their last little drop of wine, to poor mothers whose children were famishing with thirst and hunger; peasant women fed other women's babies when their own were satisfied.

It was a tragic road. At every mile of it there were

people who had fainted on the roadside and poor old men and women who could go no farther, but sat on the banks below the hedges, weeping silently or bidding younger ones go forward and leave them to their fate. Young women who had stepped out jauntily at first were so footsore and lame that they limped along with lines of pain about their lips and eyes.

Many of the taxicabs, bought at great prices, and many of the motor cars had broken down as I passed, and had been abandoned by their owners, who had decided to walk. Farmers' carts had bolted into ditches and lost their wheels. Wheelbarrows, too heavy to be trundled, had been tilted up, with all their household goods spilled into the roadway, and the children had been carried farther, until at last darkness came, and their only shelter was a haystack in a field under the harvest moon.

For days also I have been wedged up with fugitives in railway trains more dreadful than the open roads, stifling in their heat and heart-racking in their cargoes of misery. Poor women have wept hysterically clasping my hand, a stranger's hand, for comfort in their wretchedness and weakness. Yet on the whole they have shown amazing courage, and, after their tears, have laughed at their own breakdown, and, always the children of France have been superb, so that again and again I have wondered at the gallantry with which they endured this horror. Young boys have revealed the heroic strain in them and have played the part of men in helping their mothers. And yet, when I came at last into Paris against all this tide of retreat, it seemed a needless fear that had driven these people away.

PARIS THE BEAUTIFUL

Then I passed long lines of beautiful little villas on the Seine side, utterly abandoned among their trees and flowers. A solitary fisherman held his line above the water as though all the world were at peace, and in a field close to the fortifications which I expected to see bursting with shells, an old peasant bent above the furrows and planted cabbages. Then, at last, I walked through the streets of Paris and found them strangely quiet and tranquil.

The people I met looked perfectly calm. There were a few children playing in the gardens of Champs Elysées and under the Arc de Triomphe symbolical of the glory of France.

I looked back upon the beauty of Paris all golden in the light of the setting sun, with its glinting spires and white gleaming palaces and rays of light flashing in front of the golden trophies of its monuments. Paris was still unbroken. No shell had come shattering into this city of splendor, and I thanked Heaven that for a little while the peril had passed.

CHAPTER XXX

FACING DEATH IN THE TRENCHES

CAVE-DWELLING THE LOT OF MODERN SOLDIERS—
GERMANS HAVE LEARNED MUCH—STANDARDIZED
MODEL—FRENCH STUDY OF GERMAN METHODS—
"COMFORTS OF HOME"—BRITISH REFUGES IN
NORTHERN FRANCE—"PICNICKING" IN THE OPEN
AIR—RAVAGES OF ARTILLERY FIRE—THE COMMON
ENEMY, THE WEATHER—WHY COOKS WEAR IRON
CROSSES—"PUTTING ONE OVER" ON THE RUSSIANS.

"OTHER times, other manners" applies as accurately
to the battle-field as it does elsewhere. The cavalry
charge is nearly extinct, mass formation is going,
hand-to-hand conflict is rarely found, and now, it
appears, the old-fashioned and romantic bivouac is no
more. Trench-fighting has been carried on to such an
extent in France and Belgium, and Poland, that the
open camp, with its rows of little tents, outposts, and
sentry guard, becomes almost a forgotten picture of
warfare. Doubtless the military schools of the future
will make provision for special instruction in the
construction of commodious caverns on the battlefield, safe, warm, and containing all the comforts of a
barrack.

The modern warrior, like a mole, lives under ground
and displays his greatest activity at night. With the
coming of subterranean warfare, as trench-fighting

341

can be appropriately called, great armies have had to adopt unique methods. They have been compelled to build peculiar little forts—for a trench is a fort, in fact—wherever their soldiers meet the enemy. In consequence these rectangular excavations have been improved far beyond their original outline.

The first trench was nothing more nor less than a hole in the ground, deep enough to protect a man kneeling, standing, or sitting, as the case might be. Before the advent of the modern rifle and modern cannon, these defenses, with several feet of loose earth thrown up in front of them, served admirably. In those days the question of head-cover was of minor importance; today a protective roofing is the *sine qua non* of any well-constructed trench. Early in the European war it was discovered that the trench offered the safest haven from the bursting shells of the enemy's field artillery. To all intents and purposes, shrapnel, or, as its inventor termed it, the man-killing projectile—is practically harmless in its effect upon entrenched troops. Unless a shell can be placed absolutely within the two-feet wide excavation it wastes its destructive powers on the inoffensive earth and air. This has led to a modification of artillery methods, which, in turn, compels the elaboration of the trench and emphasizes the importance of head-cover.

GERMANS HAVE LEARNED MUCH

"The history of the great war," to quote from a French paper, "will show, among other things, how the Germans profited by the lessons of recent conflicts.

The South African, the Russo-Japanese, and the Balkan wars were studied minutely by them, and their particular preparations, their tactics, and their artifices result from the knowledge thus acquired. They learned much, especially, as regards the formation of trenches.

"After 1870 we confined ourselves to three regulation types of trenches: for men prone, kneeling, and standing. While in training, our soldiers were taught how to take shelter momentarily between advances, by digging up the soil a little and lying flat behind the smallest of mounds. They were instructed, moreover, how to protect themselves from the enemy's fire by propping up their knapsacks in front of them. This meant insufficient protection, and an extremely dangerous visibility, since the foe, by simply counting the number of knapsacks, could know the strength opposed to him. To insure the making of such shelter, a French company was equipped with eighty picks and eighty spades; that is, 160 tools for 250 men. These tools were fixed on to the knapsacks; and it took some time to bring them into use."

The German methods for defensive and offensive trench-making are quite different. Each man has a tool of his own, which is fixed on to the scabbard of his sword-bayonet. When occasion for fighting arises, the line conceals itself, and, as soon as it is engaged, it prepares for possible retreat, making strong positions assuring an unrelenting defensive and counter-attacks.

STANDARDIZED MODEL

It is on these sound principles that all the German fighting-lines are organized, on a more or less standardized model. The fighting-lines consist generally of one, two, or three lines of shelter-trenches lying parallel, measuring twenty or twenty-five inches in width, and varying in length according to the number they hold; the trenches are joined together by zigzag approaches and by a line of reinforced trenches (armed with machine guns), which are almost completely proof against rifle, machine gun, or gun fire. The ordinary German trenches are almost invisible from 350 yards away, a distance which permits a very deadly fire. It is easy to realize that if the enemy occupies three successive lines and a line of reinforced entrenchments, the attacking line is likely, at the lowest estimate, to be decimated during an advance of 650 yards— by rifle-fire at a range of 350 yards' distance, and by the extremely quick fire of the machine guns, which can each deliver from 300 to 600 bullets a minute with absolute precision. In the field-trench, it is obvious, a soldier enjoys far greater security than he would if merely prone behind his knapsack in an excavation barely fifteen inches deep. He has merely to stoop down a little to disappear below the level of the ground and be immune from infantry fire; moreover, his machine guns can fire without endangering him. In addition, this stooping position brings the man's knapsack on a level with his helmet, thus forming some protection against shrapnel and shell-splinters.

At the back of the German trenches, shelters are dug for non-commissioned officers and for the commander of the unit. The latter's shelter is connected with the communication trench; the others are not. If one adds that the bank, or, rather, the earth that is

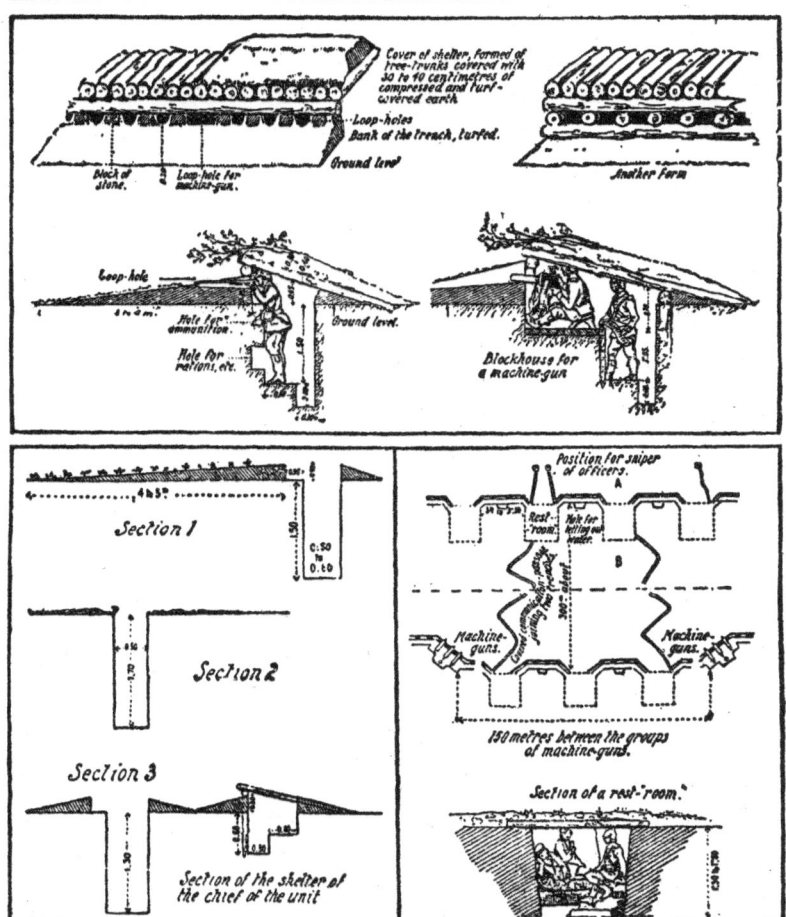

REINFORCED TRENCHES.

Upper view: Details of roofs, loop-holes, and the form of the excavations. Lower left-hand view: Vertical section of trenches and shelters. Lower right-hand view: A plan and section of trenches and rest-room.

dug from the trenches and spread out in front, extends for five or six yards, and is covered with grass, or appropriate vegetation, it will be recognized that the

345

works concealing the German lines can be seen only when a near approach is made to them.

As to reinforced trenches, the drawings show clearly their conception and arrangement. They are proof against ordinary bullets and shrapnel. Only percussion-shells are able to destroy them and to decimate their defenders. The interior details of the trenches vary according to the ingenuity and spare time of the occupants and the nature of the ground.

FRENCH STUDY OF GERMAN METHODS

The whole system, that of the rest-rooms more especially, is designed to give the men the maximum of comfort and security. Doors and wooden shutters wrenched from deserted houses are used for covers, or else turf-covered branches.

Ever since the outbreak of the war, the French troops in Lorraine, after severe experiences, realized rapidly the advantages of the German trenches, and began to study those they had taken gloriously. Officers, non-commissioned officers, and men of the Engineers were straightway detached in every unit to teach the infantry how to construct similar shelters. The education was quick, and very soon they had completed the work necessary for the protection of all. The tools of the enemy "casualties," the spades and picks left behind in deserted villages, were all gladly piled on to the French soldiers' knapsacks, to be carried willingly by the very men who used to grumble at being loaded with even the smallest regulation tool. As soon as night had set in on the occasion of a lull in the fighting, the digging of the trenches was begun. Sometimes, in the darkness, the men of each fighting nation—less than 500 yards away from their enemy—would hear the noise of the workers of the foe: the sounds of picks and axes; the officers' words of encouragement; and tacitly they would agree to an armistice during which to dig shelters from which, in the morning, they would dash out, to fight once more.

"COMFORTS OF HOME"

Commodious, indeed, are some of the present trench barracks, if we may believe the letters from the front. One French soldier writes:

"In really up-to-date entrenchments you may find kitchens, dining-rooms, bedrooms, and even stables. One regiment has first class cow-sheds. One day a whimsical 'piou-piou,' finding a cow wandering about in the danger zone, had the bright idea of finding shelter for it in the trenches. The example was quickly followed, and at this moment the —th Infantry possess an underground farm, in which fat kine, well cared for, give such quantities of milk that regular distributions of butter are being made—and very good butter, too."

But this is not all. An officer writes home a tale of yet another one of the comforts of home added to the equipment of the trenches:

"We are clean people here. Thanks to the ingenuity of ——, we are able to take a warm bath every day from ten to twelve. We call this teasing the 'bosches,' for this bathing-establishment of the latest type is fitted up—would you believe it?—in the trenches!"

FACING DEATH IN THE TRENCHES

Describing trenches occupied by the British in their protracted "siege-warfare" in Northern France along and to the north of the Aisne Valley, a British officer wrote: "In the firing-line the men sleep and obtain shelter in the dugouts they have hollowed or 'undercut' in the side of the trenches. These refuges are slightly raised above the bottom of the trench, so as to remain dry in wet weather. The floor of the trench is also sloped for purposes of draining. Some trenches are provided with head-cover, and others with overhead cover, the latter, of course, giving protection from the weather as well as from shrapnel balls and splinters of shells. . . . At all points subject to shell-fire access to the firing-line from behind is provided by communication-trenches. These are now so good that it is possible to cross in safety the fire-swept zone to the advanced trenches from the billets in villages, the bivouacs in quarries, or the other places where the headquarters of units happen to be."

"PICNICKING" IN THE OPEN AIR

A cavalry subaltern gave the following account of life in the trenches: "Picnicking in the open air, day and night (you never see a roof now), is the only real method of existence. There are loads of straw to bed down on, and everyone sleeps like a log, in turn, even with shrapnel bursting within fifty yards."

RAVAGES OF ARTILLERY FIRE

One English officer described the ravages of modern artillery fire, not only upon all men, animals and buildings within its zone, but upon the very face of nature itself: "In the trenches crouch lines of men, in brown or gray or blue, coated with mud, unshaven, hollow-eyed with the continual strain."

"The fighting is now taking place over ground where both sides have for weeks past been excavating in all directions," said another letter from the front, "until it has become a perfect labyrinth. A trench runs straight for a considerable distance, then it suddenly forks in three or four directions. One branch merely leads into a ditch full of water, used in drier weather as a means of communication; another ends abruptly in a cul-de-sac, probably an abandoned sap-head; the third winds on, leading into galleries and passages further forward.

"Sometimes where new ground is broken the spade turns up the long-buried dead, ghastly relics of former fights, and on all sides the surface of the earth is ploughed and furrowed by fragments of shell and bombs and distorted by mines. Seen from a distance, this apparently confused mass of passages, crossing and recrossing one another, resembles an irregular gridiron.

"The life led by the infantry on both sides at close quarters is a strange, cramped existence, with death always near, either by means of some missile from above or some mine explosion from beneath—a life which has one dull, monotonous background of mud and water. Even when there is but little fighting the troops are kept hard at work strengthening the existing defenses, constructing others, and improvising the shelter imperative in such weather."

FACING DEATH IN THE TRENCHES

But it is not the guns or cannon of the enemy that affect the spirits of the soldiers. It is the weather. A week of alternate rain and snow, when the ill-drained dugouts are half-filled with a freezing viscid mud; when, day after day, the feet are numbed by the frost until all sensation in them is deadened; when the coarse, scanty ration is refused by the tortured stomach —then it is that the spirits of the stoutest falter. Let the enemy attack as he will, and he must fail. It is only in fighting that the men find an outlet for their rancor.

More than thirty years ago a well-known German general declared that a book on "Seasonal Tactics" might as properly be written as those on the tactics of weapons, and of geographical conditions; and in a recent issue of the Deutsche Revue an unsigned article by a veteran of the Franco-Prussian war recounts the difficulties that arise when the Frost King holds sway. "To begin with, the precious hours of daylight are much fewer, and even these may be shortened by overcast skies and heavy fogs. Soft snow and mud seriously impede marching and at times it is impossible to take cross-country cuts, even single horsemen having great difficulty in crossing the frozen ridges of plowed fields or stubble. Moreover, even regular highways may become so slippery that they endanger both man and horse, and in hilly country such conditions make it necessary to haul heavy artillery up steep ascents by man-power. Cold head-winds also greatly impede progress.

"The necessity of bringing the troops under cover

enforces long marches at the end of the day's work, and again at its beginning, and therefore makes extra demands on energy. . . . The early dark hinders the offense from carrying out its plans completely and from utilizing any advantage won by following it up energetically. Night battles become frequent. The defense seeks to regain what it has lost by day, the offense to make use of the long nights to win what it could not achieve in the daytime. Then, too, the need of getting warmed-up makes the troops more enterprising."

All sorts of constructive work—fortification building, the erection of stations for telegraphs, telephones and wireless, etc.—is naturally much more difficult in frozen ground. General von der Goltz of the German Army is said to have recommended many years ago that in view of possible winter campaigns provision should be made in quantity of warm winter clothing, materials for the building of barracks, making double tents, etc. Another important preventive of suffering and the consequent diminished efficiency is to provide plenty of good hot food for the men.

WHY COOKS WEAR IRON CROSSES

"There isn't anything heroic about cooks," wrote Herbert Corey in the New York Globe, "and when things go wrong one either apprehends a cook as chasing a waiter with a bread-knife or giving way to tears." Yet the German army contains many a cook whose expansive apron is decorated with the Iron Cross. "And the Iron Cross," Mr. Corey reminds us, "is conferred for one thing only—for 100 per cent courage."

351

" 'They've earned it,' said the man who had seen them. 'They are the bravest men in the Kaiser's four millions. I've seen generals salute greasy, paunchy, sour-looking army cooks.'

"The cook's job is to feed the men of his company. Each German company is followed, or preceded, by a field-kitchen on wheels. Sometimes the fires are kept going while the device trundles along. The cook stands on the foot-board and thumps his bread. He is always the first man up in the morning and the last to sleep at night.

"When that company goes into the trenches the cook stays behind. There is no place for a field-kitchen in a four-foot trench. But these men in the trench must be fed. The Teuton insists that all soldiers must be fed—but especially the men in the trench. The others may go hungry, but these must have tight belts. Upon their staying power may depend the safety of an army.

"So, as the company can not go to the cook, the cook goes to the company. When meal-hour comes he puts a yoke on his shoulders and a cook's cap on his head and, warning the second cook as to what will happen if he lets the fires go out, puts a bucketful of hot veal stew on either end of the yoke and goes to his men. Maybe the trench is under fire. No matter. His men are in that trench and must be fed.

"Sometimes the second cook gets his step right here. Sometimes the apprentice cook—the dish-washer—is summoned to pick up the cook's yoke and refill the spilled buckets and tramp steadily forward to the line. Sometimes the supply of assistant cooks, even, runs short. But the men in the trenches always get their food.

" 'That's why so many cooks in the German Army have Iron Crosses dangling from their breasts,' said the man who knows. 'No braver men ever lived. The man in the trench can duck his head and light his pipe and be relatively safe. ˙ No fat cook yoked to two buckets of veal stew ever can be safe as he marches down the trench.' "

"PUTTING ONE OVER" ON THE RUSSIANS

Granville Fortescue, who visited the Russian trenches in Poland, related in the Illustrated London News a story of how the Germans, to use a slang phrase, "put one over" on the too-confiding Russians. "This happened," he wrote, "at a portion of the line where the positions ran so close that the men could communicate by shouting. It was around Christmas, and the Germans invited the Russians to come over for a hot cup of new coffee just received from home. The Russians replied to this invitation, shouting: 'Come over and try our tea. It's a special gift from the Czar.'

"The Germans then put up the white flag, and said that they would send over fifteen men to try the tea if the Russians would send over the same number to sample their coffee. The plan was carried out. When the fifteen Germans appeared in the Russian trench, the hosts remarked to one another that if these were a sample the enemy would not hold out long. They were a sick-looking lot. Suddenly the Germans pulled down their white flag and commenced firing. Then the

Russians found that they had exchanged fifteen good soldiers for fifteen typhus patients.

"It is easy to believe that the Russian soldier could be imposed upon in this way. Although extremely courageous, he is very simple-minded with it all, and certainly trusting. He is a splendid physical specimen. In the trail of trench warfare this is the great desideratum. Then, the Russians of the type that are drafted into the army have all their life been accustomed to privation and exposure. For this reason they are the only troops that I have seen who can stick six days and nights on end in a trench, under constant small arms and shell fire, with the temperature below zero, and after a day's rest be as good as ever. The Russians never grumble."

CHAPTER XXXI

A VIVID PICTURE OF WAR

THE BATTLE OF NEUVE CHAPELLE—A SURPRISE
PREPARED—"HELL BROKE LOOSE"—A HORRIBLE
THIRTY-FIVE MINUTES — TRENCHES FILLED WITH
DEAD—HOARSE SHOUTS AND THE GROANS OF THE
WOUNDED — INDESCRIBABLE MASS OF RUINS —
"SMEARED WITH DUST AND BLOOD."

ONE OF the most vivid word-pictures of what war
means in all its horror was told by an eye-witness of
the battle of Neuve Chapelle in which the British
soldiers dislodged the Germans from an important
position. He said:

"The dawn, which broke reluctantly through a
veil of clouds on the morning of Wednesday, March 10,
1915, seemed as any other to the Germans behind the
white and blue sandbags in their long line of trenches
curving in a hemicycle about the battered village of
Neuve Chapelle. For five months they had remained
undisputed masters of the positions they had here
wrested from the British in October. Ensconced in
their comfortably-arranged trenches with but a thin
outpost in their fire trenches, they had watched day
succeed day and night succeed night without the least
variation from the monotony of trench warfare, the
intermittent bark of the machine guns—rat-tat-tat-
tat-tat—and the perpetual rattle of rifle fire, with here
and there a bomb, and now and then an exploded mine.

A SURPRISE PREPARED

"For weeks past the German airmen had grown strangely shy. On this Wednesday morning none were aloft to spy out the strange doings which as dawn broke might have been descried on the desolate roads behind the British lines.

"From ten o'clock of the preceding evening endless files of men marched silently down the roads leading towards the German positions through Laventie and Richebourg St. Vaast, poor shattered villages of the dead where months of incessant bombardment have driven away the last inhabitants and left roofless houses and rent roadways. . . .

"Two days before, a quiet room, where Nelson's Prayer stands on the mantel-shelf, saw the ripening of the plans that sent these sturdy sons of Britain's four kingdoms marching all through the night. Sir John French met the army corps commanders and unfolded to them his plans for the offensive of the British Army against the German line at Neuve Chapelle.

"The onslaught was to be a surprise. That was its essence. The Germans were to be battered with artillery, then rushed before they recovered their wits. We had thirty-six clear hours before us. Thus long, it was reckoned (with complete accuracy as afterwards appeared), must elapse before the Germans, whose line before us had been weakened, could rush up reinforcements. To ensure the enemy's being pinned down right and left of the 'great push,' an attack was to be delivered north and south of the main thrust simultaneously with the assault on Neuve Chapelle."

After describing the impatience of the British

soldiers as they awaited the signal to open the **attack, and** the actual beginning of the engagement, the **narrator** continues:

"HELL BROKE LOOSE"

"Then hell broke loose. With a mighty, hideous, screeching burst of noise, hundreds of guns spoke. The men in the front trenches were deafened by the sharp reports of the field-guns spitting out their shells at close range to cut through the Germans' barbed wire entanglements. In some cases the trajectory of these vicious missiles was so flat that they passed only a few feet above the British trenches.

"There Is Nothing to Report."

"The din was continuous. An officer who had the curious idea of putting his ear to the ground said it was as though the earth were being smitten great blows with a Titan's hammer. After the first few shells had plunged screaming amid clouds of earth and dust into the German trenches, a dense pall of smoke hung over the German lines. The sickening fumes of lyddite blew back into the British trenches. In some places the troops were smothered in earth and dust or even spattered with blood from the hideous fragments of human bodies that went hurtling through the air. At one point the upper half of a German officer, his cap crammed on his head, was blown into one of our trenches.

A HORRIBLE THIRTY-FIVE MINUTES

"Words will never convey any adequate idea of the horror of those five and thirty minutes. When the hands of officers' watches pointed to five minutes past eight, whistles resounded along the British lines. At the same moment the shells began to burst farther ahead, for, by previous arrangement, the gunners, lengthening their fuses, were 'lifting' on to the village of Neuve Chapelle so as to leave the road open for our infantry to rush in and finish what the guns had begun.

"The shells were now falling thick among the houses of Neuve Chapelle, a confused mass of buildings seen reddish through the pillars of smoke and flying earth and dust. At the sound of the whistle—alas for the bugle, once the herald of victory, now banished from the fray!—our men scrambled out of the trenches and hurried higgledy-piggledy into the open. Their officers were in front. Many, wearing overcoats and carrying rifles with fixed bayonets, closely resembled their men.

TRENCHES FILLED WITH DEAD

"It was from the center of our attacking line that the assault was pressed home soonest. The guns had done their work well. The trenches were blown to

358

irrecognizable pits dotted with dead. The barbed wire had been cut like so much twine. Starting from the Rue Tilleloy the Lincolns and the Berkshires were off the mark first, with orders to swerve to right and left respectively as soon as they had captured the first line of trenches, in order to let the Royal Irish Rifles and the Rifle Brigade through to the village. The Germans left alive in the trenches, half demented with fright, surrounded by a welter of dead and dying men, mostly surrendered. The Berkshires were opposed with the utmost gallantry by two German officers who had remained alone in a trench serving a machine gun. But the lads from Berkshire made their way into that trench and bayoneted the Germans where they stood, fighting to the last. The Lincolns, against desperate resistance, eventually occupied their section of the trench and then waited for the Irishmen and the Rifle Brigade to come and take the village ahead of them. Meanwhile the second thirty-ninth Garhwalis on the right had taken their trenches with a rush and were away towards the village and the Biez Wood.

HOARSE SHOUTS AND THE GROANS OF THE WOUNDED

"Things had moved so fast that by the time the troops were ready to advance against the village the artillery had not finished its work. So, while the Lincolns and the Berks assembled the prisoners who were trooping out of the trenches in all directions, the infantry on whom devolved the honor of capturing the village, waited. One saw them standing out in the open, laughing and cracking jokes amid the terrific din made by the huge howitzer shells screeching overhead and bursting in the village, the rattle of machine guns all along the line, and the popping of rifles. Over to the right where the Garhwalis had been working with the bayonet, men were shouting hoarsely and wounded were groaning as the stretcher-bearers, all heedless of bullets, moved swiftly to and fro over the shell-torn ground.

"There was bloody work in the village of Neuve Chapelle. The capture of a place at the bayonet point is generally a grim business, in which instant, unconditional surrender is the only means by which bloodshed, a deal of bloodshed, can be prevented. If there is individual resistance here and there the attacking troops cannot discriminate. They must go through, slaying as they go such as oppose them (the Germans have a monopoly of the finishing-off of wounded men), otherwise the enemy's resistance would not be broken, and the assailants would be sniped and enfiladed from hastily prepared strongholds at half a dozen different points.

INDESCRIBABLE MASS OF RUINS

"The village was a sight that the men say they will never forget. It looked as if an earthquake had struck it. The published photographs do not give any idea of the indescribable mass of ruins to which our guns reduced it. The chaos is so utter that the very line of the streets is all but obliterated.

"It was indeed a scene of desolation into which the Rifle Brigade—the first regiment to enter the village, I believe—raced headlong. Of the church only the bare shell remained, the interior lost to view beneath

IN THE BRITISH TRENCHES

Under shell fire on the battlefield of Neuve Chepelle, where the British lines were assaulted by a merciless bombardment.

SERGEANT O'LEARY CAPTURING THE ENEMY'S POSITION.

At Cunichy, Lance-corporal Michael O'Leary was one of a party moving forward to storm the German barricades. When near the enemy he rushed to the front and himself killed five Germans who were holding the first barricade, and then went forward to the second when he killed three more of the enemy and took two others prisoners, thus practically capturing the enemy's position by himself. For this exploit Sergeant O'Leary was awarded the Victoria Cross.

a gigantic mound of debris. The little churchyard was devastated, the very dead plucked from their graves, broken coffins and ancient bones scattered about amid the fresher dead, the slain of that morning— grey green forms asprawl athwart the tombs. Of all that once fair village but two things remained intact— two great crucifixes reared aloft, one in the churchyard, the other over against the chateau. From the cross that is the emblem of our faith the figure of Christ, yet intact though all pitted with bullet marks, looked down in mute agony on the slain in the village.

"SMEARED WITH DUST AND BLOOD"

"The din and confusion were indescribable. Through the thick pall of shell smoke Germans were seen on all sides, some emerging half dazed from cellars and dug-outs, their hands above their heads, others dodging round the shattered houses, others firing from the windows, from behind carts, even from behind the overturned tombstones. Machine guns were firing from the houses on the outskirts, rapping out their nerve-racking note above the noise of the rifles.

"Just outside the village there was a scene of tremendous enthusiasm. The Rifle Brigade, smeared with dust and blood, fell in with the Third Gurkhas with whom they had been brigaded in India. The little brown men were dirty but radiant. Kukri in hand they had very thoroughly gone through some houses at the cross-roads on the Rue du Bois and silenced a party of Germans who were making themselves a nuisance there with some machine guns. Riflemen and Gurkhas cheered themselves hoarse."

CHAPTER XXXII

HARROWING SCENES ALONG THE BATTLE LINES

DRIVING BACK THE GERMANS UNDER FIRE—ON THE FIRING LINE—AMONG MANGLED HORSES AND MEN—GERMAN LOSSES FRIGHTFUL—DIXMUDE A PLACE OF DEATH AND HORROR.

SOME IDEA of the ruin wrought day after day as the battle raged in Flanders may be gained from the occasional reports of war correspondents who shared the fortunes of battle.

"The battle rages along the Yser with frightful destruction of life," wrote a correspondent of the London Daily News in October. "Air engines, sea engines, and land engines death-sweep this desolate country, vertically, horizontally, and transversely. Through it the frail little human engines crawl and dig, walk and run, skirmishing, charging, and blundering in little individual fights and tussles, tired and puzzled, ordered here and there, sleeping where they can, never washing, and dying unnoticed. A friend may find himself firing on a friendly force, and few are to blame.

"Thursday the Germans were driven back over the Yser; Friday they secured a footing again, and Saturday they were again hurled back. Now a bridge blown up by one side is repaired by the other; it is again blown up by the first, or left as a death trap till the enemy is actually crossing.

"Actions by armored trains, some of them the most reckless adventures, are attempted daily. Each day accumulates an unwritten record of individual daring feats, accepted as part of the daily work. Day by day our men push out on these dangerous explorations, attacked by shell fire, in danger of cross-fire, dynamite, and ambuscades, bringing a priceless support to the threatened lines. As the armored train approaches the river under shell fire the car cracks with the constant thunder of guns aboard. It is amazing to see the angle at which the guns can be swung.

THESE ALWAYS SURVIVE.

"And overhead the airmen are busy venturing through fog and puffs of exploding shells to get one small fact of information. We used to regard the looping of the loop of the Germans overhead as a harebrained piece of impudent defiance to our infantry fire. Now we know it means early trouble for the infantry.

"Besides us, as we crawl up snuffing the lines like

dogs on a scent, grim train-loads of wounded wait soundlessly in the sidings. Further up the line ambulances are coming slowly back. The bullets of machine guns begin to rattle on our armored coats. Shells we learned to disregard, but the machine gun is the master in this war.

"Now we near the river at a flat country farm. The territory is scarred with trenches, and it is impossible to say at first who is in them, so incidental and separate are the fortunes of this riverside battle. The Germans are on our bank enfilading the lines of the Allies' trenches. We creep up and the Germans come into sight out of the trenches, rush to the bank, and are scattered and mashed. The Allies follow with a fierce bayonet charge.

"The Germans do not wait. They rush to the bridges and are swept away by the deadliest destroyer of all, the machine gun. The bridge is blown up, but who can say by whom? Quickly the train runs back.

"'A brisk day,' remarks the correspondent. 'Not so bad,' replies the officer. So the days pass."

ON THE FIRING LINE

Another correspondent who, accompanied by a son of the Belgian War Minister, M. de Broqueville, made a tour of the battleground in the Dixmude district wrote:

"No pen could do justice to the grandeur and horror of the scene. As far as the eye could reach nothing could be seen but burning villages and bursting shells.

"Arriving at the firing line, a terrible scene presented itself. The shell fire from the German batteries was so terrific that Belgian soldiers and French marines were continually being blown out of their dugouts and sent scattering to cover. Elsewhere, also, little groups of peasants were forced to flee because their cellars began to fall in. These unfortunates had to make their way as best they could on foot to the rear. They were frightened to death by the bursting shells, and the sight of crying children among them was most pathetic.

"Dixmude was the objective of the German attack, and shells were bursting all over it, crashing among the roofs and blowing whole streets to pieces. From a distance of three miles we could hear them crashing down, but the town itself was invisible, except for the flames and the smoke and clouds rising above it. The Belgians had only a few field batteries, so that the enemy's howitzers simply dominated the field, and the infantry trenches around the town had to rely upon their own unaided efforts.

AMONG MANGLED HORSES AND MEN

"Our progress along the road was suddenly stopped by one of the most horrible sights I have ever seen. A heavy howitzer shell had fallen and burst right in the midst of a Belgian battery which was making its way to the front, causing terrible destruction. The mangled horses and men among the debris presented a shocking spectacle.

" "Eventually, we got into Dixmude itself, and every time a shell came crashing among the roofs we thought our end had come. The Hôtel de Ville (town hall) was a sad sight. The roof was completely riddled by shell, while inside was a scene of chaos. It was piled with loaves of bread, bicycles, and dead soldiers.

"The battle redoubled in fury, and by seven o'clock in the evening Dixmude was a furnace, presenting a scene of terrible grandeur. The horizon was red with burning homes.

"Our return journey was a melancholy one, owing to the constant trains of wounded that were passing."

GERMAN LOSSES FRIGHTFUL

"The German losses are frightful" wrote another correspondent. "Three meadows near Ostend are heaped with dead. The wounded are now installed in private houses in Bruges, where large wooden sheds are being rushed up to receive additional injured. Thirty-seven farm wagons containing wounded, dying, and dead passed in one hour near Middelkerke."

DIXMUDE A PLACE OF DEATH AND HORROR

From Furnes, Belgium, members of the staff of the English hospital traveled to Dixmude to search for wounded men on the firing line. Philip Gibbs, of the London Daily Chronicle, who traveled with them in reporting his experiences, said:

"I was in one of the ambulances, and Mr. Gleeson sat behind me in the narrow space between the stretchers. Over his shoulder he talked in a quiet voice of the job that lay before us. I was glad of that quiet voice, so placid in its courage. We went forward at what seemed to me a crawl, though I think it was a fair pace, shells bursting around us now on all sides, while shrapnel bullets sprayed the earth about us.

It appeared to me an odd thing that we were still alive. Then we came into Dixmude.

"When I saw it for the first and last time it was a place of death and horror. The streets through which we passed were utterly deserted and wrecked from end to end, as though by an earthquake. Incessant explosions of shell fire crashed down upon the walls which still stood. Great gashes opened in the walls, which then toppled and fell. A roof came tumbling down with an appalling clatter. Like a house of cards blown by a puff of wind, a little shop suddenly collapsed into a mass of ruins. Here and there, further into the town, we saw living figures. They ran swiftly for a moment and then disappeared into dark caverns under toppling porticoes. They were Belgian soldiers. . . .

"We stood on some steps, looking down into that cellar. It was a dark hole, illumined dimly by a lantern, I think. I caught sight of a little heap of huddled bodies. Two soldiers, still unwounded, dragged three of them out and handed them up to us. The work of getting those three men into the first ambulance seemed to us interminable; it was really no more than fifteen or twenty minutes.

"I had lost consciousness of myself. Something outside myself, as it seemed, was saying that there was no way of escape; that it was monstrous to suppose that all these bursting shells would not smash the ambulance to bits and finish the agony of the wounded, and that death was very hideous. I remember thinking also how ridiculous it was for men to kill one another like this and to make such hells on earth."

CHAPTER XXXIII

WHAT THE MEN IN THE TRENCHES WRITE HOME

SOBERING REALITIES OF BATTLE—"WAR IS TER-
RIBLE"—THE COMMON ENEMY, DEATH—"A WASTE-
FUL WAR"—"SAME PAIR OF BLUE EYES"—FIGHTING
WITHOUT HATE.

LIFE AT the front is not all marching and fighting by any means: there are long days and nights of waiting in which though it be

"Theirs not to reason why"

the soldiers have abundant time to reflect upon the grim fatality of war and the hideousness of the carnage. They are continually facing death, and though many of them, perhaps most of them, become inured to the sights of human slaughter, others cannot fail to be impressed by the stark, white faces of the fallen—friends and foes alike. Sights more horrible than perhaps they could have imagined are burned into their minds, never to be effaced.

Naturally some of their reflections find expression in the letters home, when the soldier is more or less off guard. There we get an "inside view" of the war which does much to offset the ruthlessness of rulers and restore one's faith in the essential humanity of men.

368

Only from the lips of soldiers, or from their pens when they snatch a few moments from the business of war to write to their people at home, come the most naïvely graphic accounts of trivial but illuminating incidents. Every war has thus its unknown, unhonored chroniclers, who send to their little home circles narratives that for startling realism no highly paid special correspondent could surpass. If all these letters could be assembled and arranged they would form the most essentially human account of the Great War that it is possible to conceive.

"WAR IS TERRIBLE"

The following letter, which refers to the fighting along the Aisne, was found on a German officer of the Seventh Reserve Corps:

"Cerny, South of Laon, Sept. 14, 1914.

"My dear Parents: Our corps has the task of holding the heights south of Cerny in all circumstances until the fourteenth corps on our left flank can grip the enemy's flank. On our right are other corps. We are fighting with the English Guards, Highlanders, and Zouaves. The losses on both sides have been enormous. For the most part this is due to the too brilliant French artillery.

"The English are marvelously trained in making use of ground. One never sees them, and one is constantly under fire. The French airmen perform wonderful feats. We cannot get rid of them. As soon as an airman has flown over us, ten minutes later we get their shrapnel fire in our positions. We have little artillery; without it we cannot get forward.

"Three days ago our division took possession of these heights and dug itself in. Two days ago, early in the morning, we were attacked by an immensely superior English force, one brigade and two battalions, and were turned out of our positions. The fellows took five guns from us. It was a tremendous hand-to-hand fight.

"How I escaped myself I am not clear. I then had to bring up supports on foot. My horse was wounded, and the others were too far in the rear. Then came up the guards jäger battalion, fourth jäger, sixth regiment, reserve regiment thirteen, and landwehr regiments thirteen and sixteen, and with the help of the artillery we drove the fellows out of the position again. Our machine guns did excellent work; the English fell in heaps.

"In our battalion three Iron Crosses have been given, one to C. O., one to Captain ——, and one to Surgeon ——. [Names probably deleted.] Let us hope that we shall be the lucky ones next time.

"During the first two days of the battle I had only one piece of bread and no water. I spent the night in the rain without my overcoat. The rest of my kit was on the horses which had been left behind with the baggage and which cannot come up into the battle because as soon as you put your nose up from behind cover the bullets whistle.

"War is terrible. We are all hoping that a decisive battle will end the war, as our troops already have got round Paris. If we beat the English the French resistance will soon be broken. Russia will be very quickly dealt with; of this there is no doubt.

"Yesterday evening, about six, in the valley in which our reserves stood there was such a terrible cannonade that we saw nothing of the sky but a cloud of smoke. We had few casualties."

THE COMMON ENEMY, DEATH

How foe helps foe when the last grim hour comes is revealed in the letter which a French cavalry officer sent to his fiancée in Paris:

"There are two other men lying near me, and I do not think there is much hope for them either. One is an officer of a Scottish regiment and the other a private in the Uhlans. They were struck down after me, and when I came to myself, I found them bending over me, rendering first aid.

"The Britisher was pouring water down my throat from his flask, while the German was endeavoring to stanch my wound with an antiseptic preparation served out to them by their medical corps. The Highlander had one of his legs shattered, and the German had several pieces of shrapnel buried in his side.

"In spite of their own sufferings they were trying to help me, and when I was fully conscious again the German gave us a morphia injection and took one himself. His medical corps had also provided him with the injection and the needle, together with printed instructions for its use.

"After the injection, feeling wonderfully at ease, we spoke of the lives we had lived before the war. We all spoke English, and we talked of the women we had left at home. Both the German and the Britisher had only been married a year. . . .

371

"I wonder, and I supposed the others did, why we had fought each other at all. I looked at the Highlander, who was falling to sleep, exhausted, and in spite of his drawn face and mud-stained uniform, he looked the embodiment of freedom. Then I thought of the Tri-color of France, and all that France had done for liberty. Then I watched the German, who had ceased to speak. He had taken a prayer book from his knapsack and was trying to read a service for soldiers wounded in battle."

"SAME PAIR OF BLUE EYES"

Sergeant Gabriel David, of the French infantry, who saw seven months of continuous service in the trenches of the Argonne Forest, described the odd effect of peeping over the top of a trench for weeks into the same pair of German blue eyes.

"I don't know who this man was or what he might have been," he said, "but wherever I go I can yet see those sad-looking eyes. He and I gazed at each other for three weeks in one stretch; his watch seemed to always be the same as mine. We came to respect each other. I am sure that I would always know those blue eyes, and I would like to meet that man when the war has ended."

FIGHTING WITHOUT HATE

There is yet to appear an authentic letter from a private or officer on either side that contains a tithe of the virulence and bitterness shown in the statements and writings of many non-combatants.

"One wonders," runs a letter of a British officer,

"when one sees a German face to face, is this really one of those devils who wrought such devastation—for devastation they have surely wrought. You can hardly believe it, for he seems much the same as other soldiers. I can assure you that out here there is none of that insensate hatred that one hears about.

"Just to give you some idea of what I mean, the other night four German snipers were shot on our wire. The next night our men went out and brought one in who was near and get-at-able and buried him. They did it with just the same reverence and sadness as they do to our own dear fellows. I went to look at the grave the next morning, and one of the most uncouth-looking men in my company had placed a cross at the head of the grave, and had written on it:

> " 'Here lies a German.
> We don't know his name.
> For he died bravely fighting
> For his Fatherland.'

"And under that, 'got mitt uns' (sic), that being the highest effort of all the men at German. Not bad for a bloodthirsty Briton, eh? Really that shows the spirit."

CHAPTER XXXIV

BOMBARDING UNDEFENDED CITIES

THE GERMAN RAID ON THE ENGLISH COAST —
MRS. KAUFFMAN'S DESCRIPTION—CANNONADING AT
WHITBY—FREAKISH EFFECT OF SHELLS—FLIGHT OF
SCHOOL CHILDREN.

THE NINTH Hague Convention of 1907, to which
both Germany and Great Britain gave their assent
upon identical conditions, expressly forbids "the bombardment by naval forces of undefended ports, towns,
villages, dwellings or buildings," and by inference
requires notice to be given previous to any such operations. Neither of these stipulations was observed by
the German naval raiders who on December 16, 1914,
bombarded the historic English towns of Hartlepool,
Whitby and Scarborough. Appearing in the early
morning, the Germans rained deadly shells upon these
coast towns, none of which was of strategic importance,
and only one protected by fortifications. The immediate result was the useless slaughter of many noncombatants—men and women and children, and the
ruin of buildings, churches and historic monuments,
including the ancient abbey of St. Hilda at Whitby.

The raid on Scarborough was described by Ruth
Kauffman, the wife of the novelist, Reginald Wright
Kauffman, in an interesting communication. The

374

Kauffmans had been living for several years just outside of Cloughton, a village near Scarborough.

MRS. KAUFFMAN'S DESCRIPTION

"It's a very curious thing to watch a bombardment from your house.

"Everybody knew the Kaiser would do it. But there was a little doubt about the date, and then some-

WHERE THE WAR WAS BROUGHT HOME TO ENGLAND.

how the spy-hunting sport took up general attention. When the Kaiser did send his card it was quite as much of a surprise as most Christmas cards—from a friend forgotten.

"Eighteen people were killed in the morning between eight and eight-thirty o'clock in the streets and houses of Scarborough by German shrapnel, two hundred were wounded and more than two hundred houses were damaged or demolished.

"From our windows we could not quite make out the

contours of the ruined castle, which is generally plainly visible. Our attention was called to the fact that there was "practicing" going on and we could at 8.07 see quick flashes. That these flashes pointed directly at Scarborough we did not for a few moments comprehend, then the fog slowly lifting, we saw a fog that was partly smoke. The castle grew into its place in the six miles distance.

"It seemed for a moment that the eight-foot thick Norman walls tottered, but no, whatever tottered was behind the keep. Curiously enough, we could barely hear the cannonading, for the wind was keen in the opposite direction, yet we could, as the minutes crept by and the air cleared, see distinctly the flashes from the boats and the flashes in the city.

"After about fifteen minutes there was a cessation, or perhaps a hesitation, that lasted two minutes; then the flashes continued. Ten minutes more and the boats began to move again. One cruiser disappeared from sight, sailing south by east.

CANNONADING AT WHITBY

"The other two rushed like fast trains north again, close to our cliffs, and in another half hour we heard all too plainly the cannonading which had almost escaped our ears from Scarborough. We thought it was Robin Hood's Bay, as far north of us as Scarborough is south, but afterward we learned that the boats omitted this pretty red-roofed town and concentrated their remaining energy on Whitby, fifteen miles north; the wind blowing toward us brought us the vibrating boom.

THE BOMBARDMENT OF THE EAST COAST OF ENGLAND.

This scene, painted in Hartlepool, shows the effect of a bursting German shell in the unfortified British town. Several women and many other civilians were killed by the German raiders.

ZEPPELIN DEVICE FOR DROPPING BOMBS.

An armored car is suspended by three cables from the Zeppelin airship
to a distance of several thousand feet below the monster air-craft, which
is concealed in the clouds above. (*Sphere copr.*)

"We drove to Scarborough. We had not gone one mile of the distance when we began to meet people coming in the opposite direction. A small white-faced boy in a milk cart that early every morning makes its Scarborough rounds showed us a piece of shell he had picked up, and said it had first struck a man a few yards from him and killed the man. A woman carrying a basket told us, with trembling lips, that men and women were lying about the streets dead.

"We did not meet a deserted city when we entered. The streets were thronging. There was a Sunday hush over everything, without the accompanying Sunday clothes, but people moved about or stood at their doorways. Many of the shop fronts were boarded up and shop windows were empty of display. The main street, a narrow passage-way that clambers up from the sea and points due west, was filled with a procession that slowly marched down one side and up the other. People hardly spoke. They made room automatically for a group of silent Boy Scouts, who carried an unconscious woman past us to the hospital. There was the insistent honk of a motor-car. As it pushed its way through, all that struck me about the car was the set face of the old man rising above improvised bandages about his neck, part of the price of the Kaiser's Christmas card.

"The damage to property did not first reach our attention. But as we walked down the main street and then up it with the procession we saw that shops and houses all along had windows smashed next to windows unhurt. At first we thought the broken windows were from concussion; but apparently very few were so broken; there was not much concussion, but the shells, splintering as they exploded, had flown red hot in every direction. The smoke, we had seen, had come from fires quickly extinguished.

FREAKISH EFFECTS OF SHELLS

"We left the main business street and picked our way toward the foreshore and the South Cliff, the more fashionable part of the town as well as the school section. Here there was a great deal of havoc, and we had to climb over some of the debris. Roofs were half torn off and balancing in mid-air; shells had shot through chimneys and some chimneys tottered, while several had merely round holes through the brick work; mortar, brick and glass lay about the streets; here a third-story room was bare to the view, the wall lifted as for a child's doll house and disclosing a single bedroom with shaving materials on the bureau still secure; there a drug-store front lay fallen into the street, and the iron railing about it was torn and twisted out of shape.

"A man and a boy had just been carried away dead. All around small pieces of iron rail and ripped asphalt lay scattered. Iron bars were driven into the woodwork of houses. There were great gaps in walls and roofs. The attack had not spent itself on any one section of the city, but had scattered itself in different wards. The freaks of the shells were as inexplicable as those of a great fire that destroys everything in a house except a piano and a mantelpiece with its bric-a-brac, or a flood that carries away a log cabin and leaves a rosebush unharmed and blooming.

378

"Silent pedestrians walked along and searched the ground for souvenirs, of which there were plenty. Sentries guarded houses and streets where it was dangerous to explore and park benches were used as barriers to the public. All the cabs were requisitioned to take away luggage and frightened inhabitants. During the shelling hundreds of women and children, breakfastless, their hair hanging, hatless and even penniless, except for their mere railway fares, had rushed to the station and taken tickets to the first safe town they could think of. There was no panic, these hatless, penniless women all asserted, when they arrived in York and Leeds.

FLIGHT OF SCHOOL CHILDREN

"A friend of mine hurried into Scarborough by motor to rescue her sister, who was a pupil at one of the boarding schools. But it appeared that when the windows of the school began to crash the teachers hurried from prayers, ordered the pupils to gather hats and coats and sweet chocolate that happened to be on hand as a substitute for breakfast and made them run for a mile and a half, with shells exploding about them, through the streets to the nearest out-of-Scarborough railway station. My friend, after unbelievable difficulties, finally found her sister in a private house of a village near by, the girl in tears and pleading not to be sent to London; she had been told that her family's house was probably destroyed, as it was actually on the sea-coast."

CHAPTER XXXV

GERMANY'S FATAL WAR ZONE

THE WARNING TO NEUTRAL NATIONS—UNITED STATES REFUSED TO RECOGNIZE WAR ZONE—A VIOLATION OF INTERNATIONAL RIGHTS—AIMED AT NEUTRAL SHIPPING—AN INHUMAN POLICY.

THE GERMAN imperial decree making all of the waters surrounding the British Isles a war zone and threatening to destroy ships and crews found therein after February 18, 1915, whether they were English or neutral, raised a storm of protest in the United States. The decree read:

"The waters around Great Britain and Ireland, including the whole English Channel, are declared a war zone from and after February 18, 1915.

"Every enemy ship found in this war zone will be destroyed, even if it is impossible to avert dangers which threaten the crew and passengers.

"Also, neutral ships in the war zone are in danger, as in consequence of the misuse of neutral flags ordered by the British government on January 31 and in view of the hazards of naval warfare it cannot always be avoided that attacks meant for enemy ships shall endanger neutral ships.

"Shipping northward, around the Shetland Islands, in the eastern basin of the North Sea, and in a strip

380

of at least thirty nautical miles in breadth along the Dutch coast, is endangered in the same way."

As plainly as words could state it, this was a warning that American and other neutral vessels might be sunk by German submarines and that Germany would repudiate responsibility for such action. The American press denounced the declaration and its intent, and the United States government made public a note to Germany, containing the following paragraph:

UNITED STATES REFUSED TO RECOGNIZE WAR ZONE

"If the commanders of German vessels of war should act upon the presumption that the flag of the United States was not being used in good faith and should destroy on the high seas an American vessel, or the lives of American citizens, it would be difficult for the government of the United States to view the act in any other light than as an indefensible violation of neutral rights which it would be very hard indeed to reconcile with the friendly relations now happily subsisting between the two governments."

Frederick R. Coudert, of New York, an authority on international law, said in discussing the war zone:

"From the beginning the United States government always maintained the right to treat the open sea as a public highway, and refused to acquiesce in one attempt after another to establish a closed sea. It refused to submit to an imposition of the Sound dues by Denmark, or to recognize the Baltic as a closed sea. It refused to pay tribute to the Barbary powers for the privilege of navigating the Mediterranean, and gave notice to Russia that it would

381

disregard the claim to make the North Pacific a closed sea.

A VIOLATION OF INTERNATIONAL RIGHTS

"No one has ever pretended to assert a claim to control the navigation of the North Sea, and Germany has no more right to plant mines in the open sea between Great Britain and Belgium and France than she would have to do so in Delaware Bay, or than a property owner, who was annoyed by automobiles, would have to plant torpedoes in a turnpike.

"The right to plant mines as a defense to a harbor, from which all vessels might lawfully be excluded, is one thing, but to destroy the use of the open sea as a highway, by sowing mines which might indeed destroy British ships, but might also destroy American ships, is an act of hostility which, if persisted in, would constitute a casus belli, and if we had Mr. Webster, or Mr. Marcey, or Mr. Evarts in Washington as Secretary of State, prompt notice would be given that for any damage done Germany would be held responsible."

A representative quotation from the newspapers of the United States is the following:

"The imperial decree making all of the waters surrounding the British isles a 'war zone,' and threatening to destroy ships and crews found therein after February 18, whether they be English or neutral, is surely the maddest proposal ever put forth by a civilized nation.

AIMED AT NEUTRAL SHIPPING

"This excessively efficient method of warfare, however, is one that most concerns England and France

The interest of the United States lies in the fact that the threat is aimed emphatically at neutral shipping.

"Neutral nations were loath to accept the sinister meaning of the order when it was first published; but its intent was emphasized by Bismarck's old organ, the Hamburger Nachrichten:

" 'Beginning on February 18 everybody must take the consequences. The hate and envy of the whole world concern us not at all. If neutrals do not protect their flags against England, they do not deserve Germany's respect.'

"The misuse of the American flag is annoying to this country as well as exasperating to Germany, but no government in its senses would seriously threaten to make that an excuse for piratical operations. A merchant ship has a right to fly any flag the skipper has in his locker, particularly if thereby he can deceive an enemy and evade capture. The custom is as old as maritime warfare, and has been resorted to numberless times by every nation.

"But this issue is trifling compared to the German effort to exclude neutral shipping from an arbitrarily decreed 'war zone.' It is officially admitted that this does not comprise a formal blockade, but it is clear that Germany is attempting to achieve the benefits of a blockade without its heavy responsibilities.

AN INHUMAN POLICY

"It is understood that she has a perfect right to hold up and search neutral ships in her declared 'war zone,' and to make prizes of such as carry contraband. But it is the possession of this very right which forbids the inhuman policy she proclaims. She cannot plead ignorance of a vessel's identity, or attack it unless it refuses to stop when signaled. The burden of proof is upon the submarine, and to torpedo a vessel on suspicion merely would be unredeemed piracy and murder.

"This is distinctly a case in which the convenient doctrine of 'military necessity' is not to be invoked. Nor would an occasional misuse of a neutral flag by belligerent vessels, as a ruse of war, justify a mistaken act of destruction. If every British merchantman approaching England flew the American colors, that would not excuse the torpedoing of one American ship.

"These facts are stated with convincing clearness in the official protest sent from Washington to Berlin. We do not know who framed this document, although it bears distinct literary marks of revision by President Wilson. But whoever the men actually responsible for it, they produced a state paper which is a model of terseness, lucidity, dignified courtesy and force, an irrefutable presentation of the relevant principles of international law and justice. No loyal American wants trouble, but the blood of the most pacific citizen must move a little faster on reading the German decree and the restrained but perfectly straightforward reply sent by our government."

CHAPTER XXXVI

MULTITUDINOUS TRAGEDIES AT SEA

TWENTY-NINE VESSELS SUNK IN ONE WEEK—
EIGHTY-TWO NON-COMBATANT VESSELS DESTROYED
IN GERMAN WAR ZONE—THE ATTACK ON THE
GULFLIGHT.

THE FACT that the Lusitania was the twenty-ninth
vessel to be sunk or damaged in one week in May in the
war zone established by Germany around the British
Isles throws into grim relief the ruthlessness of modern
war. The naval battles of the past were engagements
of dignity in which, when a vessel was lost, it went down
with a certain tragic magnificence after a fair fight;
but most of the vessels lost in the European war have
been the victims of torpedoes, struck by stealthy blows
in the dark. In less than three months, from February
18 to May 7, 1915, no less than eighty-two merchant
vessels belonging either to the Allies or to neutral
nations were torpedoed or mined in the war zone, with
a loss of life estimated at 1,704 non-combatants—a
terrible sacrifice to modern warfare.

Naturally the greater number of these merchant ships
were British, but the fact that the war zone was proclaimed by Germany with a view to stopping neutral
shipping as well is established by the figures which show
that among the eighty-two non-combatant vessels

destroyed there were French, Russian, Norwegian, Swedish, Dutch, Danish, Greek and three American vessels, the latter being the Evelyn, sunk by a mine explosion February 20; the Carib, sunk by a mine explosion February 22, and the Gulflight, torpedoed May 1.

In addition to these eighty-two cases of non-combatant vessels destroyed, there have been innumerable instances of unsuccessful attacks, of which a notable example was the double attempt to sink the American tank steamship Cushing, once by a Zeppelin which aimed three bombs at the vessel, and once by a submarine which placed a contact mine directly in the path of the ship; her bow narrowly missed the mine, and her stern struck it a glancing blow, but not with sufficient force to explode it.

THE ATTACK ON THE GULFLIGHT

It would require many hundreds of pages to recount the details of all of these crimes against non-combatant merchant ships, and to show the relentless severity with which neutral commerce has been attacked, but the organized military measures even against neutral ships are well illustrated by the case of the American ship Gulflight, as described by the second officer, Paul Bower:

"When the Gulflight left Port Arthur, Texas, on April 10, bound for Rouen, France," said Bower, "we were followed by a warship of some description, which kept out of sight, but in touch by wireless and warned us not to disclose our position to any one.

"At noon Saturday, May 1, we were twenty-five

miles west of the Scilly Islands, a small group about
thirty miles southwest of England. The weather was
hazy, but not thick. About two and one-half miles
ahead I saw a submarine.

"Twenty-five minutes later we were struck by a

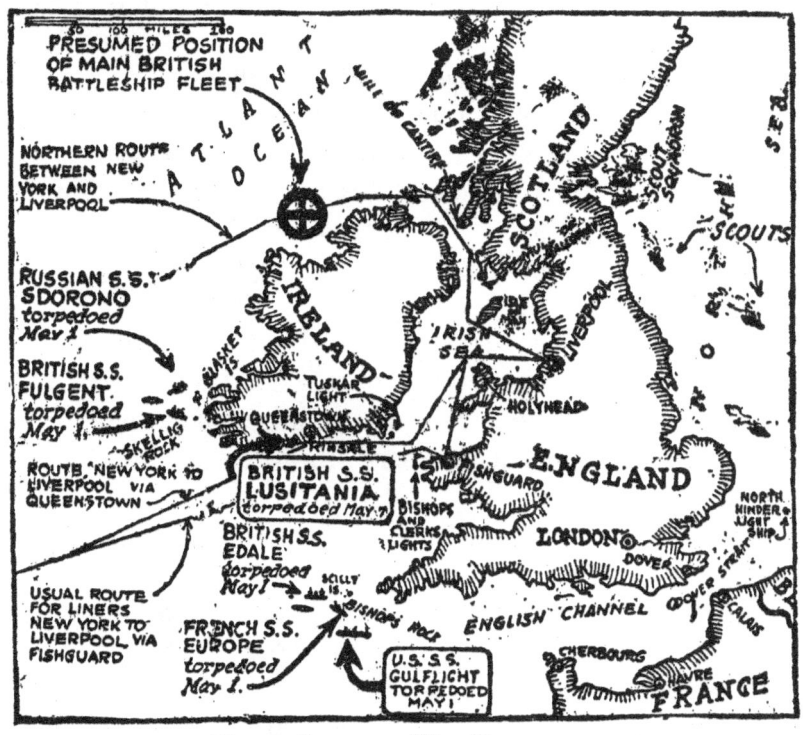

WHERE LUSITANIA WAS TORPEDOED.
Kinsale, on South Coast of Ireland, close to Cork Harbor.

torpedo on the starboard side, and there was a tremendous shock. The submarine had not reappeared on
the surface before discharging the torpedo.

"Previous to this, we had been met by two patrol
boats, which accompanied us on either side. The boat

on our starboard side was so badly shaken by the explosion that her crew imagined that she also had been torpedoed. We immediately lowered the boats and left our ship and were quickly taken on board the patrol boats. But the fog increased and we drifted about all night and did not land at Scilly until 10.30 o'clock Sunday morning.

"At midnight of Saturday, while still on board the patrol boat, Captain Gunter summoned me. I found him in bed and he said he wanted some one to roll a cigarette for him. He then tossed up his arms and fainted. From then until the time of his death, which occurred about 3.30 o'clock Sunday morning, he remained unconscious.

"Captain Gunter's speech was thick and indistinct, but we could distinguish that he wished some one to take care of his wife. The crew had always regarded Captain Gunter as a healthy man and had never heard him complain."

Second Assistant Engineer Crist, of the Gulflight, said:

"I was on watch in the engine room when we were torpedoed, and so terrible was the blow that the Gulflight seemed to be tumbling to pieces. She appeared to be lifted high in the air and then to descend rapidly. I told the boys to beat it as quickly as possible and shut the engines down.

"Reaching the deck, I found them launching both life-boats. We got safely into them, with the exception of wireless operator Short and a Spanish seaman, who had dived overboard when they felt the shock, and were drowned."

388

CHAPTER XXXVII

THE TERRIBLE DISTRESS OF POLAND

A LONG-TORTURED NATION AGAIN BLIGHTED BY
WAR — DESOLATION AND FAMINE THROUGHOUT
LAND—RICH AND POOR ALIKE DESTITUTE—PLIGHT
OF RUSSIAN POLAND—NO BREAD FOR WEEKS IN
LODZ—THREE TIMES A BATTLE-FIELD—UNABLE TO
HELP HERSELF—NO SEED AND NO DRAFT ANIMALS.

"IF YOU imagined all the people of New York State
deprived of everything they owned, left a prey to
starvation and disease, and hopelessly crushed under
the iron heels of contending armies, you might form a
slight idea of what the Poles are enduring at present,"
declared the great pianist, Paderewski, while visiting
America in 1915 in the interests of the afflicted nation.
"One of the worst phases of the situation lies in the
inability of the inhabitants of one-half of the country
to communicate with those in the other. Compared
with their lot, even that of the Belgians loses some of
its horror, for my unhappy countrymen have no France,
Holland, or England in which they can seek refuge."

Girt by a ring of war, Poland in the winter and spring
of 1915 was in the most terrible straits. Her cities
and villages had been captured and recaptured by
both Germans and Russians, her fields had been laid
waste, and her inhabitants were slowly dying of
starvation.

TERRIBLE DISTRESS IN POLAND

"If figures can give any idea of the immensity of this disaster," pleaded the great musician, "then these may convey a slight impression of what has gone on in Poland: An area equal in size to the states of Pennsylvania and New York has been laid waste. The mere money losses, due to the destruction of property and the means of agriculture and industry, are $2,500,000,000. A whole nation of 18,000,000 people, including 2,000,000 Jews, are carrying the burden of the war in the east on their backs, and their backs are breaking under the load. The great majority of the whole Polish people, about 11,000,000 men, women and children, peasants and workmen, have been driven into the open, their homes taken from them or burned, and they flee, terror-stricken, hungry and in confusion, whither they know not. In ruins, in woods or in hollows they are hiding, feeding on roots and the bark of trees. It is Christian humanity that calls for help for succumbing Poland."

"From the banks of the Niemen to the summits of the Carpathians," wrote the novelist, Henryk Sienkiewicz, in his plea to the American people, "fire has destroyed the towns and villages, and over the whole of this huge, desolated country the specter of famine has spread its wings; all labor and industry have been swept away; the ploughshare is rusted; the peasant has neither grain nor cattle the artisan is idle; all works and factories have been destroyed; the tradesman cannot sell his wares; the hearth fire is extinguished, and disease and misery prevail. To such starving people, crying out for aid, listen, Christian nations."

390

TERRIBLE DISTRESS IN POLAND

All points within the sphere of the German offensive offered a picture of utter desolation. The people fled in horror before the advancing enemy, leaving their homes and their property to sure destruction. An uninterrupted line of arson fire shone on the sorrowful path of the exiles. Their fields have been devastated and furrowed by the trenches, their animals have been taken away, their savings have been wasted, and all their chattels destroyed.

RICH AND POOR ALIKE DESTITUTE

The Polish Relief Committee, headed by Madame Sembrich, published this word from the great tenor, Jean de Reszké, whose home is in Paris:

"My poor brother was unable to get away from the war zone in time. He wrote this letter several weeks ago, and now I fear he may never survive the terrible hardships. He had plenty of money and a splended estate, but all were swept away."

The letter referred to shows that there is no leveler like war. It runs:

"My dear brother, whether this will ever get through the lines and reach you I do not know. I am sure no man could get through alive, with all this fighting and the continual bombardment going on on every hand.

"The war broke with such suddenness that it was impossible to escape. I was forced to remain here on my estate in Garnesk. This part of Poland has been reduced to worse than a desert. All is desolate and every one is suffering. My beautiful estate has met the common fate and been reduced to ashes. I am now living in a cellar with scanty covering. If a shell should drop in it would afford no protection. So fierce has been the fighting here that there have been days when I could not venture forth. We have been between two fires. All Poland needs relief.

"I have no coal, oil, coffee, and only a handful of grain left. Through the cold and the rain I have had but poor shelter, but my lot is the same as that of my fellow countrymen here. Every one is in want; every one is suffering. Many are dead, and many more will die unless aid reaches them soon. Prince Lukouirski and his wife recently reached here and are sharing my cellar with me. Their own beautiful estate has been destroyed, and even the cellar blown to atoms by the shells."

PLIGHT OF RUSSIAN POLAND

Mr. Herbert Corey, writing from Berlin to the New York Globe, in the spring of 1915, declared that unless something was done the world would be horrified—if the world had not lost its capacity for horror—by the sufferings of the Poles. "Soon cholera will come to Poland. Famine is there now. Scarlet fever and typhoid and smallpox and enteric and typhus are old settlers." The million now in utter want only live at all because "humanity has a wonderful capacity for adjustment to wretchedness.

"There are 6,000,000 Poles in the portion of Russian Poland that is being fought over. Of these, according to the Red Cross men, 1,000,000 are absolutely destitute. They are without food or the means to buy food. They are living on the charity of others who are but slightly better off. That charity must come to an end soon—because food is coming to an end. It is not merely that money is lacking. Flour is lacking. It must be imported or starvation follows.

"Russian Poland is a conspicuous example of Russian rule. No measure of self-government is permitted the people. All governing officials are appointed from Petrograd. Lodz, for example, a city which contains from 500,000 to 750,000 people—all statistics in Poland are mere guesses—is ruled by a mayor and four assistants, all sent out from Russia. No city may expend more than $150, American money, for its own purposes, except permission is secured from Petrograd. That permission is rarely given. Petrograd needs the taxes that Lodz pays. When permission is given it is long delayed. Therefore, Lodz, a town as large as St. Louis, has unpaved streets that are ankle-deep in mud in winter and ankle-deep in dust in summer. It has a privately owned and paid fire department that responds only to calls from its own clients. Ninety per cent of its residents live in sties on streets that are mere stenches.

"And yet Lodz is the second cotton-manufacturing town in Europe. It is excelled only by Manchester in its manufacturing totals. Isolated on the bleak plains of Poland, at a distance from a seaport, served by two railroads only, it is an anomaly in the commercial world.

NO BREAD FOR WEEKS IN LODZ

"For two weeks Lodz had no bread at all. For months it has had no meat at all—so far as the poorer classes are concerned. During those two weeks the mass of the population lived on potatoes.

"Conditions were slightly worse in Czenstochow, the second city in Russian Poland. Here 90,000 people live. It has no street-lights It has no attempt at street-paving. It has no sewers. It has no city water. It has no publicly maintained fire department, though a few of the merchants have a department of their own. It is pre-middle-ages in everything—morals, discomfort, filth, darkness, disease, death-rate. Cholera is there all the time. Most of its people exist in reeking hovels, smoke-filled when they can afford fires, wet and cold at other times.

"As the towns grow smaller, conditions grow worse."

THREE TIMES A BATTLE-FIELD

If the war had not come, these people would have prospered after a fashion. Potatoes were plentiful, and they had few other wants. A woman earned thirty cents a day in the mills and a man three cents more. Children worked as soon as they were old enough. Sixty-five per cent are wholly illiterate. Then—

"Russia struck at Germany. The German armies invaded Poland in retaliation. They swept almost to Warsaw—and an invading army sweeps fairly clean. There were some things left when they passed over. They were driven back, and the Russian armies covered this territory—and they gleaned what was left. Then the Russians were driven back—sacking as they went—and the Germans covered the ground once more. Three times unhappy Poland has been fought over. It had little at the beginning. It has nothing now. For months Poland has been starving, not merely going hungry. That is a commonplace of war. Poles have been dying because they cannot get food.

UNABLE TO HELP HERSELF

"Poland is quite unable to help herself. Most of the mills—probably all of the mills—are owned by Russian and German and French capitalists. The banks are all branches of foreign institutions. These concerns are all conducted by resident managers. Some of the managers have—on their own responsibility—given their work people two and a half and three cents a day each for food. Some have added a trifle for the children also. But this has practically come to an end. The managers have exhausted their supply of cash. They cannot get more. There are no mails. The towns of Poland are each printing their own paper money—not by consent of the Russian bureaucrats, but in defiance of them—but this money circulates only within the town's borders. It is highly improbable it will ever be redeemed in real money. Meanwhile the price of food commodities has risen fifty per cent in two months. By the time this reaches America the prices may have doubled.

NO SEED AND NO DRAFT ANIMALS

"Conditions are slightly better in the agricultural sections. The farmers have no seed and no draft animals, it is true. But they have fairly good supplies of potatoes. Last year's potato-crop was an enormous one.

"There is a Jewish question in every city of Poland. Where there is a Jewish question in Russia there are riots. There will be more rioting in Poland unless Providence intervenes. Russia has always confined her Jews to the pale. Being forced to make their living by trading, their naturally sharp wits have been whetted. Today they are—broadly speaking—owners of every shop in Poland. There may be Christian shopkeepers here and there. People who know Poland doubt it.

"Beggars follow the stranger in the Polish cities. Some of them are mute. They only look at the stranger through hollow eyes and hold out skinny hands. Others are vociferous. They cling to the garments of the passer-by. They cry for aid in an uncouth dialect. They run out from darkened doorways. The man who gives is pursued by a cue of them."

CHARGING THROUGH BARBED-WIRE ENTANGLEMENTS.

The King's Regiment of the British Army suffered heavily while trying to penetrate the enemy's wire entanglement at Givenchy. Three lines of a perfect thicket of barbed-wire lay between them and the enemy. Only one brave officer even managed to penetrate the wire. *Il. L. News copr.*)

The Charge of the 4th Canadian Battalion at Ypres in the Face of a Murderous German Shell Fire.

During one of the most terrible and deadly engagements of the whole war, when a powerful German outflanking movement was being rapidly developed, the 4th Canadian Battalion, to save the day, forced a counter-attack in the face of a withering fire. Lieutenant-Colonel Birchall, leading his men, fell dead at the moment when it seemed that the attack could not succeed. With a cry of anger the attack was renewed, the German trenches were taken and the

CHAPTER XXXVIII

CANADIAN CONQUERORS IN THE TRENCHES

EARLY CANADIAN EXPECTATIONS—THE BATTLE OF
GIVENCHY—FROM DIVISION TO ARMY CORPS—REAL
FIGHTING IN THE TRENCHES—RAIDING "THE GREAT
NORTHWEST"—MOVE TOWARDS ST. ELOI—IN THE
YPRES SALIENT—CAUGHT IN A RAIN OF SHELLS.

IN FEBRUARY, 1915, when the First Canadian
Contingent, after a winter of training on Salisbury
Plain, proceeded to France there was universal confidence that it had gone to take part in the great drive
that was to hurl the Germans back to the Meuse and
back to the Rhine. The only nervousness of the
Canadian soldiers was lest they should be too late to
share in the decisive battles.

The experiences of the Canadians at Langemarck,
and Ypres have already been described elsewhere.

THE BATTLE OF GIVENCHY

In June there came another outstanding fight in
which the Canadians took a prominent part—the
Battle of Givenchy. The Seventh British Division was
ordered to make a frontal attack on a strong enemy
position known as "Stony Mountain," and the First
Battalion, from Ontario, commanded by Lieut.-Colonel
Hill, was directed to secure the lines of German
trenches stretching from "Stony Mountain" to another

397

German position known as "Dorchester." The Ontario troops were reinforced by men from the Edmonton Fusiliers. The Canadians knew some hours before that they were picked for this dangerous advance, and waited in their trenches, eager for the onslaught. Two 18-pound guns were planted in their own front trench, and played havoc in the German ranks for a quarter of an hour before the advance began. "We could see portions of their trenches falling in and accoutrements flung in the air," said some of the men when describing the scene afterwards. Two minutes before the hour fixed for the advance a mine exploded under the first German trench. As the débris and dust were still in the air, the Canadians leaped from their trenches and rushed straight across the seventy yards between them and the enemy. The German guns fired among them, but nothing could stop them. They had agreed on a battle-cry, "Gas devils!" and they hurled the words out in bitter shouts as they rushed along. The Germans fired on the Canadians until they were quite near; then some tried to escape while others remained, and as the Canadians jumped into the trenches threw their arms up with the call of "Kamerades!" The trench was soon in our hands. The Germans now concentrated their artillery fire on this captured front trench. From it the Canadians rushed the second trench and captured it. The German fire grew heavier and heavier, and our men in the trenches attempted in vain to secure some shelter for themselves. Their supply of bombs ran short, and one lad, Private Smith, son of a Methodist minister of Southampton, Ontario, volunteered to go back for some more. He went back singing, was caught by a mine explosion and buried. He dug himself out, gathered a number of bombs from dead and wounded bomb-throwers around him, and returned to the second trench with them. He repeated this five times. It is said that the fire was so hot that several times he could not get into the trenches of the men who needed them most, and had to lie down and toss the bombs to them. But even with the work of such as Smith, enough bombs could not be had. Men who tried to bring them up were nearly all of them killed. The British advance had been held up by the strength of "Stony Mountain." The Canadians held their position as long as they could, but in the end had to go back.

FROM DIVISION TO ARMY CORPS

From the Battle of Givenchy for many weary months to come the Canadian troops now found themselves engaged in the routine of what was virtually siege warfare. It was their business to hold a section—an ever-growing section—of the British lines, to keep the enemy engaged, to prevent surprises, and wherever possible to surprise the enemy. The one original division grew, as further reinforcements were sent to the front after training in England, to a Canadian army corps.

REAL FIGHTING IN THE TRENCHES

Each brigade pitted the excellence of its trenches against all comers. The old shallow, muddy, irregular lines of earth that in the earlier months had done work for our troops as trenches, gave way to splendidly arranged lines, giving the maximum of protection. Dug-outs were so solidly constructed that they would stand anything save direct blows from heavy shells, and some of them, it was claimed, would stand even that. Trenches were so well drained that the troops stood on firm emplacements even in the wettest weather. A trench school was established, where selected men from the different battalions went for training. Every new device was examined, tested, and, if of any use, adopted.

At the beginning many Canadians were victims of German snipers, whose ingenuity and resource drew unwilling admiration even from our men. But before many months the Canadians turned the tables here also. They developed special groups of snipers, adepts at concealing themselves, men who never fired but to hit; who would lie hour after hour, and if necessary day after day, for a single sure shot. The Canadians, like every other part of the British Army, developed bomb-throwing to an amazing extent.

In one special line of trench warfare the Canadians gave a lead to the whole of the allied armies. Colonel Odlum, who had distinguished himself prominently in the fighting at Ypres, worked out a system of night raids on the enemy lines that for some time kept the Germans very uneasy.

RAIDING "THE GREAT NORTHWEST"

The British and the German lines were separated by a space of land generally known as No Man's Land, and called by some Canadians "the Great Northwest." In this long stretch, varying in depth from thirty or forty yards at some points to two hundred yards and more at others, both British and Germans had protected themselves by long stretches of barbed-wire—thick, strong, and deep. In some threatened points the Germans had two tangles of wire, the first sixteen feet deep, the other forty feet deep, and between these two their patrols would move at night-time to prevent the possibility of their being surprised. Colonel Odlum planned a regular method by which raiding parties would go out at night, wriggle silently to the enemy wires, make a way through the entanglements with wire-cutters, throw themselves into the enemy trenches before the Germans had realized that they were there, capture the men, destroy the machine-guns, and go back with their prisoners before it was possible to capture them. These reconnaissances were repeated time after time by the different brigades at the front. They gave opportunity for the display of great individual heroism. In one case a young officer led his men into the trenches, emptied his automatic pistol twice, firing from the hip, then sprang at a German, wrenching his dagger out of his hand and flinging it in the face of another, and finally returned with his men and his prisoners, himself the last to leave the trench.

MOVE TOWARDS ST. ELOI

Early in April the Canadians moved up towards St. Eloi from positions they had held farther south. A British division immediately on the left of the Canadians exploded several mines under the German lines and advanced, capturing two lines of German trenches for a length of about six thousand yards. One of these lines of trenches was about twenty yards behind the other. There was a third line of trenches some eight hundred yards behind these, with communicating trenches connecting them. This third line remained in German hands. On the night of April 2d–3d the Sixth Canadian Infantry Brigade relieved the British troops in the new line.

Day after day and night after night the ding-dong fight continued, swaying now this way and now that. The Canadians would advance through the mud at every opportunity, bombing the enemy; the enemy would rush back, bombing them. Now a crater would belong to one, now to another. Time after time the Germans made rushes forward, only to be met, as they drew near, with our machine-gun fire, which swept them wholesale away. Soldiers who witnessed some of these rushes declared afterwards that they would retain to their last days impressions of men staggering, reeling, rushing into inevitable death.

If the German shell fire was terrible, that of the British was soon more so. As the fight developed the British brought more and more artillery strength on this point. "This seems like heaven," said one German prisoner when dragged into our lines. "If you want to know what gun fire is, go into our lines when your shells are coming in."

IN THE YPRES SALIENT

Soon afterwards the Canadians were to face a still more dreadful experience. They had now moved up to the foremost point in the Ypres salient, and they were holding the line between Hooge and the Ypres-Menin railway. Shortly after nine o'clock on the morning of June 2d, Major-General Mercer, accompanied by Brigadier-General Williams, was visiting the front lines held by the Fourth Canadian Mounted Rifles when an artillery fire of the most severe nature covered the entire Canadian front of some three thousand yards. Simultaneously a great line of shells fell continuously far behind the front lines, making it impossible to bring up reserves. The artillery fire at St. Eloi had been severe, but it was almost as nothing to the rain of shells here. Men who had been in both called the first "child's play." The Germans had carefully and secretly accumulated a great force of guns—such strength of guns as probably never previously existed in the history of war. The Canadian troops caught in the front lines could do nothing to reply. They could not advance. They could not retire. For any man to show himself was to seek immediate death, and had he shown himself he could have done nothing against the enemy. In this rain of shells trenches disappeared, parapets were wiped out, and the British front was reduced to little more than a blurred and broken line. Some of the troops got into tunnels and into dug-outs waiting for the fire to die away. Other troops in reserve, some eight hundred yards behind, were hastily called upon to dig themselves in, for it was seen that the front lines would form little protection against the enemy.

After several hours of this artillery fire the Germans came up to our lines. They were so satisfied that no

403

man could be living that they approached without any great haste, some smoking cigarettes and all carrying heavy packs. One Canadian corporal and a few men had got into an excavation at the bottom of a trench and had dragged in a machine-gun with them. Here they lay low during the firing. When the German shell fire suddenly ceased they crawled out and looked around. They saw the Germans coming up. They placed their machine-gun in position, waited until the enemy were comparatively close, and then poured their fire into them. The Germans fled and very many fell.

THE EYE OF A SUBMARINE.

British submarine officer looking through the periscope in the hope of finding an enemy target.

Copyright by The Sun News Service.   ESCAPING A TORPEDO BY RAPID MANEUVERING

This destroyer escaped a torpedo from a hunted submarine by quick turning. Generally the torpedo travels at about

CHAPTER XXXIX

RUTHLESS SUBMARINE WARFARE

PRISONERS ON A SUBMARINE—LIFE ON A U-BOAT—
THE RETURN TO GERMANY—GERMAN ATROCITIES—
PLUCKY ENGLISHMEN—OLD MEN AND CHILDREN

AMONG THE many atrocities perpetrated by German submarines the following story by eight Spanish sailors from the British steamship Gravina, which was sunk by a submarine on February 7, 1917, seems to be a fair sample. It will tell the American people just what can be expected of German ruthlessness should any of our sailors fall into German hands. Their treatment will certainly not be any more merciful than was meted out to these helpless representatives of a neutral nation because of Germany's hatred of America and all things American.

PRISONERS ON A SUBMARINE

The Gravina was struck by a torpedo amidships, and broke in halves. The fifteen survivors were able to keep afloat by clinging to two bales of corkwood. In about half an hour's time we saw a submarine coming toward us. We shouted, "We are Spaniards, we are Spaniards! Save us!" The submarine came near to us, and many of the crew were on its platform looking at us and laughing at our struggles.

We expected to be picked up quickly, but, no, we still had to remain in the water another ten minutes while

SEA-ZONES THAT GERMANY CLAIMED TO RULE FROM BENEATH.

The waters barred to all shipping after February I, 1917, included the whole of the Mediterranean (except a lane twenty miles wide leading to the Greek coast), the whole of the North Sea, and an area extending from the Faroe Islands to 260 miles west of Ireland, and twenty miles north of Cape Finisterre to the French frontier.

the submarine officers prepared their cameras to photograph us. Having done this, they proceeded to save us. They threw lifebelts attached to ropes and got us on board. We had been fighting against death for three-quarters of an hour.

We were immediately made to go below through the afterhatch to the part of the submarine used for discharging torpedoes and storing ammunition. In this floating prison we found two companions in misfortune, the Captains of two English steamers sunk by the same submarine.

LIFE ON A U-BOAT

The monotonous but not tranquil life was disturbed from time to time by a rapid manoeuvre. Some vessel was in sight, and it was necessary to sink it. They forced us to load the torpedo, an operation which was performed with all the repugnance of honorable men. They opened the chamber of the tube, made us lift the torpedo and put it in. Afterward they gave the order to fire, and after a few seconds of anxiety we heard a formidable explosion. The German seamen jumped, laughed, and sang. They had hit the target. During the twelve days that we were on board they sank five vessels, among them a Swedish sailing ship which was sunk by cannon shots. Generally speaking, we went down at night time, and, although submerged, we always navigated. In the daytime we came up on to the surface of the sea, which, however, they never allowed us to see. We were aware of it by the change of motors. Our region of operation (that is, of the submarine) was for nine days south of Ireland.

THE RETURN TO GERMANY

"On February 15, 1917, we started on the home-ward trip to the naval base, as the German seamen informed us. We went up the west side of England, round the north, and then to Jutland, always on the surface, and in three days arrived in the waters of Heligoland. One of us managed to see the engineer's diary, where the following particulars appeared: "Eighteen miles speed on the surface and thirteen miles submerged; 12,000 tons. Crew of thirty," and in each page was noted U-81. Four hours before arriving at the Island of Heligoland they made all the prisoners go up on the deck platform, and they photographed us. They then ordered us down below again to the torpedo room. The port where we landed was not very large. There were about a dozen submarines and four or five destroyers there, but all the quays and jetties bristled with seamen with bayonets fixed. * * *

GERMAN ATROCITIES

"Three days after our arrival in prison camp we were awakened by cries from the Russians who slept in the hut. Fire had broken out in one hut apart from the others, which served as a dungeon where they shut up prisoners who were rebellious. That day six Russians, one Frenchman, and one English-man were undergoing this punishment. The prisoners naturally called to be let out, but in vain. The sentry remained unmoved. No doubt he was awaiting orders from his superiors. Those inside the dungeon were being stifled. The Englishman broke the panes

408

of a small window, with the idea of freeing himself and his companions. The sentry, seeing him leaning out of the window, gave him a tremendous bayonet thrust in the chest. The wounded man fell like lead. A small but revolting struggle then took place. The prisoners attempted to get out, and the German soldier reddened his bayonet again and again with the blood of the men shut up, who saw with horror that the fire was increasing. The conflagration could not be extinguished by the other prisoners until it had done its work. The eight unhappy individuals who occupied the dungeon were corpses. For an hour afterward nothing was heard but shouts of indignation. It looked as if a formidable outbreak would take place. The guards were immediately reinforced, and we were surrounded by a number of German soldiers. The commander of the camp issued an order stating that he was sorry for what had occurred, and that on the following day he would allow the funeral of the victims to take place with ceremony.

PLUCKY ENGLISHMEN

"It was not all the prisoners who resigned themselves to suffer what was imposed on them. The English, above all, were the most rebellious. One day we were present at a scene which was celebrated with great rejoicing in all the camp. An English seaman, who already had one eye blind as a result of blows they had given him on a previous occasion, refused to obey two officers who ordered him to go to work. They reviled one another mutually, and finally the Englishman invited them to fight, giving them such punches that as a consequence we saw them for days afterward with their heads bandaged. The German soldiers were the first to scoff at the cowardice of their superiors. The English sailor was condemned to bread and water until the end of the war.

OLD MEN AND CHILDREN

"What saddened me most were the seventy old men and thirty children of 12 to 14 years of age, all English except one, who was French; they were youngsters who had been captured on board the vessels sunk, and ran from hut to hut asking for sweets and tobacco. Another day I also suffered a great shock on seeing the English Captain of our steamer Gravina, who had so far received no news from his family, who came up to us to beg bread. 'I have always been good to you. Have compassion on me. Give me a little piece of bread, if you can spare it.' We certainly had no reason to complain of his treatment of us, and we respected him. We gave him all we could."

CHAPTER XL

THE TERRIBLE WORK OF ARTILLERY IN WAR

SEVENTY PER CENT OF CASUALTIES DUE TO ARTILLERY FIRE — INCREASED RANGE—MODERN GUNS—HOW A BIG GUN IS AIMED—AWFUL DESTRUCTIVENESS OF MODERN GUNS.

A FULL century ago, Napoleon the Great, himself an artillery officer, had developed the fighting power of artillery of his day so as to make its fire a dominant factor on the battle-field. In the present war its action is even more important, since we learn from the front that seventy per cent of the casualties are due to artillery fire. It was the gun that took Liège and Antwerp, and it is the gun which held the contending armies pent up within a semicircle of fire. Once massed formations were abandoned, the gun lost its terrors to a great extent, and did not regain its place in military estimation till the introduction of the shrapnel shell.

This is a hollow steel projectile, packed with bullets, and containing a charge of powder in the base. (See Fig. 1.) It is exploded by a time-fuse, containing a ring of slowly burning composition which can be set so as to fire the powder during the flight of the shell, when it has traveled to within fifty yards of the enemy. The head is blown off, and the bullets are projected

411

forward in a sheaf, spreading outwards as they go. The British eighteen-pounder shell covers a space of ground some three hundred yards long by thirty-five yards wide with its 365 heavy bullets.

INCREASED RANGE

In 1885 the British brought out the twelve-pounder high-velocity field-gun, which remained for some years

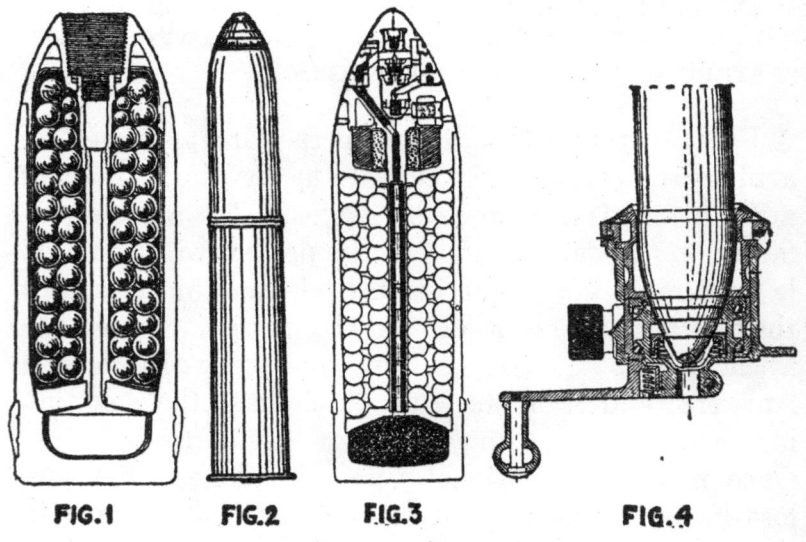

FIG. 1   **FIG. 2**   **FIG. 3**   **FIG. 4**

TYPES OF SHELLS

Fig. 1.—Shrapnel shell, packed with bullets that spread. Fig. 2.—A French quick-firer shell, like an enlarged rifle cartridge. Fig. 3.—The "Universal" shell, combining the action of shrapnel and high explosives. Fig. 4.—A fuse-setting machine.

the best gun in Europe. Its power was afterwards increased by giving it a fifteen-pounder shell, and, as a fifteen-pounder, it did good work in South Africa. Then came another development, the quick-firing gun now being used in the war, with a steel shield to protect the detachment. The quick-firing gun is badly named; its high rate of fire is only incidental, and is rarely of use in the combat. The essential feature of the "Q.F." gun, as it is generally styled, is that the carriage does not move on firing, so that the gunners can remain safely crouched behind the shield.

MODERN GUNS

The French gun as it was originally brought out has now been improved by the addition of a steel plate which closes the gap between the shields; and a steel shield is also provided to protect the officer standing on the upturned ammunition-wagon.

The carriage does not move, and the men remain in their positions behind the shield while the gun recoils between them. The carriage is prevented from sharing the movement of recoil by the spade at the end of the trail, which digs into the ground so as to "anchor" it.

RAPID FIRING

The gun-recoil carriage, as the new invention was called, increases the rate of fire, since there is no delay in running up. The French were quick to develop this new feature, and set to work to make the rate of fire as high as possible. Up till then the ammunition fired from a field-gun had consisted of a shell, a bag of powder, and a friction-tube introduced through the vent to fire the charge. This was called a round of ammunition, and its complexity was increased by the fuse, which was carried separately and screwed into the shell when the round was prepared for loading, and afterwards set with a key to burst the shell at the required distance. The French combined the whole of these separate parts into one, so that a round of "fixed" ammunition, as now used, looks exactly like an enlarged rifle cartridge. (See Fig. 2.)

Further, they did away with the cumbrous process of setting the fuse by hand, and introduced a machine which sets fuses as fast as the shell can be put into it. One of these machines is shown in Fig. 4. It is of a later pattern than that of the French service gun, being the one used by the Servians with their new gun made by the famous firm of Schneider of Creusot. The machine is set to the range ordered by the battery commander, the shell is dropped into it, and a turn of the handle sets the fuse.

HOW A BIG GUN IS AIMED

The independent line of sight is another modern device for facilitating the service of a gun. With this the gear for giving the gun the elevation necessary to carry a shell to the required distance is kept entirely separate from that used for pointing the gun at the target. The gun-layer has merely to keep his sighting telescope on the target, while another man puts on the range-elevation ordered by the battery commander.

The result of all these improvements is that the best quick-firing guns (among which the French gun is still reckoned) are capable of firing twenty-five rounds a minute. The German field-gun is hardly capable of twenty rounds a minute, being an inferior weapon converted from the old breech-loader.

But these high rates of fire are used only on emergency, as a gun firing twenty-five rounds a minute would exhaust the whole of the ammunition carried with it in the battery in three minutes.

One of the first consequences of the introduction of the shielded gun was the reappearance of the old common shell in an improved form. , The common shell is almost as old as Agincourt, and consisted simply of a hollow shell filled with powder, which exploded on striking the object. When shrapnel came into use most nations abandoned the common shell. But shrapnel proved almost ineffective against the shielded gun, and the gunners were indifferent to the bullets pattering on the steel shield in front of them. The answer to this was the high-explosive shell, a steel case filled with high explosive, such as melinite, which is the same as lyddite, shimose, or picric acid. This, when detonated upon striking a gun, can be relied upon to disable it and to kill the gunners behind it.

AWFUL DESTRUCTIVENESS OF MODERN GUNS

Of late years a shell which combines the action of the shrapnel and the high-explosive shell has been introduced. This is the "Universal" shell (see Fig. 3) invented by Major van Essen, of the Dutch Artillery. It is a shrapnel with a detachable head filled with high explosive. When burst during flight it acts like an ordinary shrapnel, and the bullets fly forward and sweep the ground in front of it; at the same time the head, with its explosive burster, flies forward and acts as a small but efficient high-explosive shell. These projectiles have been introduced for howitzers and for anti-aircraft guns, and some of the nations with new

415

equipments, such as the Balkan States, have them for their field-guns. Their introduction has, however, been delayed in Western Europe, as they are less efficient as such than the ordinary shrapnel, which is considered the principal field artillery projectile.

CHAPTER XLI

WHOLESALE DEATH BY POISONOUS GASES

CANADIAN VICTIMS — TRENCH GAS AT YPRES — AWFUL FORM OF SCIENTIFIC TORTURE—REPORT OF MEDICAL EXPERT — KIND OF GAS EMPLOYED — ALLIES FORCED TO USE SIMILAR METHODS.

KILLING by noxious gases may be, as the Germans claim, no more barbarous than slaughter by shrapnel, but it has been denounced in America as a violation of all written and unwritten codes and as a backward step toward savagery. Certainly the descriptions of responsible persons who have witnessed the pernicious work of the gas only deepens the horror with which all peace-loving citizens look upon "civilized" warfare.

The following description of the effect is told by a responsible British officer who visited some Canadians who were disabled by gas:

"The whole of England and the civilized world ought to have the truth fully brought before them in vivid detail, and not wrapped up as at present. When we got to the hospital we had no difficulty in finding out in which ward the men were, as the noise of the poor devils trying to get breath was sufficient to direct us.

CANADIAN VICTIMS

"There were about twenty of the worst cases in the ward, on mattresses, all more or less in a sitting position, strapped up against the walls. Their faces, arms, and hands were of a shiny, gray-black color. With their mouths open and leaden-glazed eyes, all were swaying slightly backward and forward trying to get breath. It was a most appalling sight. All these poor black faces struggling for life, the groaning and the noise of the efforts for breath was awful.

"There was practically nothing to be done for them except to give them salt and water and try to make them sick. The effect the gas has is to fill the lungs with a watery frothy matter, which gradually increases and rises until it fills up the whole lungs and comes to the mouth—then they die. It is suffocation, slow drowning, taking in most cases one or two days. Eight died last night out of twenty I saw, and the most of the others I saw will die, while those who get over the gas invariably develop acute pneumonia.

"It is without doubt the most awful form of scientific torture. Not one of the men I saw in the hospital had a scratch or wound. The Germans have given out that it is a rapid, painless death—the liars. No torture could be worse than to give them a dose of their own gas."

"TRENCH GAS" AT YPRES

Asphyxiating gases seem to have been first used by the Germans in the fighting around Ypres in April, 1915. The strong northeast wind, which was blowing from the German lines across the French trenches, became charged with a sickening, suffocating odor which was recognized as proceeding from some form of poisonous gas. The smoke moved like a vivid green wall some four feet in height for several hundred yards, extending to within two hundred yards of the extreme left of the Allies' lines. Gradually it rose higher and obscured the view from the level.

Soon strange cries were heard, and through the green mist, now growing thinner and patchy, there came a mass of dazed, reeling men who fell as they passed through the ranks. The greater number were unwounded, but they bore upon their faces the marks of agony.

The retiring men were among the first soldiers of the world whose sang-froid and courage have been proverbial throughout the war. All were reeling like drunken men.

AWFUL FORM OF SCIENTIFIC TORTURE

"The work of sending out the vapor was done from the advanced German trenches. Men garbed in a dress resembling the harness of a diver and armed with retorts or generators about three feet high and connected with ordinary hose-pipe turned the vapor loose toward the French lines. Some witnesses maintain that the Germans sprayed the earth before the trenches with a fluid which, being ignited, sent up the fumes. The German troops, who followed up this advantage with a direct attack, held inspirators in their mouths, these preventing them from being overcome by the fumes.

In addition to this, the Germans appear to have

fired ordinary explosive shells loaded with some chemical which had a paralyzing effect on all the men in the region of the explosion. Some chemical in the composi-

Right-hand figure: British soldier wearing respirator with air valve on top.

Left-hand figure: German with respirator and goggles armed with burning-oil-distributor.

USING DEADLY GAS AS A WEAPON IN WAR.

The German use of poisonous gases that asphyxiate soldiers of the enemy against whom they are directed, has made it necessary to devise a new defense. The pictures show the devices used by those who direct the use of the gases and those who have to meet their deadly vapors.

tion of these shells produced violent watering of the eyes, so that the men overcome by them were practically blinded for some hours.

The effect of the noxious trench-gas seems to be

slow in wearing away. The men come out of their violent nausea in a state of utter collapse. How many of the men left unconscious in the trenches when the French broke died from the fumes it is impossible to say, since those trenches were at once occupied by the Germans.

REPORT OF MEDICAL EXPERT

Dr. John S. Haldane, an authority on the physiology of respiration, who was sent by the British government to France to observe the effect of the gases, examined several Canadians who had been incapacitated by the gases.

"These men," he said, "were lying struggling for breath, and blue in the face. On examining their blood with a spectroscope and by other means I ascertained that the blueness was not due to the presence of any abnormal pigment. There was nothing to account for the blueness and their struggles for air but one fact, and that was that they were suffering from acute bronchitis, such as is caused by the inhalation of an irritant gas. Their statements were to the effect that when in the trenches they had been overwhelmed by an irritant gas produced in front of the German trenches and carried toward them by a gentle breeze.

"One of the men died shortly after our arrival. A post-mortem examination showed that death was due to acute bronchitis and its secondary effect. There was no doubt that the bronchitis and accompanying slow asphyxiation was due to irritant gas.

"Captain Bertram, of the eighth Canadian battalion, who is suffering from the effects of gas and from wounds, says that from a support trench about six hundred yards from the German lines he observed the gas. He saw first of all white smoke rising from the German trenches to a height of about three feet. Then in front of the white smoke appeared a green cloud which drifted along the ground to our trenches, not rising more than about seven feet from the ground.

"When it reached our first trenches, the men in these trenches were obliged to leave, and a number of them were killed by the effects of the gas. We made a counter-attack about fifteen minutes after the gas came over, and saw twenty-four men lying dead from the effects of the gas on a small stretch of road leading from the advanced trenches to the supports. He, himself, was much affected by the gas, and felt as though he could not breathe.

"These symptoms and other facts so far ascertained point to the use by the German troops of chlorine or bromide for the purpose of asphyxiation. There also are facts pointing to the use in German shells of other irritant substances. Still, the last of these agents are not of the same brutality and barbarous character as was the gas used in the attack on the Canadians.

"The effects are not those of any of the ordinary products of combustion of explosives. On this point the symptoms described left not the slightest doubt in my mind."

KIND OF GAS EMPLOYED

Various have been the opinions of chemists as to the kind of gas employed. Sir James Dewar, President of the Royal Institution, was of the opinion that it was liquid chlorine. Dr. F. A. Mason, of the Royal College of Science, considered it to have been bromine. Dr. Crocker, of the South-Western Polytechnic, said it may have been either carbon monoxide or liquid peroxide. Dr. W. J. Pope, Professor of Chemistry, Cambridge, and Sir E. Rutherford, Professor of Physics, Manchester University, agreed in thinking the gas to have been phosgene, a compound of carbon monoxide and chlorine, largely used in dye production in Germany.

"For some years," stated Sir James Dewar, "Germany has been manufacturing chlorine in tremendous quantities. . . . The Germans undoubtedly have hundreds of tons available. If several tons of liquid are allowed to escape into the atmosphere, where it immediately evaporates and forms a yellow gas, and if the wind is blowing in a favorable direction, it is the easiest thing for the Germans to inundate the country with poison for miles ahead of them.

"The fact that the gas is three times heavier than air makes escape from its disastrous effects almost impossible, for it drifts like a thick fog-cloud along the surface of the ground, overwhelming all whom it overtakes."

ALLIES FORCED TO USE SIMILAR METHODS

Of the German attack on the allied front near Ypres, Secretary of War, Earl Kitchener, speaking in the House of Lords on May 18, said:

"In this attack the enemy employed vast quantities of poisonous gases, and our soldiers and our French allies were utterly unprepared for this diabolical method of attack, which undoubtedly had been long and carefully prepared."

It was at this point that Earl Kitchener announced the determination of the Allies to resort to similar methods of warfare.

"The Germans," said Earl Kitchener, "have persisted in the use of these asphyxiating gases whenever the wind favored or other opportunity occurred, and His Majesty's government, no less than the French government, feel that our troops must be adequately protected by the employment of similar methods, so as to remove the enormous and unjustifiable disadvantage which must exist for them if we take no steps to meet on his own ground the enemy who is responsible for the introduction of this pernicious practice."

CHAPTER XLII

"USAGES OF WAR ON LAND": THE OFFICIAL GERMAN MANUAL

CRIMES IN BELGIUM EXPLAINED BY INSTRUC-
TIONS TO GERMAN OFFICERS—UNLIMITED DES-
TRUCTION THE END OF WAR—RULES OF CIVILIZED
WARFARE CLEARLY STATED—OTHER EXCELLENT
RULES.

THE BLACK crime of Louvain, the world-lamented destruction of the cathedral of Rheims, the denudation of the fair land of Belgium, with all its horrible attendant crimes, is explained, in part at least, by "Usages of War on Land," the official manual of instructions to military officers compiled by the general staff of the German army. It is an authoritative exposition of the rules of war as practiced by the Germans.

Two general principles bearing directly on the question of the invasion of Belgium are clearly stated in this guide:

"A war conducted with energy cannot be directed merely against the combatants of the enemy state and the positions they occupy, but it will and must in like manner seek to destroy the total intellectual and material resources of the latter. Humanitarian claims, such as the protection of men and their goods, can only be taken into consideration in so far as the nature and object of the war permit.

"The fact that such limitations of the unrestricted and reckless application of all the available means for the conduct of war, and thereby the humanization of the customary methods of pursuing war, really exist, and are actually observed by the armies of all civilized states, has in the course of the nineteenth century often led to attempts to develop, to extend, and thus to make universally binding these pre-existing usages of war; to elevate them to the level of laws binding nations and armies; in other words, to create a law of war. All these attempts have hitherto, with some few exceptions to be mentioned later, completely failed. If, therefore, in the following work the expression 'the law of war' is used, it must be understood that by it is meant not a written law introduced by the international agreements, but only a reciprocity of mutual agreement—a limitation of arbitrary behavior, which custom and conventionality, human friendliness and a calculating egotism have erected, but for the observance of which there exists no express sanction, but only 'the fear of reprisals' decides."

UNLIMITED DESTRUCTION THE END OF WAR

Put in plain language, these passages mean that there is no law of war which may not be broken at the dictates of interest. Unlimited destruction is the end, and only fear of reprisals need limit the means. The sentimental humanitarianism and flabby emotion which prevail elsewhere have no place in the bright lexicon of the German officer. "By steeping himself in military history," the manual clearly states, "an officer will be able to guard himself against excessive humanitarian notions" and learn that "certain severities are indispensable in war," and that "the only true humanity often lies in a ruthless application of them." Then there is laid down this comprehensive general rule:

"All means of warfare may be used without which the purpose of war cannot be achieved. On the other hand, every act of violence and destruction which is not demanded by the purpose of war must be condemned."

Interpreted by other passages in the volume, this implies that the end justifies the means. Barbarities may be forgiven if only they are useful. Thus "international law is in no way opposed to the exploitation of the crimes of third parties—assassination, incendiarism, robbery and the like—to the prejudice of the enemy."

RULES OF CIVILIZED WARFARE CLEARLY STATED

It must not be assumed, of course, that the German war manual is a defense of unlimited rapine. The rules of civilized warfare are usually stated clearly enough. But there are so many exceptions to the application of them that a zealous officer might well be pardoned if he regarded them as not binding whenever it was to his interest to ignore them. Thus, after a careful statement of the right of the inhabitants of an invaded country to organize for its defense, the advantages of "terrorism" are candidly set forth as outweighing these considerations in many instances. That policy has been illustrated in Belgium

427

very significantly. The difference between precept and practice is also seen in the prohibition of the bombardment of churches and unfortified towns. Regarding the latter the manual says:

"A prohibition by international law of the bombardment of open towns and villages which are not occupied by the enemy or defended was, indeed, put into words by The Hague regulations, but appears superfluous, since modern military history knows of hardly any such case."

Military history has been made since then, particularly by the German air raids on English seashore resorts.

OTHER EXCELLENT RULES

Several other excellent rules in the manual may be contrasted with German practice in the present war.

"No damage, not even the smallest, must be done unless it is done for military reasons.

"Contributions of war are sums of money which are levied by force from the people of an occupied country. They differ in character from requisitions in kind because they do not serve an immediate requirement of the army. Hence, requisitions in cash are only in the rarest cases justified by the necessities of war.

"The military government by the army of occupation carries with it only a temporary right to enjoy the property of others. It must, therefore, avoid every purposeless injury, it has no right to sell or dispose of the property."

"Usages of War on Land" makes interesting reading throughout, though the conclusions that the impartial reader will draw from it will not be in every case those which the German military authorities would have him draw.

CHAPTER XLIII

A GREAT FIGHT IN THE AIR

SETTING THE TRAP—A RING OF ENEMIES—FIRST
BLOOD—TO THE RESCUE—RETRIBUTION—A VIC-
TORIOUS FINISH.

THIS IS the story of how five British airplanes fought
twenty-seven Germans and beat them, sending eight to
earth crashing, crippled or in flames. It was on Saturday, May 5, 1917, a day of great heat, when there was
a haze so thick that you could hardly see the ground
from a height of 2,000 feet. Our men had started fairly
late in the afternoon, and at 5 o'clock were well over in
enemy country, when, with the sun at their backs, they
saw two enemy machines ahead. They tried to close
with the enemy, who made some show of giving fight.
It was only a show, however, for as our leading
machine drew near the Germans turned and made
with all speed for home.

SETTING THE TRAP

The tactics suggested that the two enemy machines
were only decoys, intended to lure our little flotilla as
far as possible from its base—and the suspicion was
soon confirmed. Even as we started to chase the two
flying enemies, out of the haze and void on all sides new
fleets came closing in.

430

The new arrivals flew in three formations, two of which contained eight machines, and the third contained nine, making twenty-five German airplanes, all of a uniform fighting type, to whom the other two, which now ceased to run away, joined themselves, making twenty-seven enemy machines in all.

A RING OF ENEMIES

One of the enemy fleets, taking advantage of the thick air, had passed behind our little squadron and came at it, as from the direction of our own lines, straight between it and the sun—an awkward direction from which to have an enemy flying at you in the late afternoon, when the sun is getting fairly low. The other two fleets came from the southeast and northeast. As they approached they spread out so that our men were ringed around with enemies on every side.

The fight began at about 11,000 feet; but in the course of the things that followed it ranged anywhere from 3,000 to 12,000 up and down the ladders of heaven. And an extraordinary fact is that, all the while that it went on, the German anti-aircraft guns below kept at work. Usually, as soon as airplanes engage overhead, the "Archies" are silent for fear of hitting the wrong man; and whether the German gunners were drunk with excitement at what was going on above them, or whether it was that our machines formed so isolated and compact a mass in the heart of the great maelstrom that it seemed still possible to shoot at them in safety, is not known, At all events, the tumult in the skies was increased by the constant pumping into the tangled mass of shells from the ground.

431

FIRST BLOOD

The actual fighting lasted for a full hour, from 5 to 6 o'clock, an extraordinary time for such a thing, and during all that hour our men fought tooth and nail. And the fight had lasted but a few minutes when we drew first blood, and an enemy machine which Captain A. had attacked went down in flames, with the wings of one side shot away. Then it was Lieutenant B.'s turn. He caught his adversary at close range fairly, and the German airplane went down, turning over and over as it fell straight down 11,000 feet, leaving a trail of smoke behind. Lieutenant C. scored next, his enemy's machine spinning plumb down to where, somewhere below the haze, it must have crashed.

Then, for a moment, it seemed that our luck was turning. Lieutenant B.'s engine gave out and he was "compelled to leave the formation." It is a simple phrase, but what it means is that, helpless and with engine still, the airplane dropped out of the fight from 11,000 feet down to 3,000 feet. It was a dizzying drop, and as he fell, an enemy, seeing him defenseless and scenting easy prey, went after him.

TO THE RESCUE

But other eyes were watching. Lieutenant C. saw his crippled comrade slipping downward and saw the German diving after. Quick as a flash he followed, and before the German could do his work the British airplane was almost touching the tail of his machine, and in another second the German turned

432

clean over in the air and then crashed nose foremost down into the abyss.

Then, almost by a miracle, B.'s engine caught its breath again. Once more the machine was under control, and B., who was one of those who were new to the game, climbed and rejoined formation. Some 8,000 feet he had to climb, with the baffled "Archies" blazing at him from below, up into the inverted hell above, where his four comrades were fighting enemies who outnumbered them six to one. Just as he "rejoined" another German fell. It was A.'s second victim of the day, and friend and foe alike saw the machine go, sheeted in flames, down into the gulf.

RETRIBUTION

Then once again it seemed that a throw had gone against us, for, still under control, but with flames bursting from its reserve petrol tank, one of our machines began to drop. Again an enemy, glimpsing an easy quarry, dived for the flaming ruin as it fell, but, quicker than he, A. also dived, and while our crippled machine, still belching flames, slid off, with its nose set for home, the German, mortally hit, dropped like a stone.

It was just retribution. The unwritten laws of this marvelous game prescribe that no honorable fighter attack an enemy in flames. Such an enemy is out of the fight, and has trouble enough for a brave man. The German who dived for our burning machine knew that he was doing an unchivalrous thing, and it may be that that knowledge unnerved him so that he paid the penalty.

Strangely enough, our burning airplane got home. I have seen the wreckage, with the reserve petrol tank on the roof bearing two bullet holes on one side and great ragged tears on the other where the bullets passed out. The whole tank is scorched and crumpled. The flames had burned away the whole central span of the upper plane. The thick rear main spar was charred and burned through, and two ribs were completely severed and hung with loose, blackened ends. Yet, like a great blazing meteor, it crossed our lines and came to earth, not, indeed, at its own home, but on safe and friendly ground; and, as another airman said to me in admiration, "He made a perfectly topping landing."

A VICTORIOUS FINISH

Meanwhile the wonderful fight was drawing to a close. The British pilot, Lieutenant D., emptied a belt from his machine gun into an enemy when so close that his wings almost brushed the other's rudder; and the enemy turned turtle, clear over on his back, and, spurting out a thick column of black smoke, went down.

Some of the enemy were already drawing off, but our men were in no mood to let them go. It is harder to get out of a losing fight than it is to begin it, and before the enemy mob could disentangle itself from the battle two more of their machines had gone to earth—one, his third in the fight, falling to Lieutenant C. and one to Lieutenant E.

Then the last four of our machines, still lords of the air, came home.

CHAPTER XLIV

WAR'S REPAIR SHOP: CARING FOR THE WOUNDED

EFFICIENCY OF THE RED CROSS SERVICE—THE
BANDAGING CAMP—THE SANITATION COMPANY—
THE HOSPITAL BARGE.

AMID THE dreadful welter of carnage and its attendant agony which spells modern warfare one ray of brightness appears in the universal gloom in the shape of the highly organized efficiency of the Red Cross Service, which waits upon battle. Die Umschau, of Berlin, printed an admirable description of its activities from the pen of Professor Rupprecht, one of the chief organizers of the German Military Hospital Service, of which we give an abstract:

"The stretcher-bearers of the infantry—four to each company—who bear the Red Cross symbol on the arm, when a battle is on hand, gather at the end of the battalion (sixteen men with four stretchers) and then proceed to the Infantry Sanitation Car. As soon as the 'bandaging camp' is made ready . . . they go to the front with stretchers and knapsacks in order to be ready to give aid to the wounded as soon as possible. Musicians and others are employed as assistant stretcher-bearers. These wear a red band on the sleeve but do not come under the provisions of the Geneva Treaty."

THE BANDAGING CAMP

Similar arrangements are made for the cavalry. The so-called "bandaging camp" is for the purpose of gathering the wounded and examining and classifying them. It should be both protected and accessible, and if possible near a water supply. At the end of a battle it is the duty of the troops to search trenches, woods, houses, etc., for the wounded, protect them

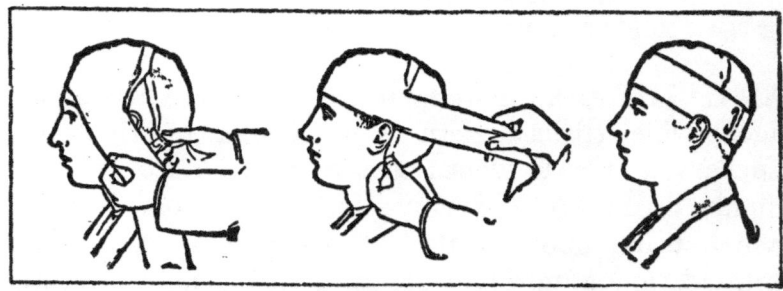

QUICKER AND EASIER THAN BANDAGES: THE "TABLOID" ADJUSTABLE HEAD-DRESSING.

This dressing for head-wounds in the form of a cap, can be applied in a few seconds, and remains comfortably in position. It can be washed, sterilized, and used repeatedly. The diagrams show the method of adjusting and the dressing in position.

against plunderers and carry them to the bandaging camp, as also to bury the dead.

"At the bandaging camp the surgeons and their assistants must revive and examine the men and make them ready for transport. Operations are seldom practicable or necessary here. The chief concern is to bandage wounds of bones, joints, and arteries carefully. . . . Severe hemorrhages usually stop of themselves, on which account it is seldom desirable to bind the limb tightly above the wound. The wound itself must never be touched, washed, or probed. After the clothing is removed or cut away it must merely be covered with the contents of the bandage package."

Every soldier carries two of these packages in a pocket on the lower front corner of his left coat-tail. Each package contains a gauze bandage enclosed in a waterproof cover. There is sewed to this bandage a gauze compress saturated with sublimate and of a red color. It is so arranged that the bandage can be taken hold of with both hands without touching the red compress.

It is strongly impressed upon the stretcher-bearers and all assistants that cases having wounds in the abdomen are not transportable and must on no account be given food or drink; also that bleeding usually stops of itself. They are taught, too, that touching, washing, or probing the wound is injurious, and that only *dry* bandages must be placed on the wound— never those that are damp or impervious.

"The wounded who are capable of marching leave their ammunition, except for a few cartridges, at the bandaging camp, are provided if need be with a simple protective bandage, and march first to the nearest 'camp for the slightly wounded,' or to the nearest 'resting-camp.' The rest of the wounded are removed as soon as possible directly to the field hospitals or lazarets. If obliged to remain for a while before removal they are protected by portable tents, wind-screens, etc. . . . If it is impossible to carry the wounded along in a retreat they are left in care of the hospital staff under the protection of the Red Cross."

437

THE SANITATION COMPANY

In case of a big battle a sanitation company remains near the bandaging camp. Every army corps has three of these companies, which, together with the twelve field lazarets of the corps, form a sanitation battalion.

As soon as it is apparent that the troops will remain in one locality for some length of time the smaller bandaging camps or stations are supplemented by a chief bandaging station some distance in the rear, and if possible, near a highway and near houses. At this spot there are arranged places for the entry and exit of the wagons carrying the wounded, for the unloading of the wounded, for the dying and the dead, for cooking, and a "park" for wagons and horses.

Each field lazaret is capable of caring for two hundred men, but this capacity may be extended by making use of local aid. The supplies carried are very comprehensive, including tents, straw mattresses and woolen blankets, lighting materials, clothing and linen, tools, cooking utensils, soap, writing materials, drugs and medical appliances, sterilization ovens, bandages, instruments, and an operating-table. As fast as possible the patients treated are sent home on furlough or removed to permanent military hospitals. The very perfection of this system but deepens the tragic irony that occasions it.

THE HOSPITAL BARGE

One very important development in the care for the wounded is the introduction of the hospital barge. The rivers and canals of France offer splendid opportunities for conveying wounded from point to point. This new method of transport was foreshadowed in an article in the London Times, in which the writer, in describing the hospital barges, said:

"The north of France, as is well known, is exceedingly rich in waterways—rivers and canals. The four great rivers, the Oise, the Somme, the Sambre, and the Escaut (Scheldt), are connected by a network of canals—quiet and comfortable waterways at present almost free of traffic. So far as the reaching of any particular spot is concerned these waterways may be said to be ubiquitous. They extend, too, right into Belgium, and have connection with the coast at various points—for example, Ostend. Here, then, is a system of 'roads' for the removal of the wounded, a system which, if properly used, can be made to relieve greatly the stress of work imposed upon the ambulance motor cars and trains. Here also is the ideal method of removal.

"The Ile de France is lying at present at the Quai de Grenelle, near the Eiffel Tower. This is a Seine barge of the usual size and type, blunt-nosed, heavily and roomily built. You enter the hold by a step-ladder, which is part of the hospital equipment. This is a large chamber not much less high from floor to ceiling than an ordinary room, well lighted, and ventilated by means of skylights. The walls of the hold have been painted white; the floor has been thoroughly scrubbed out for the reception of beds, of which some forty to fifty will be accommodated.

"The forward portion of the barge can accommodate more beds, and there is no reason why a portion of it

439

should not be walled in and used as an operating room, more especially since in the bow a useful washing apparatus is fitted. The barge is heated by stoves, and a small electric plant could easily be installed. The barges are used in groups of four, and a small tug supplies the motive power. In favorable circumstances about fifty kilometers a day can be traveled."

The barges employed are big, roomy barges one hundred and twenty feet long, sixteen feet broad, and ten feet high. Care is taken to use only fairly new and clean barges which have been used in the conveyance of timber or stone or other clean and harmless cargoes.

CHAPTER XLV

THE TERRIBLE DISASTER AT HALIFAX

WAR'S HORRORS BROUGHT HOME—PLACING THE
BLAME—A FATAL MISUNDERSTANDING—A SUDDEN
CATACLYSM—A FRIGHTFUL SCENE OF DEATH AND
DESTRUCTION — RICHMOND BEARS THE BRUNT —
CURIOUS FREAKS OF THE BLAST—"WORSE THAN
THE BATTLEFIELDS OF FRANCE"—THE PEOPLE FLEE
FOR SAFETY—RELIEF WORK BEGINS—A BLIZZARD
BRINGS ADDED MISERY.

WE MUST look to the battlefields of Europe to find
a parallel for the Horror of Halifax which resulted in
the snuffing out of the lives of 1,200 men, women and
children, the maiming of 3,000 additional human
beings, and the destruction of property valued at more
then $25,000,000.

And even in European battle areas it would be
difficult to find a parallel, for in the direct business of
war only men are concerned—men who go knowingly
into the maw of death with a fighting chance. But
hundreds of the victims of the Halifax disaster were
women and children who did not have a fighting
chance. Like a bolt from the blue came the Grim
Specter, Death, mercilessly swinging his saber, cutting
down the young and the old, and the strong and the
weak without discrimination.

THE DISASTER AT HALIFAX

The disaster sent a shudder through the civilized world, and gave America her first "closeup" of the great war, for it was the explosion of a munitions ship that brought ruin, suffering and grief indescribable to ill-fated Halifax.

Probably the exact cause of the disaster will never be known, but here are the facts that investigating officials have thus far been able to drag from the chaos:

The Norwegian steamship Imo, commanded by Captain From, and bound for Rotterdam with a relief cargo for the Belgians, was moving toward the sea in the Narrows leading from the harbor to Bedford Basin. The French munitions ship Mont Blanc, loaded with 5,000 tons of explosives was coming into the harbor. The vessels collided, and in a few minutes descended the blow which wiped out a portion of Halifax.

PLACING THE BLAME

Members of the crew of the Imo declared that the Mont Blanc was to blame for the collision, while the captain of the latter ship put the blame upon the Imo. A statement made by the crew of the Imo, follows:

"Our ship was moving toward the sea when the Mont Blanc was seen coming in our direction. The French vessel blew two blasts on her whistle, indicating that she was going to the starboard. The Imo replied with two blasts, and the Mont Blanc turned. We thought that the French ship could pass in safety, but the

442

distance was too short and the Imo rammed the Mont Blanc on the starboard side.

"Captain From was standing on the bridge when the explosion came; his head was blown off. The body of William Hayes, our pilot, was hurled to the beach, and the Imo was dashed upon the rocky shore."

Captain Lamedoc, of the Mont Blanc, gave his version of the causes of the collision, as follows:

"We had on board 5,000 tons of freight, mostly explosives. The ballast tanks were filled with water. In the forward hold was stored picric acid; then came a steel bulkhead, and in the next hold was T. N. T., a high explosive. We also had T. N. T. in the third hold, and on the top of the forward deck was stored about twenty barrels of benzol over the picric acid, with a steel deck in between.

"It was a clear morning; the water was smooth and we were at half speed on the starboard side toward the Bedford Basin. There were no vessels in our course until we sighted the Belgian relief ship Imo coming out of Bedford Basin and heading for the Dartmouth shore. She was more than two miles away at the time. We signaled we would keep the Mont Blanc on the starboard tack going up to the basin, where we were to anchor.

"We headed a little more inshore so as to make clear our purpose to the Imo. She signaled that she was coming on the port, which would bring her on the same side with us. We were keeping to the right or starboard, according to pilotage rules, and could not understand what the Imo meant. But we kept on our course, hoping that she would come down, as she should, on the starboard, which would keep her on the Halifax side of the harbor and the Mont Blanc. The next thing we knew the Imo had rammed us."

A FATAL MISUNDERSTANDING

Perusal of these statements shows that the collision resulted from a misunderstanding of some sort, and just who was to blame will have to be determined by marine experts. Both Captain From and the pilot Hayes are dead, and can never speak in their own defense.

The business life of Halifax had just begun for the day at nine o'clock on the morning of December 6, 1917, when the town was shaken to its foundations by an explosion which baffles all description.

THE SUDDEN CATACLYSM

Persons in the streets were picked up bodily as if by a giant hand and hurled to the ground; occupants of office buildings cowered under showers of falling glass and plaster.

An area of about two miles square known as Richmond, in the northeastern section of the city, was laid in ruins; hundreds of men, women and children were crushed to death as buildings collapsed, and many others were pinned in the débris and died a terrible death before they could be released. The Richmond section became a veritable inferno when fire swept the ruins, cutting off the escape of scores buried in the wreckage.

Large numbers were injured by the collapse of the Arena Rink, the Military Gymnasium, the sugar

444

refinery and grain elevator. The walls of the Armory crashed inward, killing six soldiers; the buildings of the Protestant Orphanage crumpled up like so much pasteboard; the matron and all but two of the children were killed. The plant of the Richmond Printing Company fell like a house of sand and thirty girl-workers were shot into eternity. The great trainshed of the Candian Pacific Railway swayed as if in the clutches of an earthquake, and then, with a grinding roar, collapsed like a structure of matchwood, burying a hundred or more persons in an entanglement of steel girders, sheet metal and glass. The Military Hospital, Admiralty House, Government Dock Yards, Garrison Chapel, Province Parliament Building, Post Office, Deaf and Dumb Asylum, Home for the Aged and nearly all the department stores, rocked and crumbled under the blow.

A FRIGHTFUL SCENE OF DEATH AND DESTRUCTION

Cries of fear, the moans of the injured, the shrieks of the dying and the frantic voices of frightened children could be heard above the din of grinding girders, falling timbers and breaking glass. A great, uncontrollable terror seized the inhabitants of Halifax, and held them in the grip of helplessness for the time being.

The explosion was heard more than a hundred miles away, and the jar of the detonation crippled electric installations in all telephone, telegraph and cable stations within a radius of forty miles, preventing Halifax from summoning aid in her great hour of need.

The damage along the waterfront was severe, many

men composing crews of ships in the harbor being killed or injured.

RICHMOND BEARS THE BRUNT

But the heaviest force of the blow fell at Richmond, where most of the dwellings were frame structures. A western tornado could not have flattened these wooden houses more quickly and effectually. The lives of mothers and housewives were cut off while they busied themselves with their home duties, and the chatter of little children was stopped forever by falling walls and beams. Kitchen stoves were dashed to pieces, the live coals setting fires simultaneously in many places. In scores of cases occupants of houses who had escaped without injury, or who were only slightly injured, were baffled by the flames in their search for members of their families, and were forced to stand impotently by while what had once been their homes became funeral pyres for their loved ones. A number of children of the Richmond section were killed by the collapse of public school buildings; teachers who escaped injury, worked heroically to save their pupils

CURIOUS FREAKS OF THE BLAST

The explosion brought forth a crop of freak occurrences some of them so remarkable as to be almost unbelievable. The case of Mayers, a third officer of the British transport Middleton Castle, stands out almost in the light of a modern miracle. The transport was not more than 200 yards from the Mont Blanc when the crash came. Mayers was on deck, ready to step into a small boat, to go ashore. When he regained consciousness, he was prone on high ground a half mile away. There was not a piece of clothing on his body, but he was not seriously injured.

M. L. Backer, a telegraph operator, entered his home to find his baby in a cradle, safe under a blanket which was covered with broken glass. Part of a shell, weighing eighteen pounds had ploughed through the wall of his home, two feet above where the baby slept.

As the town rocked under the terrific blast, Lola Burns, eight-year-old daughter of John Burns, of Granville Street, was on her knees by her cot saying her prayers. The house collapsed, and hours later little Lola was found in the midst of the wreckage, hemmed in by fallen timbers, but quite unharmed, still on her knees and praying fervently.

In a cellar at Richmond a soldier in uniform was seen digging frantically. It was Private Henneberry, who had been overseas with the Sixty-third Battalion and returned home on furlough.

"Here was my home," explained the soldier briefly. "I am sure I heard a moan a moment ago."

Others gave him a hand and presently Hanneberry's eighteen-months-old daughter Olive was taken out alive from under a kitchen stove. Her wounds were superficial, but the soldier's joy was shortlived. A little more digging exposed the bodies of his wife and five other children.

"WORSE THAN THE BATTLEFIELDS OF FRANCE"

A graphic description of the explosion and the terrifying scenes that followed were furnished by Duncan Gray, a lieutenant in the Canadian Army. He was

447

engaged in inspecting shells in a shed on the water-front when the devastation began, and barely escaped before the building collapsed. Here is his story:

"A few seconds after the roar of the explosion, a gust of wind swept through the shed, and then down came pillars, boards and beams. I rushed to the open, and the sight that met my gaze filled me with horror.

"I have been in the trenches in France, I have gone over 'the top', and friends and comrades have been shot in my presence. I have seen scores of dead men lying upon the battlefield; I am familiar with the horror of 'No Man's Land' but the sight that greeted me in Halifax was a thousand times worse than any of these, and a thousand times more pathetic.

"I saw people lying around under timbers, stones and other débris, some battered beyond recognition, and others groaning in their last agonies.

"Rushing here and there I struggled to assist them, and, as near as I can remember, I pulled twenty-two men and children from under the wreckage. I was right in the middle of the district the hardest hit and therefore witnessed the full horror of the situation.

"Partly blinded by smoke from burning dwellings, I groped around assisting some of the poor mothers and little ones who were running about screaming and searching vainly for lost ones, in many instances never to be seen by them again. I struggled on, coming across more and more bodies of dead men, women and children. Death was everywhere. The district became a living hell as the fires gained headway. I saw many men who acted as if they had gone mad. Thinking only of their wives and children, they dashed

448

about in the burning débris, hazarding their lives with the single thought of rescuing their loved ones."

Investigators for the Canadian government have established that it was twenty-five minutes after the collision of the Imo and the Mont Blanc that the explosion took place.

THE PEOPLE FLEE FOR SAFETY

At the first shock houses rocked, vessels broke from their moorings and bits of shell whistled through the air. The first thought of the terrified populace was that Halifax was the subject of a German air raid. With buildings tottering and falling on every side, hundreds of persons, many of them insufficiently clad, rushed into the streets. The police gave orders that everybody should flee to the south of the city, and in a brief space of time Barrington Street resembled a road of Belgium or Serbia when the inhabitants of those afflicted countries fled before invading German armies.

Every variety of vehicle was pressed into service for the sick and the infirm. Men, women and children, many of them carrying hastily snatched belongings, hurried along the pavements and overflowed the streets. Stores were deserted, houses were forsaken, and the entrance to Point Pleasant Park was soon black with human beings, some massed in groups and others running frantically about. The wildest rumors were in circulation and every new bearer of tidings was immediately surrounded and besieged with anxious inquiries. Then came the word that the danger was under control, and the fugitives flocked back to their homes only to find them in ruins.

RELIEF WORK BEGINS

The work of rescue and relief was promptly organized. The Academy of Music and many other public buildings were thrown open to house the homeless. Five hundred tents were erected on the common and these were occupied by troops who surrendered their barracks to homeless women and children.

A score of morgues were improvised and these were soon filled with the dead. The first contribution to the morgues from the ruined districts was twenty-five wagonloads of corpses, many of them crushed or charred beyond recognition.

Relief parties searched the ruins for persons imprisoned under timbers and other débris. Many rescues were made.

At noon of the fatal day, telegraph wires were mended, and the news of the Halifax Horror flashed over the North American continent. Fire-fighting companies arrived from Truro, Amherst, Moncton and Windsor on special trains and they came in good time to save the principal British port in the western hemisphere from complete destruction. After several hours of heroic work the fire-fighters placed the flames under control.

A BLIZZARD BRINGS ADDED MISERY

As if Halifax had not suffered enough, the next day a howling blizzard swooped down from the north, covering the stricken city with three feet of snow. A

450.

biting wind added to the misery of the thousands of homeless. The explosion had broken nearly all of the window glass in the town, so that even houses that had not been wrecked were exposed to the bitter blasts.

But relief was now on the way from all sections of the United States and Canada. The American Red Cross set its great relief machinery into motion, with the result that tons of supplies were quickly en route to the city of misery. Boston sent a relief train and a food ship, and money, food and clothing poured in from New York, Philadelphia, Chicago, Montreal, Toronto, and other cities.

With courage and enterprise characteristic of the Anglo-Saxon, residents of Halifax recovered quickly from the effects of the blow and began the work of rehabilitation. Precautions were instituted to prevent repetition of the catastrophe.

CHAPTER XLVI

THE WONDERFUL CAMPAIGN FOR JERUSALEM

THE HOLY CITY AT LAST RESTORED TO CHRISTIAN-
ITY—TURKEY'S FUTILE EFFORT AGAINST THE SUEZ
CANAL—THE BRITISH FORCES INVADE PALESTINE
—THE TURKS DRIVEN NORTH—SMASHING THE
TURKISH CHARGE—TERRIFIC DIFFICULTIES CON-
FRONT THE BRITISH—SAVING SACRED BETHLEHEM
—THE FALL OF THE CITY—DISTRESS IN EARLY
DAYS OF THE WAR—AMERICAN ENTERPRISE AIDS
—A HISTORIC CITY.

THE FALL of Jerusalem to the British forces under General Allenby on December 9, 1917, was hailed as a good omen in all of the Allied countries which were fighting German military autocracy so that democracy might be saved.

Following as it did the serious Allied reverses in Italy, and the collapse of military resistance in Russia, the capture of the birthplace of Christianity caused new hope to flame in the breasts of depressed millions in America, England, France and Italy.

THE HOLY CITY AT LAST RESTORED TO CHRISTIANITY

The capitulation of the Holy City marked the end, with two brief interludes, of more than 1,200 years' possession of the seat of the Christian religion by the Mohammedans.

On the Road to Jerusalem.

The Imperial Camel Corps gave valuable aid in the capture of the Holy City.

THE TERRIBLE HAVOC WROUGHT BY THE GREAT EXPLOSION AT HALIFAX.

This photograph tells the story of the suffering and misery caused by the explosion with graphic realism. The great piles of debris from razed homes, intermingled with the dead and wounded, presented a sight worse than the battlefields of Europe. The wrecked building on the hill was a printing plant in which a great number of girls and men were killed.

THE CAMPAIGN FOR JERUSALEM

For 673 years the Holy City had been in control of the Turks, the last Christian ruler of Jerusalem being the German Emperor Frederick, whose short-lived domination lasted from 1229 to 1244. Hence the joy of millions upon millions of Christians that the mystic city amid the hills of Palestine, where stood Solomon's Temple, where rested the Roman legions, and close by, where died Christ, rests again under the cross.

TURKEY'S FUTILE EFFORT AGAINST THE SUEZ CANAL

But, apart from its religious significance and apart from its connection with the campaign being waged against Turkey by the British in Mesopotamia, the fall of Jerusalem marked the definite collapse of the long-protracted efforts of the Turks to capture the Suez Canal and invade Egypt.

Almost the first move made by Turkey after her entrance into the war was a campaign against Egypt across the great desert of the Sinai peninsula.

In November, 1914, a Turkish army, variously estimated at from 75,000 to 250,000 men marched on the Suez Canal and succeeded in reaching within striking distance of the great artificial waterway at several points. For a number of months there was bitter fighting, the canal being defended by an Anglo-Egyptian army aided by Australians and New Zealanders, and French and British forces.

For the greater part of 1915 conflicting reports of the situation were received from the belligerents, but in December of that year definite information showed that the Turks had been driven back as far as El Arish, about eighty-five miles east of the canal. A lull occurred which lasted for six months and in June, 1916, the Turks again advanced as far as Katieh, about fifteen miles east of the canal.

THE BRITISH FORCES INVADE PALESTINE

Here, they were decisively defeated, losing more than 3,000 prisoners and a great amount of equipment. Another period followed in which the situation was greatly confused through the vagueness and contradictory character of the official statements, but in December, 1916, the British stormed El Arish, and a few days later severely defeated the Turks at Maghdabah, about sixty miles to the south on the same front. Within two weeks the invaders were driven out of Egypt, and the British forces crossed the border into Palestine.

There had been no hint from either official or unofficial sources as to a British intention to undertake a definite invasion of the Holy Land, and it was with intense surprise that the world learned on March 7th that the British forces had captured El Khulil, fifteen miles south of Jerusalem. El Khulil is the modern name of ancient Hebron.

The campaign lapsed into stagnancy through the heated period, but was actively renewed with the setting in of cooler weather last fall.

THE TURKS DRIVEN NORTH

Early in November the British activity resulted in the capture of Beersheba, forty miles south of Jerusalem. Simultaneously a coastal column became active. By November 7th, the city of Gaza was in

British hands, and the English were pursuing the Turks northward after having inflicted casualties estimated as in excess of 10,000. In the meantime, the British inland force was again up in the neighborhood of Hebron, where the Turks were reported organizing for the defense of Jerusalem.

General Allenby, the British commander, kept his forces near the coast in rapid motion, and pushed on to Jaffa, the port of Jerusalem, in mid-November. On November 22d, the British had arrived within five miles of Jerusalem, on the northwest, and on December 7th, General Allenby announced that he had definite possession of Hebron. Jerusalem was thus virtually cut off on all sides but the east. Then began the gigantic British encircling movement, which enfolded on the south the little town of Bethlehem, where Christ was born.

SMASHING THE TURKISH CHARGE

In attacks preceding the surrender of Jerusalem, the Turks employed storming troops in successive assaults on Nebi Zamuel, northwest of the Holy City, then held by London troops. The final Turkish assault was preceded by terrific shelling, and as the cannonade died away the Turks rushed forward, yelling and brandishing their long sabers.

The British poured a fearful machine-gun fire into the advancing line, which melted away like snow before an April sun. Then the English, with leveled bayonets, charged the disordered mob of heathen; jabbing, stabbing and cutting, they hewed their way through the masses of the enemy until, after a few moments of terrific hand-to-hand fighting, a panic seized the Sons of Mohammed, and they fled in terror from the battlefield. Hundreds were cut down while they were trying to escape.

The Turks had a strong line west, south and north-east of Jerusalem, and they were well provided with machine-guns. Their artillery dominated the crests over which the British would have to advance. Some Turkish guns were placed just outside the city walls, making it impossible to reply to their fire without endangering the town.

TERRIFIC DIFFICULTIES CONFRONT THE BRITISH

And that was not all; a torrential rain made the roads impassable, while a chilly east wind pierced the soldiers to the bone. The problems of supply and transport nearly drove the English officers to despair; the camels could not keep a foothold on the slippery paths. Nevertheless, British bulldog persistency won, for the food and ammunition supply was maintained fully in spite of all obstacles.

The attack began on the night of December 7th, when the British moved up under the cover of darkness. The assault pivoted on Nebi Zamuel, from which the Londoners advanced eastward toward Jerusalem, while another British column ascended the Hebron road, threatening the town from the south.

SAVING SACRED BETHLEHEM

They found Hebron evacuated, but encountered resistance around Bethlehem, where the unscrupulous Turks had also posted guns, so that the counter-battery work would endanger the sacred village. The British had the disagreeable experience of being shelled without the ability to reply. But they pressed bravely forward, and by noon of December 8th, were two miles north of Bethlehem.

In the meantime the Londoners had a hard task on the steep slopes of the historic Judean Hills, where it was impossible to bring field guns to their support, but some mountain batteries and howitzers rendered magnificent service, and by seven o'clock in the morning the intrepid Britishers had stormed and captured all enemy works west of the town. In the face of galling fire, they swept over hill after hill, clubbing and bayoneting as they went. Nothing could stop their enthusiastic rush.

Single-handed, a British corporal captured an entire Turkish battery; yelling like a madman, he leaped over the breastwork behind which the battery was concealed, killed three Mohammedan gunners with his automatic pistol, bayoneted another, and beat out the brains of a fourth with the flat side of his saber. The remainder of the Mohammedan gunners did not wait for their turn, but took to their heels.

But the Turks still held the last line on the ridge overlooking Jerusalem, having posted numerous machine-guns in the houses of Jewish and German colonists in the farthest outskirts of the town.

THE FALL OF THE CITY

The position was charged late in the afternoon of the 8th, and old campaigners thrilled as the Londoners, with leveled bayonets and ringing English yells,

457

rushed into the nest of machine guns. Seemingly unmindful of the storm of lead and steel, the Britons raced forward with faces grim with determination. It was a magnificent exhibition of courage, and it was crowned with success. The fierceness of the assault undermined the morale of the Turks, and they broke ranks and fled, abandoning their guns.

During the night the Turks withdrew to the north and the east of the city, and at 8 o'clock on the morning of the 9th, the mayor and the chief of police came out with a flag of truce and surrendered. Acceptance of the surrender was made formally at noon, without actually entering the city, only pickets being posted to prevent surprises. While these events were transpiring, British troops swept through the suburbs northward, being subjected to machine-gun fire from the Mount of Olives and Mt. Scopus. The ridge of Mt. Scopus was stormed with the bayonet, and the Turks were cleared from the Mount of Olives.

Further north, the Turks were established in a long series of trenches around the village of Beltikes. These trenches were carried with a rush, and the British lines advanced beyond the village. Welsh troops, advancing from the south, pushed across the road east of Jerusalem leading to Jericho, and thrust back Turkish reinforcements advancing along this road to succor Jerusalem. In the course of these operations, the Welsh captured more than 1,000 prisoners, besides 700 wounded Turks in the hospitals of Jerusalem.

There was a great demonstration of joy when General Allenby advanced to take the surrender of the Holy City. Flowers were showered on the British troops, and the populace wept and shouted with joy at their deliverance from the hands of the oppressors.

In the House of Commons on December 12th, Premier Lloyd George read the following telegram from General Allenby, telling of the capture of the Holy City:

"I entered the city officially with a few of my staff, the commanders of the French and Italian detachments, the heads of the political missions, and the military attachés of France, Italy and America.

"The procession was all afoot, and at Jaffa gate I was received by the guards representing England, Scotland, Ireland, Wales, Australia, New Zealand, India, France and Italy. The population received me well.

"Guards have been placed over the Holy places. My military Governor is in contact with the acting custodians and the Latin and Greek representatives. The Governor has detailed an officer to supervise the Holy places. The Mosque of Omar, and the area around it, have been placed under Moslem control, and a military cordon of Mohammedan officers and soldiers has been established around the Mosque.

"Orders have been given that no non-Moslem is to pass within the cordon without permission of the military Governor and the Moslem in charge."

The telegram also announced that a proclamation in Arabic, Hebrew, English, French, Italian, Greek and Russian, had been posted in the citadel, and on all the walls, proclaiming martial law, and intimating that all Holy places should be maintained and protected according to the customs and beliefs of those to whose faith they are sacred.

THE CAMPAIGN FOR JERUSALEM

DISTRESS IN EARLY DAYS OF THE WAR

In the early days of the war and the abortive Turkish attacks against the Suez Canal, the people of Jerusalem were so famished they would fight for the bodies of animals that died in and about the town. On every side there was suspicion and persecution. Every one suspected of sympathizing with the Allies were imprisoned or killed. Hundreds of persons were executed. Among these was the Mufti of Gaza, belonging to a distinguished Arab family, who, after an attempt to escape, was captured and hanged with his son outside the Jaffa gate.

The American colony of about 300 souls was not molested. It did noble work in relieving distress, aided by funds from America. When the United States broke off relations with Turkey these funds were discontinued. Nevertheless, members of the colony persisted in the work to the best of their ability, and between January and March of 1917, they assisted more than 25,000 persons. They also took charge of the hospitals and performed splendid service in the care of the sick. The Germans attempted to obtain the exile of all Americans from Jerusalem, but the Turks would not listen to the proposal, but a number of the younger Americans were sent to Damascus. It was intended to deport the remainder, but the arrival of the British army defeated the intention.

Early in November, Enver Pasha, the Turkish minister of war, came to Jerusalem, and upon his return to Constantinople, recommended that the Holy City be evacuated. Three days later, however,

The "Stirrup-charge" of the Scots Grays and Highlanders at St. Quentin.

The Scots Grays and the Highlanders together took part in Flanders not in one charge, but in a series of charges as at Waterloo, bursting into the thick of the enemy, the Highlanders holding on to the stirrup leathers of the Grays as the horsemen galloped, and attacking hand to hand. The Germans had the surprise of their lives and broke and fled before the sudden and unexpected onslaught, suffering severe losses alike from the swords of the cavalry and the bayonets of the Highland infantrymen.

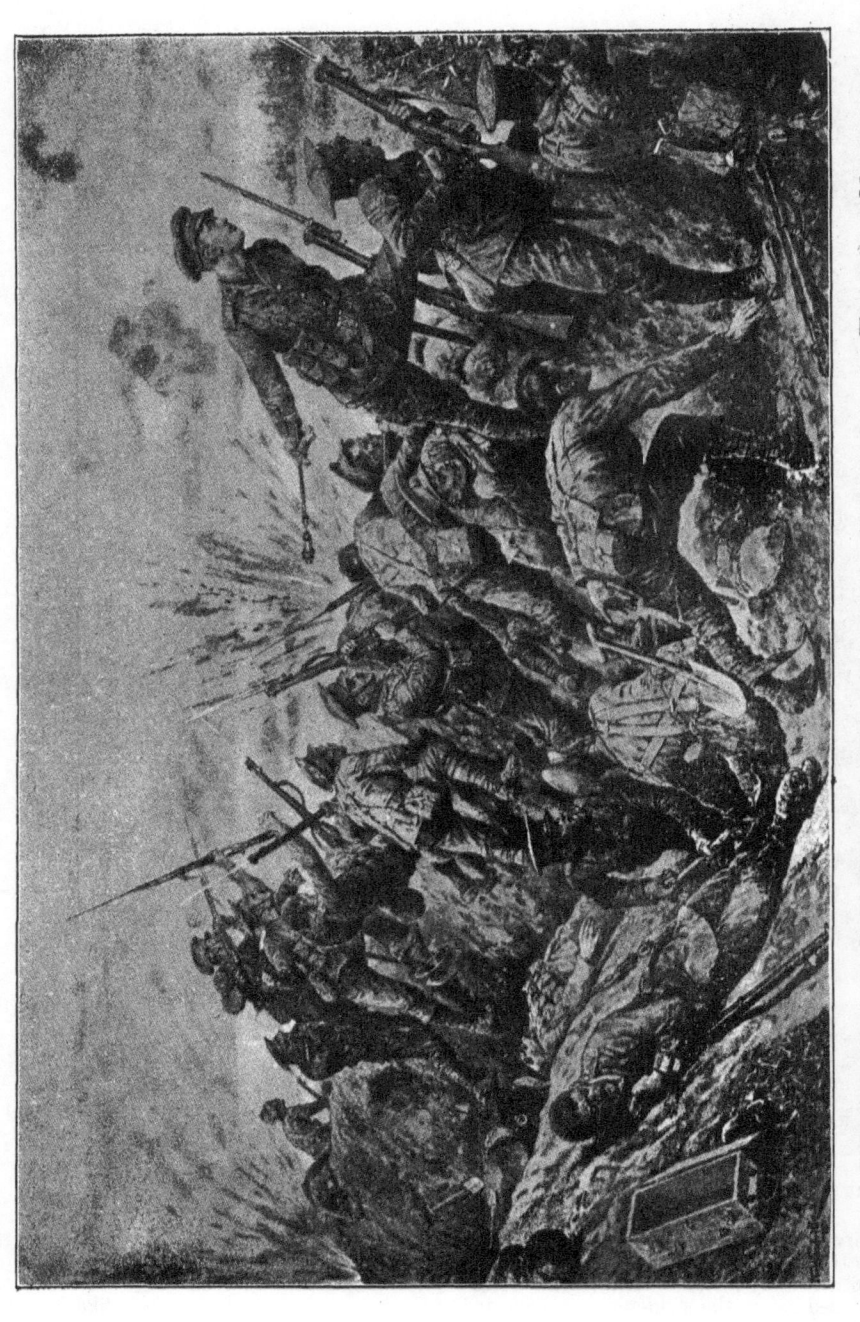

SECOND LIEUTENANT G. H. WOOLLEY'S HEROIC DEFENSE OF "HILL 60" WITH A HANDFUL OF MEN

They resisted all attacks made on their trench, the Lieutenant throwing bombs and encouraging his men through the

he changed his mind and sent reinforcements. A proclamation was issued, saying that the Turks would hold out to the last. Some of the sacred edifices were mined, it is said.

Later General von Falkenhayn, a pompous German, arrived and took control of the defense measures; the day before the entry of the British, workmen were still engaged in fitting the headquarters with electric lights. The German general fled to a place of safety in the hills when he saw that the city would surely fall.

According to Turkish estimates, there are in Palestine nearly 25,000 Arabs and Jews who deserted the army to avoid military service under the Mohammedans and Germans.

AMERICAN ENTERPRISE AIDS

Major-General F. B. Maurice, Director of Military Operations of the British War Office, declared in an interview that the capture of Jerusalem was due in no small measure to American enterprise.

"In the campaign as a whole," he said, "the greater accomplishment has not been the defeat of the Turks, but the conquest of the Sinai desert. The troops who fought at Gaza, drank water from Egypt, pumped through an American pipe line. They were supplied over a broad-gauge railroad, laid clear across the one hundred and fifty miles of desert, which has defeated almost everyone that tried to conquer Egypt for centuries. Every ounce of material for this pipe line, the railroad and the other works came either from Great Britain or the United States."

461

THE CAMPAIGN FOR JERUSALEM

A HISTORIC CITY

In sentimental and romantic aspect, the capture of Jerusalem far exceeds even the fall of the fable-crowned Bagdad. The modern city of Jerusalem contains about 60,000 inhabitants, and is the home of pestilence, filth and fevers, but in historic interest it naturally surpasses to the Christian world all other places on earth.

Since the days when David wrested it from the hands of the Jebusites to make it the capital of the Jewish race, Jerusalem has been the prize and prey of half the races of the world. It has passed successively into the hands of the Assyrians, Babylonians, Greeks, Romans, Persians, Arabs, Turks, the motley crowds of crusaders, finally to fall before the descendants of that Richard the Lion-Hearted, who strove in vain for its possession more than seven hundred years ago.

NOTE:—There are 63 pages of illustrations in this book, which, added to the 462 pages of text, make a total of 525 pages.

www.ingramcontent.com/pod-product-compliance
Lightning Source LLC
Chambersburg PA
CBHW020605040726
47498CB00003B/649